Difference and Pathology

SANDER L. GILMAN

Difference and Pathology

STEREOTYPES OF
SEXUALITY, RACE,
AND MADNESS

Cornell University Press

ITHACA AND LONDON

First published 1985 by Cornell University Press.
Second printing, 1986.
Cornell Paperbacks edition first published 1985.
Second printing, 1988.

International Standard Book Number 0-8014-1785-6 (cloth)
International Standard Book Number 0-8014-9332-3 (paper)
Library of Congress Catalog Card Number 85-7809
Printed in the United States of America
*Librarians: Library of Congress cataloging information
appears on the last page of the book.*

*The paper in this book is acid-free and meets the guidelines
for permanence and durability of the Committee on Production
Guidelines for Book Longevity of the Council on Library Resources.*

This volume is dedicated to Marianne Horney-Eckardt,
who listened with patience to many of the ideas in it

Contents

Plates

Preface

IN THE ESSAYS in this book I examine stereotypes ranging in currency from the Middle Ages to the twentieth century, with a primary focus on the turn of the century. Geographically, I survey the Western European tradition as reflected in Germany, France, England, and Italy and as imported into the United States. The volume is "comparative" in that it deals with texts from a number of sources—science, popular literature, the fine (and not so fine) arts, and medical illustration.

The kind of information that can be gleaned by visiting a tavern or attending an informal dinner party is for the most part lost to us for the turn of the century and before. But the examples presented in this volume show that texts— loosely speaking, literature and illustration consciously committed to public scrutiny—are a rich source of enlightenment in the study of Western stereotypes. Every Western society has generated a seemingly endless series of texts as a means of fixing stereotypes within a world of constant forms (whether aesthetic or scientific), and these texts provide a very good basis for analyzing the historical forces at work in the shaping of stereotypes.

All of these essays reflect my personal fascination with our need to create stereotypes. That need has given rise to a fantastic variety of images of the Other, some of them quite remote from observable fact but all of them at one time or another solemnly accepted as veritable truth. In this volume I show that the most powerful stereotypes in nineteenth-century Western Europe and the United States were those that associated images of race, sexuality, and the all-pervasive idea of pathology, and I attempt to trace the historical evolution of these stereotypes. One important general finding is that such major categories of stereotypes can be (and regularly have been) freely associated, even when their association demands a suspension of common sense. Stereotypes can assume a life of their own, rooted not in reality but in the myth-making made necessary by our need to control our world.

Stereotyping is clearly in evidence in the life of every civilization of which we have records. Its ubiquity and its immense influence on culture and history have not passed unnoticed by thoughtful people before our time, but events in this century have thrust some awareness of it on even the least willing among us. Like many other innate and ungovernable human needs, the need to stereotype has acquired increased catastrophic potential at a pace roughly in step with technological advances in our ability to harm one another. That we did not kill ourselves off at an uncontrolled rate and without pausing for breath as soon as we had the means to do so is proof that our dangerous tendencies are not unopposed by a very strong instinct for survival. The formal recognition and study of stereotyping, which in the years since the Holocaust has taken many forms in fields as diverse as psychology and literary criticism, is an important token of our wish to live.

I believe that stereotyping is a universal means of coping with anxieties engendered by our inability to control the world. Refining on that broad understanding, which is the task I undertake in the Introduction, is of course a very different thing from puzzling out how a multitude of historical and social strands lend a given stereotype its particular form. The latter is the main burden of this book.

The need for stereotypes runs so deep that I do not think it will ever be thwarted; nor do I think that it will ever be converted to purely harmless expression. But I believe that education and study can expose the ideologies with which we structure our world, and perhaps help put us in the habit of self-reflection.

While some of these essays have appeared earlier, they have been rewritten and edited to form a cohesive whole. For useful comments at various stages in the book's preparation, my thanks go to my colleagues at the Cornell Medical College, especially Eric T. Carlson, Jacques Quen, Lawrence Friedman, Robert Michels, and Otto Kernberg; at Cornell University, Ithaca, especially James Boon, Dominick LaCapra, Mary Jacobus, I. V. Hull and Henry L. Gates, Jr.; at the Wellcome Institute for the History of Medicine, William Bynum, Roy Porter, and

William Schupach; at the University of Cologne's Medical Faculty, U. H. Peters; at the University of California, Berkeley, Winfried Kudszus; at the University of Wisconsin, Madison, George Mosse; at Princeton University, Laura Engelstein, Elaine Showalter and Ruth Angress; and at Columbia University, Nancy Stepan. I especially wish to thank Davydd Greenwood, director of the Center for International Studies at Cornell, and Walter Lippincott, director of Cornell University Press, for their informed comments. The manuscript for this book was prepared by Kate Bloodgood, it was edited by Brian Keeling, and the index was done by Jane Marsh Dieckmann.

Versions of chapters 1, 2, 5, 6, and 7 previously appeared in the following sources and are used with the permission of the editors and publishers. Chapter 1: *Journal of the American Academy of Psychoanalysis* 9 (1981): 337–60; Chapter 2: *New Literary History* 14 (1983): 359–72; Chapter 5: Sander L. Gilman, *On Blackness without Blackness: Essays on the Image of the Black in Germany* (Boston: G. K. Hall, 1982), pp. 1–18; Chapter 6: *Journal of the History of the Behavioral Sciences* 20 (1984): 150–59; Chapter 7: *Modern Judaism* 1 (1981): 90–100.

SANDER L. GILMAN

Ithaca, New York

Introduction: What Are Stereotypes and Why Use Texts to Study Them?

"Stereotypes"

The celebrated Didot, the French printer, with a German named Herman, have announced a new discovery in printing, which they term stereotype.

Annual Register (London), 1798

WE ALL CREATE IMAGES of things we fear or glorify. These images never remain abstractions: we understand them as real-world entities. We assign them labels that serve to set them apart from ourselves. We create "stereotypes."

Reviewing the early history of the term *stereotype* can usefully introduce the concerns of this book. In the late eighteenth century *stereotype* was coined as a technical designation for the casting of multiple papier-mâché copies of printing type from a papier-mâché mold.[1] By the mid-nineteenth century the term had already achieved the level of abstraction we find in such phrases as "a stereotyped expression." For, just as a series of unvarying casts could be made from one mold, so too were commonplaces seen as unchanging. When, during the early twentieth century, social psychologists adopted *stereotype* to designate the images through which we categorize the world, they were perhaps more conscious than are we that "immutable structure" was essential to the meaning of the term they were appropriating. They saw stereotypes, much like commonplaces, as rigidly structured. Doubts about the appropriateness of that connotation have led recently to attempts to replace the term *stereotype* with *image*.[2] Investigators of literary stereotypes have even called the literary representations of our images of the world *mirages*. But the term *stereotype* seems to me particularly apt inasmuch as its origin is in the manufacture of texts. The link this term gives us to the world of the text more than compensates for its dubious stress on the immutability of our images. For indeed it is within texts that we can best examine our representations of the world through our articulation of what seems, on the most superficial level, the rigid structures of the stereotype.

How and why do we create stereotypes? The discussion below, which is the theoretical background for the chapters that follow, is necessarily a very abbreviated treatment of a large subject. For readers who wish to learn more about the topic I recommend my *Introducing Psychoanalytic Theory* (New York: Brunner/Mazel, 1982) as well as the general theoretical introduction to my *Seeing the Insane* (New York: John Wiley, 1982; paperback, 1985).

The Deep Structure of Stereotypes

> The organization of intrapsychic reality in terms of love and hate is more important for our understanding of the continuity in intrapsychic development, unconscious conflict and object relations themselves than the fact that these contradictory states are originally directed toward the same object—mother—or that, in the oedipal phase, a male and female object are the recipients of the child's dominant needs and strivings.
>
> Otto Kernberg
> *Severe Personality Disorders:*
> *Psychotheraputic Strategies*

Everyone creates stereotypes. We cannot function in the world without them.[3] They buffer us against our most urgent fears by extending them, making it possible for us to act as though their source were beyond our control.

The creation of stereotypes is a concomitant of the process by which all human beings become individuals. Its beginnings lie in the earliest stages of our development. The infant's movement from a state of being in which everything is perceived as an extension of the self to a growing sense of a separate identity takes place between the ages of a few weeks and about five months.[4] During that stage, the new sense of "difference" is directly acquired by the denial of the child's demands on the world. We all begin not only by demanding food, warmth, and comfort, but by assuming that those demands will be met. The world is felt to be a mere extension of the self. It is that part of the self which provides food, warmth, and comfort. As the child comes to distinguish more and more between the world and self, anxiety arises from a perceived loss of control over the world. But very soon the child begins to combat anxieties associated with the failure to control the world by adjusting his mental picture of people and objects so that they can appear "good" even when their behavior is perceived as "bad."[5]

But even more, the sense of the self is shaped to fit this pattern. The child's sense of self itself splits into a "good" self, which, as the self mirroring the earlier stage of the complete control of the world, is free from anxiety, and the "bad" self, which is unable to control the environment and is thus exposed to anxieties. This split is but a single stage in the development of the normal personality. In it lies, however, the root of all stereotypical perceptions. For in the normal course of development the child's understanding of the world becomes seemingly ever more sophisticated. The child is able to distinguish ever finer gradations of "goodness" and "badness," so that by the later oedipal stage an illusion of versimilitude is cast over the inherent (and irrational) distinction between the "good" and "bad" world and self, between control and loss of control, between acquiescence and denial.

With the split of both the self and the world into "good" and "bad" objects, the "bad" self is distanced and identified with the mental representation of the "bad" object. This act of projection saves the self from any confrontation with the contradictions present in the necessary integration of "bad" and "good" aspects of the self. The deep structure of our own sense of self and the world is built upon the illusionary image of the world divided into two camps, "us" and "them." "They" are either "good" or "bad." Yet it is clear that this is a very primitive distinction which, in most individuals, is replaced early in development by the illusion of integration.

Stereotypes are a crude set of mental representations of the world.

They are palimpsests on which the initial bipolar representations are still vaguely legible. They perpetuate a needed sense of difference between the "self" and the "object," which becomes the "Other." Because there is no real line between self and the Other, an imaginary line must be drawn; and so that the illusion of an absolute difference between self and Other is never troubled, this line is as dynamic in its ability to alter itself as is the self. This can be observed in the shifting relationship of antithetical stereotypes that parallel the existence of "bad" and "good" representations of self and Other. But the line between "good" and "bad" responds to stresses occurring within the psyche. Thus paradigm shifts in our mental representations of the world can and do occur. We can move from fearing to glorifying the Other. We can move from loving to hating. The most negative stereotype always has an overtly positive counterweight. As any image is shifted, all stereotypes shift. Thus stereotypes are inherently protean rather than rigid.

Although this activity seems to take place outside the self, in the world of the object, of the Other, it is in fact only a reflection of an internal process, which draws upon repressed mental representations for its structure. Stereotypes arise when self-integration is threatened. They are therefore part of our way of dealing with the instabilities of our perception of the world. This is not to say that they are good, only that they are necessary. We can and must make the distinction between pathological stereotyping and the stereotyping all of us need to do to preserve our illusion of control over the self and the world. Our Manichean perception of the world as "good" and "bad" is triggered by a recurrence of the type of insecurity that induced our initial division of the world into "good" and "bad." For the pathological personality every confrontation sets up this echo. Stereotypes can and often do exist parallel to the ability to create sophisticated rational categories that transcend the crude line of difference present in the stereotype. We retain our ability to distinguish the "individual" from the stereotyped class into which the object might automatically be placed. The pathological personality does not develop this ability and sees the entire world in terms of the rigid line of difference. The pathological personality's mental representation of the world supports the need for the line of difference, whereas for the non-pathological individual the stereotype is a momentary coping mechanism, one that can be used and then discarded once anxiety is overcome. The former is consistently aggressive toward the real people and objects to which the stereotypical representations correspond; the latter is able to repress the aggression and deal with people as individuals.

The Natural History of the Stereotype

The yearning for rigidity is in us all. It is part of our human condition to long for hard lines and clear concepts. When we have them we have either to face the fact that some realities elude them, or else blind ourselves to the inadequacy of the concepts.

Mary Douglas
Purity and Danger: An Analysis of
the Concepts of Pollution and Taboo

While the deep structure of the stereotype seems simple, its realization is much more complex. The complexity of the stereotype results from the social context in which it is to be found. This context parallels, but is not identical to, the earlier symbiotic context in which the child begins to differentiate himself from the world. The deep structure of the stereotype reappears in the adult as a response to anxiety, an anxiety having its roots in the potential disintegration of the mental representations the individual has created and internalized.[6] The sense of order the adult maintains is much like the structure of order which precedes the earliest stage of individuation. It is an unconscious sense of symbiosis with the world, a world under the control of the self. Anxiety arises as much through any alteration of the sense of order (real or imagined) between the self and the Other (real or imagined) as through the strains of regulating repressed drives.

The models for control are linked to structures in society which provide status and meaning for the individual. Self-esteem is linked to the image of the self and of the meaningful objects or Others in the social world. Our self-image not only reflects our mental representation of the external world, but, by influencing our perception of objects and their integration into that mental representation, shapes it as well. The objects exist, we interact with them, they respond to (or ignore) our demands upon them. But when we relate to them, we relate to them through the filter of our internalized representation of the world. This representation centers around our sense of control.

The objects in our world are reduced to images. No matter how well articulated, these images are constantly altered by our interaction with the realities upon which they are based. We may momentarily perceive an individual as aggressive, but the absence of a constant pattern of aggression enables us to resolve the conflict between the "bad" image and the complex reality and perceive the individual as possessing both "good" and "bad" aspects. When, however, the sense of order and control undergoes stress, when doubt is cast on the self's ability to control the internalized world that it has created for itself, an anxiety appears which mirrors the earlier affective coloring of the period of individuation. We project that anxiety onto the Other, externalizing our loss of control. The Other is thus stereotyped, labeled with a set of signs paralleling (or mirroring) our loss of control. The Other is invested with all of the qualities of the "bad" or the "good." The "bad" self, with its repressed sadistic impulses, becomes the "bad" Other; the "good" self/object, with its infallible correctness, becomes the antithesis to the flawed image of the self, the self out of control. The "bad" Other becomes the negative stereotype; the "good" Other becomes the positive stereotype. The former is that which we fear to become; the latter, that which we fear we cannot achieve.

The models we employ to shape the stereotype are themselves protean. As we seek to project the source of our anxiety onto objects in the world, we select models from the social world in which we function. The models are thus neither "random" nor "archetypal." It is evident that stereotypes are not random or personal; nor is there some universal soul, a black box that generates these categories of difference. Every social group has a set vocabulary of images for this externalized Other. These images are the product of history and of a culture that perpetuates them.[7] None is random; none is isolated from the historical context. From the wide range of the potential models in any society, we select a model that best reflects the common presuppositions about the Other at any given moment in history. While all of these images exist simultaneously, the ones that are invested with relatively greater force vary over time. An image can gain in potency partly as a result of actions by the corresponding real entities. When, for example, a group makes demands on a society, the status anxiety produced by those demands characteristically translates into a sense of loss of control. Thus a group that has been marginally visible can suddenly become the definition of the Other. But stereotypes can also be perpetuated, resurrected, and shaped through texts containing the fantasy life of the culture, quite independent of the existence or absence of the group in a given society.

Each society has a distinct "tradition," to use Gordon Allport's term, that determines its stereotypes.[8] A rich web of signs and references for the idea of difference arises out of a society's communal sense of control over its world. No matter how this sense of control is articulated, whether as political power, social status, religious mission, or geographic or economic domination, it provides an appropriate vocabulary for the sense of difference. Difference is that which threatens order and control; it is the polar opposite to our group. This mental representation of difference is but the projection of the tension between control and its loss present within each individual in every group. That tension produces an anxiety that is given shape as the Other. The Other is protean because of its source, the conflicts within the individual as articulated in the vocabulary of the group. Qualities assigned to the Other readily form patterns with little or no relationship to any external reality. Since all of the images of the Other derive from the same deep structure, various signs of difference can be linked without any recognition of inappropriateness, contradictoriness, or even impossibility. Patterns of association are most commonly based, however, on a combination of real-life experience (as filtered through the models of perception) and the world of myth, and the two intertwine to form fabulous images, neither entirely of this world nor of the realm of myth. The analogizing essential to this process functions much like systems of metaphor.[9] Since analogies are rooted in a habitual perception of the world, they are understood as an adequate representation of reality. The mental representation that results, of course, divides the world into categories in accordance with stereotypical perception. All experience can thus be measured against this "reality," and since this experience is structured through a system of mental representations in precisely the same way as was the overall structure of the world, the experience reifies the stereotypical image of the world. Analogy thus becomes the basis for the association between otherwise disparate categories.

Categories

I am suggesting that the appearance in the culture of a philosophical tendency which was hypnotized by the success of science to such an extent that it could not conceive of the possibility of knowledge and reason outside of what we are pleased to call the sciences is something that was expected given the enormously high prestige that science has in the general culture, and given the declining prestige of religion, absolute ethics, and transcendental metaphysics. And I am suggesting that the high prestige of science *in the general culture* is very much due to the enormous instrumental success of science, together with the fact that science seems free from the interminable and unsettleable debates that we find in religion, ethics and metaphysics.

Hilary Putnam
Reason, Truth and History

How do we learn to see?

Oscar Wilde half ironically suggested that the world is perceived through the prism of art. "External nature," according to Wilde, "imitates Art. The only effects that she can show us are effects that we have already seen through poetry, or in paintings."[10] While stated in the vocabulary of aestheticism, Wilde's thesis turns on our basic need to structure the world in familiar terms. Stephen Pepper has called models of explanation that reflect this need *root metaphors:*

A man desiring to understand the world looks about for a clue to its comprehension. He pitches upon some area of commonsense fact and tries to see if he cannot understand other areas in terms of this one. This original area becomes then his basic analogy or root-metaphor. He describes as best he can the characteristics of this area, or, if you will, discriminates its structure. A list of its structural characteristics becomes his basic concepts of explanation and description. We call them a set of categories. In terms of these categories he proceeds to study all other areas of fact whether uncriticized or previously criticized. He undertakes to interpret all facts in terms of these categories. As a result of the impact of these other facts upon his categories, he may qualify and readjust the categories, so that a set of categories commonly changes and develops.[11]

However, the use of analogy in the creation of such categories does not guarantee their validity. Indeed, the moment of creation of such categories is one of the moments when the vocabulary of stereotypes crystallizes. We learn to perceive in terms of historically determined sets of root-metaphors, and they serve as the categories through which we label and classify the Other. These categories are not mutually exclusive. Often they contradict or supplement one another.

It is the ability to hold simultaneously two (or more) images of the Other which makes it possible to link them. All such images reflect projections of anxiety, and it is in the context of this commonality that the moment of homeostatic thinking takes place and the root metaphors underlying the basic categories are associated. Thus when models for perception are built, these models are heuristic structures that the self uses to integrate the various stereotypes associated by analogy.

The categories into which stereotypes can be divided, however, are not arbitrary. They are bipolar but are mutable and constantly shifting. They reflect certain basic perceptual categories, which are in turn projections of internalized, often repressed models of the self and the Other. All of the categories reflect the cultural categories of seeing objects as a reflection or distortion of the self. The resulting basic categories of difference reflect our preoccupation with the self and the control that the self must have over the world. Because the Other is the antithesis of the self, the definition of the Other must incorporate the basic categories by which the self is defined. I believe that three basic categories of this kind are generated by our sense of our own mutability, the central role of sexuality in our nature, and our necessary relationship to some greater group. To use a rather crude shorthand, I will speak of illness, sexuality, and race, since these are labels that have been given to broad characteristics essential to definitions of the self at various points in history.[12]

Our understanding of the pathological is rooted in an awareness of the human organism's fragility—not simply its mortality, though that has always and everywhere inspired fear of the ultimate loss of control, but its susceptibility to disease, pollution, corruption, and alteration, things that we experience in our own bodies and observe in others. Every group has laws, taboos, and diagnoses distinguishing the "healthy" from the "sick." The very concept of pathology is a line drawn between the "good" and the "bad." This accounts for the power that metaphors of illness have. Whether we turn to Bartolome de las Casas's sixteenth-century restructuring of the metaphor of syphilis to describe not the infection of Europe by the inhabitants of the New World, but the action of the Europeans as an agent of destruction in the New World, or to Susan Sontag's discussion of the function of metaphors of "tuberculosis" and "cancer" in the nineteenth and twentieth centuries, the idea of the pathological is a central marker for difference.[13] The potential illness, age, and corruption of the self is projected onto others so that the world becomes seen as both corrupt and corrupting, polluted and polluting. The threat and its result become one.

Of all the models of pathology, one of the most powerful is mental illness.[14] For the most elementally frightening possibility is loss of control over the self, and loss of control is associated with loss of language and thought perhaps even more than with physical illness. Often associated with violence (including aggressive sexual acts), the mad are perceived as the antithesis to the control and reason that define the self. Again, what is perceived is in large part a projection: for within everyone's fantasy life there exists a play of aggression not essentially different from that of the initial moment of individuation, an incipient madness that we control with more or less success. This is not to say that mental illness does not exist (any more than that syphilis and cancer, both fruitful of metaphors, do not exist), but that the function of the idea of mental illness within the sign systems of our mental representations shapes our "seeing the insane."

The old "platonic" idea of disease as a corporeal invasion of the self, a "thing" lying outside the self that enters to corrupt it, has not been shaken off by modern medicine.[15] Models of illness are commonly treated as realities. While this manner of "seeing" pathology has not gone unchallenged by empirical views of disease, its persistence into the latter twentieth century is evidence of how deep is the human disposition to structure perception in terms of binary difference. We have the "healthy" and the "pathological" self. Likewise, concepts of mental illness, no matter what "model of madness" is employed, recapitulate the "realist" definition of illness as dichotomously opposed to "health." While illness, especially mental illness, can be evaluated on a scale of debility ranging from the slightly to the greatly impaired, the poles of the scale are there in order to define difference. The concept of difference is needed to distinguish the healer from the patient as well as the "healthy" from the "sick." Order and control are the antithesis of "pathology." "Pathology" is disorder and the loss of control, the giving over of the self to the forces that lie beyond the self. It is because these forces actually lie within and are projected outside the self that the different is so readily defined as the pathological. Such definitions are an efficient way of displacing the consciousness that the self, as a biological entity subject to the inexorable rules of aging and decay, ultimately cannot be controlled.

One major category with which pathology is often associated is human sexuality.[16] The sexual dimension of human experience is one of those most commonly divided into the "normal" and the "deviant," the "good" and the "bad." Human sexuality, given its strong biological basis, not unnaturally is often perceived as out of the control of the self. Since fantasy is an innate part of human sexuality, it is not only the biological but also the psychological which can be understood as out of control. For a secure definition of self, sexuality and the loss of control associated with it must be projected onto the Other. Fantasies of impotency are projected onto the Other as frigidity, fantasies of potency as hypersexuality. Or an obverse image appears—where loss of control is defined by the label of infertility, the Other becomes overfertile. Sexual norms become modes of control. Thus deviation, either in the nature of the sexual act or in its perceived purpose, becomes "disease" or its theological equivalent, "sin." The analogy between the "ill" and the "perverse" is ubiquitous.

Group cohesiveness, like the "pathological" and the "sexual," threatens secure self-control. Here the potential for loss of control arises from demands the group places upon the individual, demands that may contradict the mental representation of the self.[17] The double bind may be so deep that the individual has to project it onto the Other. The perception of the Other as a threat to the individual's autonomy is thus a reflection of the loss of autonomy felt within the group. Group identity thereby serves as a means of defining the "healthy," that which belongs to the group and "protects" those in it, as well as its antithesis, the outsider, the Other.[18]

The labels given outsider groups are legion. One of the most fascinating is that of "race." In "seeing" (constructing a representational system for) the Other, we search for anatomical signs of difference such as physiognomy and skin color. The Other's physical features, from skin color to sexual structures such as the shape of the genitalia, are always the antitheses of the idealized self's. Here the links between "pathology," "sexuality," and "race" become even more overt: sexual anatomy is so important a part of self-image that "sexually different" is tantamount to "pathological"—the Other is "impaired," "sick," "diseased." Similarly, physiognomy or skin color that is perceived as different is immediately associated with "pathology" and "sexuality."

These associations are double-edged. They may appear as negative images, but they may also appear as positive idealizations. The "pathological" may appear as the pure, the unsullied; the sexually different as the apotheosis of beauty, the asexual or the androgynous; the racially different as highly attractive. In all of these cases the same process occurs. The loss of control is projected not onto the cause or mirror of this loss but onto the Other, who, unlike the self, can do no wrong, can never be out of control. Categories of difference are protean, but they appear as absolutes. They categorize the sense of the self, but establish an order—the illusion of order in the world.

Representations

Discourses, sign-systems and signifying practices of all kinds, from film and television to fiction and the languages of natural science, produce effects, shape forms of consciousness and unconsciousness, which are closely related to the maintenance or transformation of our existing systems of power. They are thus closely related to what it means to be a person. Indeed "ideology" can be taken to indicate no more than this connection—the link or nexus between discourses and power.

Terry Eagleton
Literary Theory

As remarked above, the implication of rigidity that attaches to *stereotype* is inappropriate when *stereotype* is used in social psychology, but the early connection of that term with text production is peculiarly apt. Texts are an ideal source for a study of the fluidity of stereotypical concepts. But "texts" must be understood in the broadest sense of that term. All structured systems of representation, no matter what the medium, can be construed as "texts" for the study of stereotypes.[19] From advertising copy to medical illustration, from popular novels to classical drama, from the academic portrait to graffiti scratched on the walls of prisons—all are texts in that they function as structured expressions of the inner world in our mental representation. Some of these systems are more complicated than others, but all of them are on some level interrelated, being as protean as the stereotypes that underlie them.

This is not to reduce the "work of art" to a system of stereotypical signifiers, but rather to stress that such systems are incorporated within the work of art, high or low, and shape the fictions that these works present. This crafting of language may be quite conscious, for example in parody of the stereotypical presuppositions of the time, or it may be quite naive, or it may be both simultaneously. The function within such systems of representation of stereotypes to represent classes of humanity has been discussed in terms of the "set roles" in classical and neoclassical drama, images of national character in literature, racial typologies in films, and the representation of groups within the history of "higher art." All of these traditional examinations attend to the stereotype as a group manifestation, but ignore its basic structure. Quite often studies of this sort, no matter how sophisticated, lose sight of the interrelationship of the patterns of stereotyping. Thus, a recent study of the sexuality of Christ in Renaissance art, brilliant as it is, manages to ignore the charges of sexual pathology brought against the Jews in the Middle Ages and the Renaissance. Christ's divine sexuality sets him apart from the "perfidious Jews."[20] Such links illuminate the interdependence of systems of stereotypical representation.

All of these systems are inherently bipolar, generating pairs of antithetical signifiers ("the noble savage" vs. "the ignoble savage"). All reflect the deep structure of the stereotype while responding to the social and political ideologies of the times. More complicated texts provide more complicated representations of difference. These texts may be complicated because they consciously form a fiction of the world. Such novels, plays, and poetry are written and marketed to fulfill certain needs of specific groups within a given society. Within the closed world they create, stereotypes can be studied as an idealized definition of the different. The closed world of language, a system of references which creates the illusion of completeness and wholeness, carries and is carried by the need to stereotype.[21] For stereotypes, like commonplaces, carry entire realms of associations with them, associations that form a subtext within the world of fiction. In the case of works claiming to create a world out of whole cloth, such a subtext provides basic insight into the presuppositions of the culture in which the work arises and for which it is created. In some works, tension incident to conflicts between the "realities" of a given culture and author's idealized sense of the audience results in parodic distortion of the stereotypes; in others, the stylized reflection of the mental representation of the world provides an acceptable matrix for the stereotypical structures that dominate the daily mental life of the culture. Reflected or unreflected, such structures exist within all texts, since the creation of the text is an attempt to provide an image of control. The fictional world as structured by the author is the world under control, in which even the loss of control is reduced to the level of a fiction directed and formed by the author.

When systems of representation are used to structure the projections of our anxiety, they are necessarily reductive. Often the very appeal to a set system of images is a sign of the observer's awareness of the absence of difference. Stephen Heath has commented that "where a discourse appeals directly to an image, to an immediacy of seeing, as a point of its argument or demonstration, one can be sure that all difference is being eluded, that the unity of some accepted vision is being reproduced."[22] This "accepted vision" is the stereotypical perception of the Other. The anxiety present in the self concerning its control over the world directly engenders a need for a clear and hard line of difference between the self and the Other.

In a parallel set of texts, those of the "human sciences," a parallel creation of fictions is undertaken.[23] Unlike the fictions of "high art," the fictions of psychology, biology, anthropology, sociology, genetics, and medicine relate, directly or tangentially, to perceived realities. Their point of departure is not the assumptions of a closed world of fiction but the nature of humanity. But the very act of perception is of course colored by our mental representations of the world. Science creates fictions to explain facts, and an important criterion for endorsing these fictions is their ideological acceptability. Science, in spite of its privileged status in the West as arbiter of reality,[24] is in this respect a blood relation of art.

The reception of a statement about reality depends on whether and how well it fits into the web of conventions which links all of the representational systems in a culture.[25] That such a web of conventions obtains within the aesthetic world is a commonplace; but parallel systems exist synchronically within other areas of representation. Medical iconography, for example, borrows from and contributes to the general pool of images found in a culture. Medicine, like other "human sciences," is a relatively powerful source of conventions since we do tend to see its semiotics as "objective" compared to the conventions of aesthetics. Medical icons are no more "real" than "aesthetic" ones. Like them they *may* be rooted in some shadow of observed reality, but when they are they represent our perceptions in a manner determined by the observer's historical context. Their relationship is to their own time, and to the history of the conventions they employ. Medicine uses its categories to structure an image of the diversity (and pathology) of humanity, and is as much at the mercy of the needs of its age to comprehend this infinite and often contradictory diversity as is any other system that classifies our perception of the world.[26] Its peculiar power lies not only in its status as science but in the overt helplessness of the individual in the face of illness (or in the face of being labeled as ill). It is owing to that power that the conventions of medicine can, as we shall see, so easily infiltrate other apparently closed representational systems.

In some cases the interdependence of stereotypical models of the world in science and in the arts is great enough to show the identity of the root metaphors that underlie both. Often, however, it is the metaphoric language of science or of the work of art which reveals their interdependence. In examining the language of science we begin to understand the underlying presupposition about human nature. The stereotypes that structure this perception are shared with other systems of representation. They reflect the basic attitudes of a given culture and epoch toward specific groups. The extent to which these generalizations obtain in the world of "scientific discourse" as well as in the discourse of other systems of representation can be judged in the following case, in which texts from "science" and "art" provide clues to the interweaving of two stereotypes in European thought of the nineteenth and twentieth centuries.

A Case for the Protean Nature of Stereotypes

Poles have never come out against Jews "because they are Jews" but because Jews are dirty, greedy, mendacious, because they wear earlocks, speak jargon, do not want to assimilate, and *also* because they *do* assimilate, cease using their jargon, are nattily dressed, and want to be regarded as Poles. Because they lack culture and because they are overly cultured. Because they are superstitious, backward and ignorant, and because they are damnably capable, progressive, and ambitious. Because they have long, hooked noses, and because it is sometimes difficult to distinguish them from "pure Poles." Because they crucified Christ and practice ritual murder and pore over the Talmud, and because they disdain their own religion and are atheists. Because they look wretched and sickly, and because they are tough and have their own fighting units and are full of *khutspah*. Because they are bankers and capitalists and because they are Communists and agitators. But in *no* case because they are Jews.

Konstantyn Jelenski
Kultura (Paris, May 1968)

It is a truism that skin color has mythic qualities. Frantz Fanon summarized the attitude of the West toward blackness, which is but the projection of Western anxiety concerning the Other in terms of skin color:

In Europe, the Black man is the symbol of Evil. . . . The torturer is the Black man, Satan is Black, one talks of shadows, when one is dirty one is black— whether one is thinking of physical dirtiness or moral dirtiness. It would be astonishing, if the trouble were taken to bring them all together, to see the vast number of expressions that make the Black man the equivalent of sin. In Europe, whether concretely or symbolically, the Black man stands for the bad side of the character. As long as one cannot understand this fact, one is doomed to talk in circles about the "black problem." Blackness, darkness, shadow, shades, night, the labyrinths of the earth, abysmal depths, blacken someone's reputation; and on the other side, the bright look of innocence, the white dove of peace, magical, heavenly light.[27]

That blacks are the antithesis of the mirage of whiteness, the ideal of European aesthetic values, strikes the reader as an extension of some "real," perceived difference to which the qualities of "good" and "bad" have been erroneously applied. But the very concept of color is a quality of Otherness, not of reality. For not only are blacks black in this amorphous world of projection, so too are Jews.

In *Carmen* (1845), a novella, Prosper Mérimée records the meeting of his narrator, a French antiquarian, with the protagonist on a parapet above the river in Cordova. Carmen is the quintessential Other—female, a gypsy possessing all languages and yet native only in her hidden tongue, proletarian, and black. For as Mérimée later notes in the tale, the gypsies are "the black ones." But when Carmen is first introduced to the reader it is not at all clear who she is. The narrator hazards a guess that she "might be Moorish or . . . (I stopped short, not daring to say Jewish)."[28] It is Carmen's appearance that leads the narrator astray. But this overlapping of images of Otherness, the Moor, the Jew, the Gypsy, is possible only from the perspective of the French narrator, for whom Otherness in Spain is an amalgam of all of these projections. Now Mérimée's image of his narrator's confusion of Others is quite blatant and has little polemical value outside the world of the fiction that is his tale of Carmen. The coalescence of structures or codes of Otherness changes considerably in character when one moves to a later text in a quite different cultural context.

Within the late nineteenth-century racist tractates published in Germany, the image of the black Jew appears with specific political implications. In Houston Stewart Chamberlain's *Foundations of the Nineteenth Century* (1899), Chamberlain, Richard Wagner's son-in-law, categorizes the Jews as "a mongrel race which always retains this mongrel character."[29] This is not merely a gratuitous insult. For Chamberlain, like many of the thinkers of the late nineteenth century, stressed the centrality of racial purity. The Jews are the least pure race, are the inferior product of a "crossing of absolutely different types." While Chamberlain does see some value in "racial mixture" as a means of strengthening racial types, he uses the Jews as the prime example of the negative results of such interbreeding. For Chamberlain the most recent "hybridization" of the Jew was the "admixture of Negro blood with Jewish in the Diaspora of Alexandria—of which many a man of Jewish persuasion at this day offers living proof." Chamberlain's choice of the Jew was not a random one. He wished to document the biological basis of the "Jewish Question," as perceived by racist thinkers at the turn of the century. He sought out the idea of Blackness, a myth that had even stronger implications within the German tradition than elsewhere because of the almost total absence of blacks in the German experience of the world. By the time Chamberlain wrote his infamous tractate, Germany had been a colonial power for little less than two decades, and the Germans were using their myth of Otherness to justify the paternalistic treatment of blacks in their colonies. This myth was then applied to the Jew, who, unlike the black, was assuming a promised status in Europe. The Jew became the "white Negro," as Otto von Bismarck's friend Hermann Wagener observed in 1862, because the demands of the Jew for political and social equality created in the privileged group, the Germans, the need to see the Jews as politically subservient and immutably different.[30] The image of the Jew as the black was not merely the product of the racist biology of the late nineteenth century, even though the examples cited above reflect the rhetoric of this pseudoscience. For the association of the Jew with blackness is as old as Christian tradition. Medieval iconography always juxtaposed the black image of the "synagogue," of the "Old Law," with the white of the Church.[31] The association was an artifact of the Christian perception of the Jew which was simply incorporated into the rhetoric of race. But it was incorporated not merely as an intellectual abstraction but as the model through which Jews were perceived and treated, and to which they thus responded as if confronted with the reflection of their own reality. Adam Gurowski, a Polish noble, observed in his 1857 memoirs that "numbers of Jews have the greatest resemblance to the American mulattoes. Sallow carnation complexion, thick lips, crisped black hair. Of all the Jewish population scattered over the globe one-fourth lives in Poland. I am, therefore, well acquainted with their features. On my arrival in this country (the United States) I took every light-colored mulatto for a Jew."[32] In the eyes of the non-Jew who defined them in Western society, the Jews became the blacks.

If the blackness of the Jew is the synthesis of two projections of Otherness within the same code, how then did the Other, the Jews, respond to their being labeled as black? Erik Homburger Erikson's first work, *Childhood and Society* (1950), contains a detailed analysis of Adolf Hitler's development based on a reading of Hitler's *Mein Kampf* (1923).[33] He presents Hitler's racial typology as "a simple racial dichotomy of cosmic dimension: the German (soldier) versus the Jew," and he goes on to characterize this typology: "The Jew is described as small, black, and hairy all over; his back is bent, his feet are flat; his eyes squint, and his lips smack; he has an evil smell, is promiscuous, and loves to deflower, impregnate, and infect blond girls. The Aryan is tall, erect, light, without hair on chest and limbs; his glance, walk and talk are *stramm,* his greeting the out-stretched arm. He is passionately clean in his habits. He would not knowingly touch a Jewish girl—except in a brothel. This antithesis is clearly one of ape man and superman." Erikson, who fled Austria to escape the Nazis, and who had earlier fled his own identity as a "Homburger" to become an "Erikson," presented very much his own reading of Hitler's racial theory. For what strikes a reader of *Mein Kampf* is that Hitler did not accept Chamberlain's hybrid theory of Jewish racial identity; rather he relied on a much more primitive conspiracy theory.[34] For Hitler the linkage between the Jew and the black was a political one. It was the Jews who inspired the French to station black troops along the Rhine following the 1919 armistice and it was therefore the intent of the Jew to set loose these "barbarians belonging to a race inspired by Nature . . . with a tremendous sexual instinct," quoting the British radical E. D. Morel, "into the heart of Europe."[35] Erikson simply recreates the image of the Jew as black with which he himself grew up. Erikson's image of the "black" Jew is a hyperbolic summary of the Nazi image of the Jew. For the Aryan "superman" had been destroyed and his perfection had been shown to be chimerical. Erikson's integration and projection of his own inner anxiety about his identity is present in his parody of Nazi racial theory.

Erikson begins his discussion of the nature of the Jew by dismissing Oswald Spengler's argument that anti-Semitism is merely "a matter of projection." Erikson argues that, on the contrary, while such projections are distortions there is always a "kernel of profound meaning," meaning not in terms of the group projecting the stereotype, but in terms of the group onto which it is projected. He then tabulates three qualities of the "Jew" which trigger the projections of the anti-Semites. First is the ritual of circumcision, which is the Jew's way of " 'asking for it.' " It precipitates the fear of castration. Second are the two models of the Jew's nature, "dogmatic orthodoxy and opportunistic adaptability, the living caricatures of the bearded Jew in his kaftan, and Sammy Glick." This dichotomy is postulated as the radical split in the identity of Jews which gives rise to the third quality, their "cynical relativism" or adherence to dogma, whatever its nature.

Erikson's rejection of the blackness of the Jew present in nineteenth-

and early twentieth-century racial theory seems absolute. And yet when he turns to his own anatomy of the Jew, he simply adapts, in terms of his own projection of that which he sees himself not to be, other aspects of these same theories. Indeed it is in Hitler's *Mein Kampf* that the rootlessness of the Jews, their support of all destructive dogmas, from the Talmud to Marxism, is stressed. And most important, Erikson selects the two images of the Jew which dominate the anti-Semitic texts of his adopted home, Vienna. The Jew is either the dogmatic, illogical Eastern Jew, "the bearded Jew in his kaftan," or the *Luftmensch,* the wheeler-dealer, rootless, without morals or goals. The latter category is represented for him by the title character of Budd Schulberg's 1941 novel, *What Makes Sammy Run?* It is thus in fictions, in the world of texts and discourse, that Erikson places the "bad" Jew. While Erikson does point out that these are the extremes of what he perceives Jewish identity to be, seeing the Jewish mediation of culture within the relativity of a Jewish perception of the world, he also outlines what he is not. He is clearly not the racial stereotype of Jewish physiognomy, for that is to be like the American image of the powerless black as victim, a subject to which he devotes an entire chapter in *Childhood and Society,* nor is he the rootless Jew, without goals or morals. He sees himself as a creator of a new Jewish discourse, like his triumvirate of ideal Jews, "Marx, Freud, and Einstein," all of whom "*personify* these redefinitions of the very ground man thought he stood on." Erikson sees himself within the model of this image of the Jew; he projects his inner anxiety concerning his potential weakness, that weakness ascribed to him as a Jew by the Germans, onto the Jewish Other. One need not repeat the Nazi image of the Jew as revolutionary and destructive. Within the entire panoply of Jews invoked in Nazi rhetoric, the revolutionary triad of Marx, Freud, and Einstein, the creators of Jewish class-struggle, Jewish psychology, and Jewish physics, dominate. Alfred Rosenberg, the Nazi party ideologist, in his continuation of Chamberlain's argument in *The Myth of the Twentieth Century* (1930), makes this point quite tellingly. Erikson has shaped his image of the Jew within the confines of the anti-Semitic rhetoric that categorizes the nature of the Jew, including the labeling of the Jew as black. No longer concerned with this superficial categorization, he includes within his image of the Jews other aspects of the code of Otherness applied to the Jew, selecting some aspects as positive and applicable to himself, seeing other images as negative and existing in real Jews in the real world. Erikson's "kernel of profound meaning" found within the "Jews" turns out to be nothing more than his projection of his inner anxieties about his self-definition onto the nature of the Jew, in a rhetoric framed by his own time and place in the world. But this was not simply the fantasy of one who saw himself as different. The status of the black within Weimar Germany was extraordinarily parallel to that of the Jew under the Nazis. Much public discussion revolved about the question of what should be done with the offspring of "black" (non-European) soldiers, especially in the occupied Rhineland.[36] The proposals were all cast in the rhetoric of "eugenics," a pseudoscience that in Germany became closely allied with the suppression of Jewish identity. What was suggested most often was sterilization. Erikson's sense that the Jews were tempting fate through their public avowal of circumcision was evoked by the threat to sterilize all "Blacks." Thus Jewish "self-castration" (circumcision as a sign of difference) called forth and was called forth by the threat of the public rhetoric about the black. Seeing oneself as outside this circle became a necessity in order to retain any sense of control over one's own person.

Erikson incorporates the fear of being identified with the black into his projection of what is an acceptable or an unacceptable mask for the Jew to wear. The image of blackness projects much of the repressed anxiety surrounding the Jew's sexual identity in twentieth-century Europe. The depth of the association of the Jew with the black enabled non-Jewish Europeans during the nineteenth century to "see" the Jews as blacks. The association of blacks with revolution, a powerful one in the late eighteenth and early nineteenth century, is carried over to the role of Jewish emancipation, itself linked with Napoleon and the restructuring of the old social order in Europe. Thus change of any kind, but especially violent change, is associated with blackness. An early nineteenth-century print depicts French "revolutionary fury" in the form of a medusa-headed female attacking the "Shield of Brittanica." And the image of revolution is black![37] Here the subtext is that of the black as the revolutionary female. If the natural history of the image of the black is examined, especially in conservative sources following the Haitian Revolution in 1804, one of the most remarkable findings is the association of black revolutionaries of both sexes with sexual excess, as in Heinrich von Kleist's "Engagement in St. Domingo." As in the image of the black French soldier on the Rhine following World War I, the image of blackness becomes one with that of sexual aggression. All of these mythic aspects of the image of the black are associated by analogy with the image of the Jew. Jewish writers such as Erik Erikson, no matter how tenuous their identity as "Jewish," felt threatened once Jewishness was associated with a "disruption" of the social system (a rupture that they perceived as the fulfillment of the Enlightenment's promise of civil equality). Their anxiety occasioned by the rise of political anti-Semitism made them need to distinguish between their own self-image (based upon the idealized self-image of the "good" German) and the image of the "bad" Jew. To locate the "bad" Jew meant to place their anxiety in a world isolated from the self. Thus the association of "black" and "Jew" which grew out of the revolutionary images of change present in nineteenth-century Europe came to define "Jewishness" in the United States after World War II.

The association of the images of "blackness" and "Jewishness" is a test case for the interrelationship of images of difference. The black and the Jew were associated not merely because they were both "outsiders" but because qualities ascribed to one became the means of defining the difference of the other. The categories of "black" and "Jew" thus became interchangeable at one point in history. The line between the two groups vanished, and each became the definition of the other. The ultimate source of this identification was the need to externalize the anxiety generated by change in European (read Christian) middle-class society, a society under extraordinary tension during the course of the nineteenth century. The black no longer satisfactorily bore projections of anxiety. Too distanced, too controlled by the power of colonial empire, the black became part of the European world of myth. The Jew, however, daily present in society and demanding access into a bourgeois life seemingly so stable and well defined in terms of its Christian identity, was perceived as the radical par excellence. And the Jew was thus seen as one with the image of the black present in the fantasy world of European myth. This constant admixture of myth and unconscious deformation of reality is the basis for stereotyping.

PART I

STEREOTYPES
OF SEXUALITY

DESPITE ALL OF the biological constants of human sexuality, the image of it shifts from age to age, from location to location. The four essays that follow examine texts from late nineteenth- and early twentieth-century Europe. Other texts from other places could be used to examine the issues they raise, specifically the role of "seeing" the Other as a sexualized being and the association of this image with illness. What is fascinating to me about the set of images in the texts I have chosen is that they link certain focal points of anxiety. The black, the proletarian, the child, the woman, the avant-garde are all associated in a web of analogies. All of the images relate to some reality (there was child prostitution, Nietzsche did exist, Europeans did explore black Africa), but cultural fantasies are spun about each mimetic kernel. And in all of these fantasies human sexuality plays a large part.

The role of sexuality in shaping these fantasies (and being much of their substance) is not merely an artifact of the nineteenth and early twentieth centuries. Human sexuality is a wellspring for much of our fantasy life. What is important is that the systems of representation during this period made these references to human sexuality overt. It is not a question of "interpreting in" the role of human sexuality. In all of the stereotypes we shall examine, the sexual component is evident. In the nineteenth century (that age of supposed prudery) human sexuality became a topic of cultured discourse within both the culture of science and that of the arts. While earlier parallel stereotypes, such as images of the Other in the Enlightenment, make some reference to the fantasies of sexuality, it is only in the nineteenth century that the sexual becomes a central structuring feature of systems that relate difference to pathology. Thus the syphilophobia of the nineteenth century is an artifact of the influential authors' belief that sexually transmitted diseases were on the increase, but also of nineteenth-century European society's brooding anxiety about declining sexual power.

Illness and difference are linked when the nineteenth-century European looks at the Other. The distancing force of this association localizes the anxiety of the European concerning his (we can speak of the European voice of the nineteenth century as male) control over the world. This loosely localized anxiety becomes focused when Sigmund Freud confronts his fantasies of seduction or a judge adjudicates a sentence for a murderer. Each defines the source of his anxiety by reference to specific aspects of the world, lying outside of himself. And all of those associations to the internalized world of human sexuality are now projected onto the sexuality of the Other.

Male Stereotypes of Female Sexuality in Fin-de-Siècle Vienna

The Puzzle

WE BEGIN with a conundrum set by a master puzzle solver. Steven Marcus, in a lucid discussion of Freud's *Three Essays on the Theory of Sexuality* (1905), poses this riddle:

One can add as a piece of crowning confusion the following leap in the dark from the second essay. In his discussion of the polymorphous perverse sexuality of children Freud pauses for an illustration: "In this respect children behave in the same kind of way as an average uncultivated woman in whom the same polymorphous perverse disposition persists. Under ordinary conditions she may remain normal sexually, but if she is led on by a clever seducer she will find every sort of perversion to her taste, and will retain them as part of her own sexual activities. Prostitutes exploit the same polymorphous, that is, infantile, disposition for the purposes of their profession; and considering the immense number of women who are prostitutes or who must be supposed to have an aptitude for prostitution without becoming engaged in it, it becomes impossible not to recognize that this same disposition to perversions of every kind is a general and fundamental human characteristic." One doesn't know where to look for a handle to these remarks. It is even difficult to frame a context that might make discussion of them pertinent. Perhaps we can do no better than repeat the waggish observation that it is very difficult to know the meaning of a statement about Freud being right or wrong since he is always both.[1]

Explaining the linkage of childhood sexuality, polymorphous perversity, and prostitution in Freud's puzzling illustration requires "framing the context" in which the stereotypes of female sexuality were generated in fin-de-siècle Vienna. An understanding of the various models of female sexuality that existed side by side at the turn of the century can supply the missing interrelationship among the diverse elements in this riddle. As Marcus suggests, Freud's views are neither "right" nor "wrong," but rather reflect an amalgam of the inconsistencies and contradictions surrounding the idea of female sexuality in 1905. To pinpoint the tensions that shaped this amalgam in Vienna as well as the tensions in Freud's own life which moved him to employ it can serve a heuristic function.[2]

On the borderland between the stereotypes of childhood sexuality, proletarian sexuality, and the prostitute is the image of the child prostitute. Here the child serves as the sexual object, with all of the mystique surrounding adult sexuality, childhood, and approachability preserved. It is to this image that we can turn to begin our unraveling of Marcus's puzzle.

The Medico-Legal Background

The view that sexuality exists in early childhood permeates the medical literature of the late eighteenth century and throughout the nineteenth century, at least in the extensive literature dealing with masturbation and its results.[3] Masturbation came to be viewed as the most important problem in medical science, since it was regarded as the cause of physical collapse and, as Voltaire observed, premature death.[4] The medical literature on female masturbation, such as D. M. Rozier's monograph on the "secret habits of the woman," first published in 1825, stressed the permanent damage to the development of the psyche as well as to the organism.[5] Masturbation was viewed as a deviant sexual practice leading to other pathologies, including sexual ones.

By the 1880s the identification of masturbation as the major etiology of mental as well as physical illness had all but vanished from the medical literature. Richard von Krafft-Ebing, in his *Psychopathia sexualis* (1888), viewed the entire problem of childhood masturbation as peripheral.[6] He was able to summarize the half-dozen cases taken from contemporary sources quite cursorily. In only two was it claimed that masturbation resulted in further sexual activity. One described an eight-year-old girl "who consorted with boys of the age of ten or twelve" after a history of masturbation, and the other a girl who from the age of seven "practised lewdness with boys." Hermann Rohleder refers to the latter case in his *Lectures on the Sexual Drive* (1901), condemning the activities of this "horror of a child."[7] In a lecture held before the Viennese Psychiatric and Neurological Association in 1902 Alfred Fuchs described two cases of sexuality in children. The first was a case of masturbation in a twenty-month-old boy, the second a case of mutual masturbation which led to further sexual activity in a two-year-old girl.[8] In all of these cases the sexual activity of the child in the form of masturbation is viewed as pathological. However, it is only in the case of the female children that further sexual activity is perceived as a pathological result of early childhood masturbatory practices. Indeed Krafft-Ebing's report of the eight-year old girl who "consorted with boys of the age of ten or twelve" condemns the girl as "devoid of all child-like and moral feelings" without any comment on the sexuality of her youthful partners.

The labeling of sexual activity, whether masturbatory, heterosexual, or homosexual, as pathological when found in children reflects the stereotype of the "pure child" present in Romantic thought.[9] The early nineteenth century saw the child as almost noncorporeal, the polar opposite to the pathological sensuality of the masturbator. Jakob Christoph Santlus, in his *Psychology of the Human Drives* (1864), stressed the structure of acquisition of sexuality in the normal course of maturation. He drew a sharp distinction, too, between the development of female sexuality and that of male sexuality. The normal female was supposed to acquire sexual awareness only at the moment of menarche: "How many girls are not horrified when they begin to menstruate and with the menses the first sexual sensations are felt?"[10] In the female all sexuality existing before puberty was perceived as pathological; in the male, only masturbatory sexuality.

While the medical literature of the time either condemned or ignored early sexual activity in females, the public health texts of the nineteenth century could not treat this question quite as simply. In Viennese daily life the existence of child prostitutes could not be ignored. While references to the existence of at least two hundred regular prostitutes under the age of twelve in Liverpool during 1857 are without parallel for Vienna, available statistics concerning registered prostitutes in the last third of the nineteenth century tell a surprising story.[11] During the first decade of registration, from 1873 to 1883, the majority of registered prostitutes in Vienna were legally minors.[12] The minimum age for registration during this decade was fourteen, which meant that more than 50 percent of the approximately fifteen hundred registered prostitutes were between the ages of fourteen and twenty-one. Indeed in the first year of registration (1873) fourteen fifteen-year-old prostitutes were registered and in the following year an additional three fourteen-year-olds and four fifteen-year-olds. This evidence, and evidence for other European cities (Edinburgh, for example, where large numbers of underaged prostitutes were recorded in the same decade),[13] suggests that a trade in child prostitution may have existed in Vienna, Great Britain, and elsewhere in Europe during the mid- to latter nineteenth century.

By the first decade of the new century, Viennese laws concerning the registration of prostitutes were tightened. In the regulations dated 1 June 1911, the minimum age for registration rose to eighteen—with a caveat, however: "Minors may be assigned to supervision . . . only when complete moral indifference, without any hope of betterment, had been unmistakably ascertained."[14] In other words, the law covered all minors, even those below the legal age of registration if their actions revealed a total and innate lack of the dominant society's moral standards (a description that would have been applied to any child prostitute, of course). The nominal minimum registration age merely emphasizes the gap between the arbitrary legal definition of the child and the realities of daily life in Vienna.

Friedrich Hügel's programmatic public health study of 1865, which proposed the establishment of registration for prostitutes and the opening of licensed brothels, is further evidence that child prostitution flourished in mid-nineteenth-century Vienna. One of Hügel's central aims was the elimination of child prostitution. He wished to exclude all girls under the age of *sixteen* from his proposed houses of prostitution.[15] (In fact, when registration was introduced as a result of the 1873 Viennese World's Fair, only prostitutes younger than fourteen were excluded.) Hügel's work offers a twenty-point catalogue of the sources of prostitution.[16] This list bears examination since it reflects the dominant male Viennese view of the nature of the prostitute and the causes for her deviant behavior. It begins with the "bad education of girls in general, but especially those from the lowest classes." Girls are exposed to the "immoral speech and acts" of their parents and of the ubiquitous boarders, whose presence in most lower-class homes was an economic necessity. The home is thus the breeding ground for future prostitutes. The poverty of the home is what makes the luxurious life of the prostitute attractive. It is also in the home that the initial sexual experience is had.

Parents' seduction of children is common: "Fathers and daughters living together in concubinage; —fathers living off the ill-gotten gains of the daughters . . ." Hügel draws a parallel between the poverty, unemployment, and low wages of female workers and the biological and psychological weaknesses of the female. The lower-class, poorly educated female is by nature physically weaker and more given to "coquetry, love of pleasure, dislike of work, desire for luxury and ostentation, love of ornament, alcoholism, avarice, immorality, etc." than women of the middle and upper classes.

William Acton, in his idiosyncratic mid-Victorian study of British prostitution (1857), had prefigured Hügel's categories, seeing prostitution as being "derived from the vice of women": "Natural desire. Natural sinfulness. The preferment of indolent ease to labour. Vicious inclination strengthened and ingrained by early neglect, or evil training, bad associates, and an indecent mode of life. Necessity, imbued by the inability to obtain a living by honest means consequent on a fall from virtue. Extreme poverty. To the black list may be added love of drink, love of dress, love of amusement."[17] While Acton sees the economic pattern of nineteenth-century society as a catalyst in the creation of prostitution, he also sees the potential for prostitution as inherent in the lower-class female.

The belief that lower-class females tended by nature to enter the life of the prostitute is reflected in the image of the female as the active seductress. Acton sees the woman as the temptress and the laws punishing her putative seducer as laws that are meant to "strengthen, by the very firm abutment of the breeches-pocket, both him and his good resolutions against the temptations and force of designing women."[18] If taken seriously enough, this image of the female as sexual predator, which permeated late nineteenth-century thought,[19] would provide the ultimate rationale for considering the prepubescent female as the cause of her own seduction. Her sexuality, in such a view, is pathological and externally directed.

The ambiguous view of childhood sexual activity found in the public health literature of the nineteenth century has a remarkable parallel in late nineteenth-century Austrian law. Paragraph 127 of the *Austrian Criminal Code* makes it a crime to have sexual relations with anyone under the age of fourteen (*Nothzucht*).[20] This seems clear and absolute, corresponding as it does to the minimum age for the registration of prostitutes and the presumed age of menarche.[21] (Fourteen was also the age of consent in Austria—the lowest age of consent on the continent in the nineteenth century. As puberty and the age of consent were held to be coterminous in both Roman and Canon law, one can assume an implied legal equivalency in Austrian law.) But paragraph 128 concerning cases of sexual abuse other than penetration with children under the age of fourteen was the subject of a court decision that modified its interpretation, as well as that of the preceding paragraph. The Highest Court (*Oberster Gerichts- und Cassationshof*) held on 3 February 1858 that in order to prove a case of indecent assault it was necessary to prove that "the minor with whom the immoral act was performed had been the passive participant." This ruling seems to recognize the potential of the minor as the seductress. The law reflected at least some of the stereotypical perceptions of the female child held by medicine during the fin de siècle. Both medicine and law assumed a potential sexual pathology in the female which could manifest itself even in the child. To no little degree this view was shaped by the reality of childhood prostitution, which linked the idea of seduction (and the attendant fear of syphilitic infection) with the image of the lower-class prostitute. The dangers inherent in the child prostitute, the demonic antithesis of the image of prepubescent purity, heightened and focused the anxiety present in Viennese society concerning sexuality in general and its association with pathology in particular.

The Pornographic View

In 1906, shortly after Sigmund Freud published his *Three Essays on Sexuality,* a work appeared in Vienna which has established itself as the classic work of pornography in German. Written anonymously, but certainly by a man,[22] *Josefine Mutzenbacher, or the History of a Viennese Whore as Told by Herself* has a mock autobiographic structure typical of the numerous fictional accounts of the lives of prostitutes beginning at least as early as *Moll Flanders* (or perhaps as far back as Fernando de Rojas's *The Spanish Bawd*). In eighteenth-century Vienna a series of pornographic novels, written in the same autobiographic mode, purported to chronicle the lives of the lower-class serving girl in Vienna.[23] In these reverse *Pamela*s the seduction of the serving girl prepares her for a rich (and varied) life as a prostitute. Unlike *Josefine Mutzenbacher,* however, all of these works deal with female characters above the legal age of consent. The later work presents itself as the sexual history of a female child between the ages of five and fourteen. Indeed the novel closes at the very age and the very moment when Josefine enters into the life of a registered prostitute in Vienna. The uniqueness of the age and adventures of the most successful pornographic heroine in German letters can be judged in part by the sequels to the novel. Published during the 1930s and evidently not by the author of the 1906 novel, *My 365 Lovers* as well as *My Daughter Peperl* dealt with heroines at least at the age of consent.[24] The latter work, chronicling the pornographic adventures of Josefine's daughter, consciously rejects the pattern established by the earlier novel and begins with a pubescent protagonist. Also noteworthy is the fact that the average age at first marriage of females in Austria during the fin de siècle was the mid-twenties (from 26.3 in 1871 to 25.3 in 1910).[25] Indeed a contemporary writing on the question in 1904 sees the "natural" age for marriage for the female as twenty.[26] The youth of the protagonist in *Josefine Mutzenbacher* must, in the circumstances, have functioned as an important distancing factor.

Josefine Mutzenbacher is set in the world of the Viennese proletariat, a world that, according to a contemporary, supplied the majority of Vienna's criminals and prostitutes.[27] The tiny apartment of the family Mutzenbacher is crowded with the five-member family (the parents, Josefine, and Josefine's two male siblings) and a boarder. Like all pornographic works, the novel is a series of sexual scenes, beginning with five-year-old Josefine's "seduction" by a boarder. The seducer, part of the extended family, plays the role of a voyeur, observing but not touching the child. At first, the five-year-old "wanted to scream, but he said to her, 'Be good. I won't do anything.'"[28] Years later Josefine observes that she "[had] not [understood] any of this and as is a child's wont, I did not think about it. Today I know what it means, and I refer to the carpenter's apprentice as my first lover" (10). Fear of sexuality and the repression of that fear through feigned ignorance are implied by Josefine's dismissal of her own sexual curiosity.

If the carpenter's seduction nourishes the psychological seed of polymorphous sexuality present in the child, the second episode of the work brings her sexuality to full flower. At the age of seven she is introduced into the world of heterosexuality by a brother and sister, thirteen and nine years old respectively, who have been engaging in incestuous coupling. She observes the sexual acts of the two "with a feeling, composed of curiosity, amazement, horror, and yet an up-to-now strange excitement" (12). The world of Josefine's playmates is that of poverty. Their home has been shattered by the death of their mother and the absence of the father. The nine-year-old girl seduces Josefine's brother, who is approximately the same age. Yet their sexuality is that of adults, concluding with mutual orgasm. The child has become the adult *in nuce*.

According to Josefine's account it is at the age of seven, confronted with the sexuality of her peers, that she became aware of her own sexuality: "Since that day I have seen children and adults, men and women through other eyes. I was only seven years old, but my sexuality was fully present. It could be read in my eyes. My face, my mouth, my gait must have been a single invitation to grab me and lay me down. . . . [The] effect which emanated from me . . . made strange and, it seemed to me, prudent men after meeting me, lose all sense of prudence and risk everything without a second thought" (17). This is the voice of the woman as temptress at the age of seven. Within the opening pages of the novel, the newly discovered sexuality of the child seduces other members of her extended family, her brother and her cousins. But the author stresses Josefine's physical immaturity, her inability to engage in genital sexual contact, and opposes it to her demand for sexual stimulation. The sexual acts in which Josefine engages with her brother and cousins run the gamut of nongenital sexual variations. The polymorphous quality of Josefine's sexual interest is evident when she attempts to blackmail Horak, the beer deliveryman, into having genital sex with her. When this proves to be impossible, her desire for the sexual act encourages the adult to introduce her into anal sexuality. Within the first forty pages of the novel Josefine has various sexual misadventures with three adults, including an anonymous soldier, as well as two other children: Robert, who had earlier been seduced by his stepmother, and a nameless seven-year-old who pounces upon her in a field. Sexuality permeates Josefine's world. Her sibling, her neighbors, even the strangers on the street see her as a sexual object. All of this precoital sexuality leads to Josefine's seduction by the new boarder, Herr Ekhard. The question arises as to who is seducing whom:

When we were alone again, I became very excited, because it occurred to me that we could do everything without being disturbed. I went into the kitchen to Herr Ekhard—that was his name—let him stroke my hair again and I ran my hands through his beard, which excited me even more. And again it must have been something in my glance, something which robbed him of his rationality. He pressed his hand on my dress, at exactly the critical point. I stood in front of him, he sat on a chair, and he pressed his hand against me. If I did not know what was happening nothing would have occurred to me. But I smiled at him and my smile must have said everything. (37)

Josefine's seduction by the boarder is clearly not one of a passive, asexual being. By the end of the first half of the novel Josefine, still under ten, is completely sexual. Her mother, having herself been seduced by Herr Ekhard, summarizes the author's apparent view of the sexual potential of the child: "Children are evil. . . . One cannot supervise them enough" (104). The proletarian child, the potential lower-class prostitute, is congenitally predisposed to engage in all varieties of adult sexuality.

The second half of the novel, beginning after the sudden death of Josefine's mother, moves outside the world of the family and that of the immediate neighborhood. Josefine is seduced by her priest and her catechist. The entire world seems to sense her sexual presence and be attracted by it. Indeed after her seduction by the catechist is revealed through the report of a naïve playmate, she is seduced by her own widowed father. The introduction of a new boarder, Rudolf, moves the incestuous relationship to a new plane. Rudolf has a liaison with a young girl, Zensi, whom he had seduced at the age of eight; and Rudolf and Zensi, encouraged by Josefine's unemployed father, initiate her into the world of the Viennese demimonde. It is thus only in the final third of the novel that the economic imperative is presented. While all the social evils of poverty are reflected in the earlier segments of the novel, from the abandonment of children by working parents to the immorality of boarders, it is the inherent sexual nature of the child which is central to the novel. While Josefine's polymorphous sexuality is triggered by her seduction at the age of five, she indulges in sexual acts out of the pleasure they bring her. She is delighted when she finds that she can be paid for what she enjoys. Her move into the world of the demimonde represents the culmination of the sexual experiences that begin within her family. Here the novel stops. As in other pseudoautobiographies of prostitutes, the protagonist achieves the pinnacle of her desires. She is able to live off of that aspect of her existence which gives her the most pleasure. Here the male fantasy of the lower-class prostitute and her accessibility on the fringes of the upper class is played out.

Josefine sees her childhood experiences, in retrospect, as paramount in shaping her successful life as a whore. She ends the novel with the observation that "my childhood memories, as colorful and exciting as they are, have remained in my memory and I have reported them. In the final instance they are childhood memories, even if they are sexual and not at all childlike. But they remain in all cases more deeply and permanently engraved in our memory than everything that we later experience" (272).

The image in *Josefine Mutzenbacher* of the sexual life of the child under the age of consent reflects many of the sexual stereotypes of the female present in fin-de-siècle Viennese thought. The sexuality of the child, at least that of the proletarian child, is presupposed. The tawdriness and horror of real child prostitution is missing, as is the debauchery of the seducer present in earlier images of the seduction of the innocent female.[29] For these female children are in no way perceived as innocent. In *Josefine Mutzenbacher,* as well as in Victorian English child pornography, the child is the active participant if not the initiator of the sexual act.[30] The accessibility of the child as sexual object is emphasized. But it is not any child. It is specifically, at least in the world of Vienna, the female proletarian child. The sexuality attributed to the proletarian is the sexuality of the Other. The distance between the perceived self and this Other is equivalent to the distance perceived between the races. In Jefferson's Virginia the Otherness of the black made the black female the sexual object par excellence; in Freud's Vienna the Otherness of the proletariat gave the lower-class female the same status.[31]

The Literary View

The image of the child as sexual object in the belles lettres of fin-de-siècle Vienna is somewhat more subtle and complex than that found in *Josefine Mutzenbacher,* but the basic structure is unmistakably similar. Among the creative writers of this period whose works were intended for the parlor rather than the smoking room was Peter Altenberg (1859–1919), and in his writings the figure of the prepubescent female assumes a central role. Even a cursory glance at Altenberg's first volume of sketches, *As I See It* (1896), shows a preoccupation with the child. The first sketch, "Nine and Eleven," begins:

> Margueritta stood close to him.
> She leaned up against him.
> She took his hand in her little hands and held it tightly.
> Sometimes she pressed it softly against her breast.
> And yet she was only eleven years old.[32]

The opening of this sketch is consciously ambiguous. Only in the fifth sentence is Margueritta revealed to be a child. The physical attractiveness evoked by the opening lines belongs not to the innocent but to the seductress. Altenberg contrasts two children in the sketch, the older child (Margueritta) outgoing and responsive, the younger withdrawn and quiet. The narrator finds himself seated between the two, staring out to sea. He reflects on the younger child, Rositta, "above whom fate was poised. . . . And yet she kissed him so softly and said: 'You, Herr Alberti . . .'" (5). For Altenberg the child contains the woman, with all her seductive powers.

In the sketch "Music" the male narrator listens to the completely unself-conscious piano playing of a twelve-year-old, which brings forth a hidden level of meaning to the piece:

"What are you playing?!" The man asked.
"Why do you ask?! That is my Albert-Étude, Bertini No. 18. When I play it I always think about you—"
"Why?!"
"I don't know; it is so pretty."

It is as if a child had suddenly become a woman (57). With that self-conscious declaration of her emotions, the child loses her innocence "and the soul [is] lost from the music." Here the innocence and spontaneity of the child are destroyed by a moment of conscious reflection lacking in the first sketch. There the flirtatiousness of the nine- and eleven-year-olds is undiscriminating. They practice their unself-conscious coquetry before every male, though always within socially acceptable bounds. In the sketch "Music" innocence is lost because of the specific interest of the child in "him," the narrator. But even here, as in all the sketches that Altenberg set among the Viennese petite bourgeoisie, the role of the child as sexual object is suppressed. While the child, either actively or passively, assumes the role of innocent seductress in relationship to the narrator, there is no blatantly sexual moment, at least until the author's imagination leaves the confines of the Ringstrasse. In the epiphany entitled "The Greek," Altenberg provides a new persona for the narrator, who is now the title character. The sketch is set in a park in Greece, where the narrator observes "a white batiste dress flying by. —Ash-blond, long, loose, silken hair. Slender delicate legs in black stockings. She is thirteen years old. One sees above the knee white underpants. She flies across the path with her hoop" (119). The narrator's reaction to the sight of this child, whose description is that of a Viennese schoolgirl, is sexual. He ruminates: "Oh, you, nude, completely nude, on a perfumed, velvet field in the evening shadows, pushing your hoop and flying—flying! And then you stand there and throw in a rounded movement your blond hair backwards and we drink with our eyes, with the artist-soul's organ of love, your slender white body—in the love of beauty!" (119). Like Aschenbach's fantasy about the androgynous fourteen-year-old boy observed on the Lido in Thomas Mann's "Death in Venice" (1912), the child, in its very movement, is perceived as a sexual object.[33] The playful chasing after the hoop transforms this child into the mythological Diana of the hunt, with all of the sexual implications of that equation, just as Tadzio is associated with Hyacinthus. Altenberg, like Mann, must seek his idealized child in the south, since the stereotypical children of northern and central Europe are not to his purpose. Mann's ironic use of the Polish child in a Venetian setting underlines his awareness of this fact. Altenberg simply transplants his fantasy from Vienna to Greece. His Greek narrator is indistinguishable from his other narrators, and his child-figure is identical to the other girl-children in her appearance and in her unconscious incarnations of beauty (the dance with the hoop). But in Altenberg's Greece, as in Aschenbach's Venice, the exoticism of place, like the exoticism of class in *Josefine Mutzenbacher,* enables the character to articulate, in sexual metaphors, the narrator's vision of the child as sexual object. Altenberg's stereotypical image of the child as inherently pure but with clearly sexual overtones was evident to his more radicalized contemporaries. Ria Claassen, in her pamphlet "The Female Phantom of the Male" (1898), condemns Altenberg, among others, for having created the "phantom of the woman as virgin-mother, as a saint, as the intercessor with a transcendental principle."[34] As is evident, this stereotype simply provided another distancing technique with which the male could rationalize his attraction to the seemingly unthreatening sexuality of the female child.

In a different genre Felix Salten (1869–1947) imagined many of the same characteristics in the prepubescent female.[35] In 1911 Salten published a commentary to a volume of photographs taken by Emil Mayer at the Prater, Vienna's public amusement park. These candid photographs included a series of four entitled "Young Love" in which Mayer captured two young girls flirting their way through the park. Salten commented: "Yes, this little group also belongs here. Children . . . but there will be strict individuals who will shake their heads at this scene and say 'There aren't any children any more!' And yet they are children, evidently completely innocent children who do not know that this 'eyeplay' [*Augenspiel*] is called coquetry, that their laughter, winking, gossiping, their little graceful, as well as affected mode of presentation is the prelude to the comedy of love, toward which they are maturing."[36] For Salten, as for the general Viennese public, the coquetry, the sexual play-fulness of the female child, is the sign of her innate nature. Indeed in an article some three decades earlier an anonymous reporter in the Viennese *Illustrated Extra* condemned the casting of a twelve-year-old as an adul-teress in a Prater penny theater. "Even more appalling than the child-actress mimicking adult immorality, was her audience . . . an audience of peers, children titillated by a child imitating adult sexual misdeeds."[37] Salten in 1911, writing for a more sophisticated audience, does not sound the condemnatory note found in the earlier newspaper article, but the message remains the same. Adult sexuality is omnipresent in uncon-scious form in children: "Here [in the Prater] young beauties celebrate their first successes. Developing coquettes experience their first tri-umphs. Future fickle hearts commit their first betrayals. . . . Here there is pain, disappointment and in all the childish lack of experience, bitter experiences. Twelve-year-old girls sigh, 'I will never believe a man again.' Fourteen-year-old boys shout ironically: 'Stop already with women.' When they sit at home in the evening, childish sleepiness in their eyes, all is forgotten. And when their parents ask them, 'Where were you?' they answer innocently and simply: 'Out walking . . .'" (115).

For Altenberg and Salten the mask of the naïve child is precisely what fascinates and excites the adult. For Arthur Schnitzler (1862–1901) the image of the seductive child is embedded in a more highly colored con-text, revealing a subtle reworking of this theme.[38] In his long novella "Casanova's Return Home" (1918) the seduction of the child plays an interesting, if marginal, role. Schnitzler uses the historical character of Casanova in a totally fictional re-creation of the aged roué's attempt to return to the city of his birth, Venice, from which he had been earlier banned for his political associations. The fifty-three-year-old and pen-niless Casanova arrives on the outskirts of Venice disguised as the noble Chevalier de Seingalt. He is recognized by Olivio, whose marriage to Amalia Casanova had made possible on a whim some sixteen years before by contributing a dowry to the couple. Amalia had expressed her gratefulness to the young and handsome stranger by spending her wed-ding night with him. In the past sixteen years Olivio has managed to raise himself up into the fringe of the bourgeoisie, and his wife has borne him three daughters, the oldest of whom, Teresina, is thirteen at the time of Casanova's return to the scene. Olivio believes that his daughters, "thirteen, ten, and eight . . . [are] none of them old enough to have their heads—if I may be so bold—none of them old enough to have their heads turned by Casanova."[39] It is indeed none of the daughters who captures Casanova's fancy, but rather their cousin Marcolina, who appears to Casanova not much older than the oldest daughter. The story focuses on the fascination of the older man for the young girl. Olivio's wife Amalia sees in the aged and destitute Casanova the young, rich, and noble individual with whom she slept almost two decades earlier; Marcolina sees before her only a wreck of a man masquerading as a nobleman. When the aged Casanova is stymied in his attempt to seduce the child-woman Marcolina he turns to the oldest child, the thirteen-year-old Teresina. This episode is prefigured in the meeting of the children with Casanova in which "the oldest, Teresina, still appearing like a child, stared at the stranger with unconstrained, somewhat peasant-like curiosity" (252). Rather than kissing the children's proffered hands, he takes "each of the children around their heads and kisses each on both cheeks." This seemingly paternal act has, from Casanova's viewpoint, sexual overtones. Toward the conclusion of the novella Teresina is sent to fetch Casanova for a dinner party of the local noteworthies. Her absence is noted by the assembled group, who begin to joke to her discomfited father about her presence in Casanova's chambers. In the chambers a seduction occurs:

Olivio's oldest little daughter, the thirteen-year-old, entered [his chambers] and announced that the entire party was assembled and awaiting the Chevalier to begin their gambling. Her eyes glowed strangely, her cheeks blushed, her woman-like, thick tresses played blue-black about her temples, her childish mouth was agape. "Have you drunk some wine, Teresina?" Casanova asked and took a long step toward her. "Indeed—and the Chevalier saw that at once?" She grew even redder and as if in embarrassment she licked her lower lip with her tongue. Casanova grabbed her by the shoulders, breathed into her face, pulled her to him and threw her on the bed. She looked at him with large, helpless eyes, from which the glow had vanished. But when she opened her mouth as if to scream, Casanova threw her such a threatening glance that she almost froze and permitted him to do anything he pleased with her. He kissed her tenderly yet wildly and whispered: "You must not tell the priest, Teresina, not even in the confessional. When you have a lover or fiancé or even a husband, no one needs to know about this. You should always lie, you should lie to your father and mother and sisters, so that you shall do well here on earth. Note this." —Thus he blasphemed and Teresina must have held this for a blessing which he spoke over her for she took his hand and piously kissed it like that of a priest. He laughed loudly. "Come," he said, "My little woman, we shall appear in the salon arm-in-arm." She became a bit affected, but smiled not at all unpleased. (323)

The reader perceives Casanova's act in an unflattering light, as that of an aging roué, committed at a moment of self-doubt about his attractiveness, which violates his host's hospitality. Yet Casanova's image of the child Teresina alters the implications of this passage. She is a child-woman from a lower class (at least a class lower than that of the invented Chevalier de Seingalt) who is captivated by the myth of Casanova the lover without being completely prepared for the physical reality implied by that myth. In Casanova's eyes she initially appears the coquette, standing on the edge of maturity. She has womanlike hair but a childish mouth. Her physiognomy is that of the child-woman. While Casanova's act must be condemned, since in Schnitzler's Vienna no sexual intercourse, even by mutual consent, was legally permitted under the age of fourteen, the implicit rationale for Casanova's act lies within the nature of the child seduced. Teresina is the seductive country girl, Schnitzler's sweet girl, his woman of the suburban Viennese demimonde, at the moment of defloration. Her sexual precocity, at least as perceived by Casanova, is the extenuating factor in this seduction, and this precocity is to no little degree the result of her belonging to another class. Here Schnitzler's irony can be felt. For of course the Chevalier de Seingalt does not exist. It is a title assumed by Casanova, as he states, to show his innate nobility. Indeed it is the fecundity of the rising bourgeoisie, typified by Olivio and his family, against which the stagnant world of Venetian noble intrigue is contrasted. Casanova perceives Teresina as beneath him in class. Gordon Allport has noted that "liaisons with members of lower classes seem particularly attractive to people with higher status. The daughter of the patrician family who runs away with the coachman is almost as familiar a theme in literature as the prodigal son who wastes his substance in riotous living with lower-class women. Both reveal the same truth."[40] The truth is the implied sexual libertinage of the Other. In "Casanova's Return Home," the Other is both of a lower class and a child.

If the writers of fin-de-siècle Vienna are to be believed, the female child's most vital essence is a seductive woman she conceals within herself. The prepubescent figure of Lucile in the tale "Lucidor" (1910) by Hugo von Hofmannsthal (1847–1929), which served as the basis for Richard Strauss's opera *Arabella*, pointedly illustrates this.[41] Lucile's sexuality breaks through the barriers of both her youth and her disguise as a young boy to seduce her sister's lover. As in *Josefine Mutzenbacher,* "Death in Venice," and "Casanova's Return Home," Hofmannsthal's heroine is an attractive exotic—a Polish (albeit noble) child in imperial Vienna; and again it is the seducer who is seduced, at least as perceived by the middle-class male authors and their characters.

Return to the Puzzle

Having now "framed the context" for Freud's statement concerning infantile polymorphous perversity in terms of the fin-de-siècle Viennese understanding of the female child, we can usefully recapitulate Freud's argument. The seduction of the child leads to polymorphous perverse activity in the form of "sexual irregularities" because an "aptitude for them is innately present in [the child's] disposition." Although the child is inherently sexual, in both the narrow and the broad use of the term, because of the immaturity of this sexuality the child has not yet created "mental dams" against "sexual excesses." Freud's labels for these structures, which typify the bourgeois attitude toward sexuality, are "shame, disgust and morality." They are the precise antitheses of the qualities of the stereotyped female child. She is totally without a sense of the implications of her acts, and thus beyond proscriptive morality. Thus the child is like the adult female, whom she has concealed within her. Here Freud's association of child and adult sexuality is exposed as faulty. For it is within *all* children that the potential for polymorphous perversity is hidden. Freud has simply extended the stereotype of the female child to all children and is thus able to move from this implied equation to the adult female with ease. While in every female the act of seduction may bring forth the disguised tendency toward perversion, it is most evident in the "average uncultivated female" of the proletariat. She has not developed a strong identification with the moral system of the dominant economic and social class and can thus be seduced into a life of perversity. Her seduction releases her polymorphous nature and she becomes like the prostitute, for most women "have an aptitude for prostitution." The prostitute is therefore the natural extension of the female child.

Freud's view concerning the prostitute did not coincide with public opinion of the latter nineteenth century, which isolated and distanced the prostitute by categorizing her as a congenital degenerate. That view is well represented in Cesare Lombroso's classic study *The Delinquent Female: The Prostitute and the Normal Woman* (1893).[42] Christian Ströhm-berg, Lombroso's most vociferous German supporter, stated it quite baldly: "[The prostitute] fills her ranks from the degenerate females, who are clearly differentiated from the normal woman. Their abnormal predisposition can be seen in the gradations from occasional prostitution to moral insanity."[43] The prostitute's future is predetermined both physically and psychologically from the moment of conception. Freud, by contrast, intimates that all women possess as a tendency the characteristics that prostitutes live out.

It is in a quintessentially Viennese work of the fin de siècle that one answer to Lombroso can be found. Otto Weininger's *Sex and Character* (1903), which appeared while Freud was formulating his views on female sexuality, abandoned the older Romantic antithesis between the "virgin" and the "whore" which underlies Lombroso's theory.[44] Weininger's work is a mad diatribe against the specters of the woman and the Jew which haunted his imagination. But this work of pseudoscience had an overwhelming shaping influence on the Viennese view of woman's biological nature. "I have come to regard the prostitute element as a possibility in all women just as much as the merely animal capacity for motherhood,"[45] Weininger wrote. "We do not have to face the general occurrence of women as one or the other of two distinct inborn types, the maternal and the prostitute. The reality is found between the two" (217). Prostitution is not the result of seduction per se or of social conditions, for "where there is no inclination for a certain course, the course will not be adopted" (217). Weininger also comments on the etiology of this inclination: "Schopenhauer said that a man's existence dates from the moment when his father and mother fell in love. That is not true. The birth of a human being, ideally considered, dates from the moment when the mother first saw or heard the voice of the father of the child" (217). The female has the potential for the degenerate life of the prostitute from before the moment of conception.

Freud's enigmatic statement is consistent, then, with one important strain of Viennese beliefs about the sexuality of the female child, the female proletarian, and the prostitute, even if it also shows continuity with his own earlier understanding of the role of seduction in the etiology of hysteria and the general problem of the incestuous overtones present in hysterical patients. And this assimilation of late nineteenth-century views of the woman into Freud's theory of infantile sexuality (or at least into the language in which the theory is couched) is revealing in

more than one way. The stereotyped seductive child in turn-of-the-
century Vienna was exactly of the age of sexual latency in which overt
sexuality is missing. The male authors' need for the most reflective mirror possible for their projections is evident. In latency neither the unin-
hibited sexuality of the infant nor the emerging sexuality of puberty
conflicts with the projected sexual interests of the adult male.

There is more than a suggestion of the same mirroring effect in a letter
of Freud to Wilhelm Fliess on 31 May 1897, written around the time that
Freud was formulating his theory about infantile sexuality. In the letter
he recounted a dream concerning his ten-year-old daughter Mathilde:

Recently I dreamed of [having] overaffectionate feelings for Mathilde, only she
was called Hella; and afterward I again saw "Hella" before me, printed in heavy
type. Solution: Hella is the name of an American niece whose picture we have
been sent. Mathilde could be called Hella because she recently shed bitter tears
over the defeats of the Greeks. She is enthralled by the mythology of ancient
Hellas and naturally regards all Hellenes as heroes. The dream of course shows
the fulfillment of my wish to catch a *Pater* as the originator of neurosis and
[the dream] puts an end to my ever-recurring doubts.[46]

These "overaffectionate feelings" which Freud attributes to his desire to
make the father the seducer in his theory of neurosis are clearly sexual in
nature. He conflates his daughter with his teenaged niece, relating the
asexual to the sexual, and rationalizing this relationship in the intensity of
Mathilde's asexual feelings. Does Freud's intense desire to find seductiveness in the child reflect his wish to escape recognizing the seducer in
himself? Indeed the reality of the adult male's sexual interest in the prepubescent female is the basis for a trauma theory that Freud initially
acknowledged but then replaced with an antithetical structure connected
with infantile sexuality, the oedipal triangle.[47] The two theories exist
simultaneously, both as reflections of the male perception of female sexuality. Freud's rejection of the symmetry between male and female sexuality has its evident locus in the sexual projections of the adult male. This
in itself does not vitiate the validity of Freud's formulation of infantile
sexuality, but it does alter our understanding of the reason for its "discovery." That is seen to be the adult male's need to establish the innocence of the male seducer. One can relate the operative structure of
projection to the general anxiety concerning *female* sexuality as the origin
of *male* disease, but on a more private level this may well relate to the

"seduction" of the child Sigismund Freud by his lower-class nanny. The residue of this image of the woman as seductress present in *The Interpretation of Dreams* (1900) reflects the sexualized image of the servant.[48] Freud has simply reversed the ages of the participants as well as their roles—the adult male is seduced by the young servant girl. The awareness of such fantasies of seduction is coupled with an awareness of the crude reality of the child prostitutes who haunted the Viennese streets. No credence can be given to any view, such as that of Jeffrey Masson, which attempts to isolate reality from fantasy.[49] Freud himself never denied the possibility of actual seduction. What he stressed was the ubiquitousness of fantasies of seduction. These fantasies are present whether or not an actual seduction takes place. Freud's assimilation of the stereotypes of female sexuality of fin-de-siècle Vienna provided a vocabulary in which to clothe his personal anxieties and fantasies.

The other aspects of the sexual attractiveness of the Other, her exoticism and concomitant availability, are also amalgamated by Freud into his understanding of the Viennese middle-class female's self-image. In a note to Fliess, he commented that female sexual neurosis derives largely from the presence of the serving girl in the middle-class family:

An immense load of guilt, with self-reproaches (for theft, abortion), is made possible by identification with these people of low morals who are so often remembered, in a sexual connection with father or brother, as worthless female material. And, as a result of the sublimation of these girls in fantasies, most improbable charges against other people are contained in the fantasies. Fear of prostitution (fear of being in the street alone), fear of a man hidden under the bed, and so on, also point in the direction of the servant girl. There is tragic justice in the circumstance that the family head's stooping to a maidservant is atoned for by his daughter's self-abasement.[50]

Freud traces female hysteria to the serving girl's seduction of the adult male. He sees unacceptable sexual contact existing across class lines, since the middle-class female accepts this sexual arrangement, which provides for a seductress as her source of self-castigation. The source of this image is the adult male's projection of his own guilt as a potential seducer of those within his extended family (here the stress is on the serving *girl*). This is parallel to the anxiety stirred by his desire to seduce his daughter. Class and family connect to provide the model for the male's projection.

The relationship between male projections of female sexuality and realities of female sexuality is, at best, tenuous. It is, however, of importance in understanding the dominant fantasies concerning the female. The seductive child and the degenerate lower-class female are both figments of the masculine imagination in turn-of-the-century Vienna, yet because they were articulated through works of art they became central metaphors for sexuality in Viennese society. They thus became the sexual fantasies, or nightmares, of an entire society.

2

The Nietzsche Murder Case; or, What Makes Dangerous Philosophies Dangerous

Who Is Nietzsche?

EVERYONE KNOWS Nietzsche. He's the crazy man whose works, if you read them, may drive you crazy. Dr. Goll, Lulu's lover in Frank Wedekind's fin-de-siècle dramas of sexual pathology, *Earth-Spirit* (1895) and *Pandora's Box* (1904), had this Nietzsche in mind when he confused him with the Dalai Lama (Wedekind's ironic title for that master of pseudo-Eastern philosophy, Arthur Schopenhauer):

> *Goll:* I've quite forgotten what your ballet is called?
> *Alwa:* Dalai Lama.
> *Goll:* I thought he was in a lunatic asylum.
> *Schön:* You're thinking of Nietzsche, Doctor.
> *Goll:* You're right. I always confuse the two.[1]

For some time after Nietzsche became known, he was widely seen as the quintessential outsider, the madman whose insanity is infectious. This moment in the history of Nietzsche's reputation is well documented, at least within the catalogue of his influence on the literary world.[2] Seeing a reputation only within such limited focus, however, removes the intricate web of implications summed up by the very concept of "reputation" from the historical context. It treats books as sentient entities, interacting in a world apart from human events. Recently, such social historians as Eugen Weber have asked heretical questions of texts, such as, Can any text (and in this context a reputation is indeed a text) be understood if that understanding is not rooted in some sense in a specific perception of the world?[3] and, Does the structural alteration of concepts have any relationship to social and political realities?[4] No idea is possible without specific reference to the world in which it is embedded; and structural shifts in complexes of ideas *may* have their roots in basic alterations (or continuities) of our perception of the world, as articulated in the sign systems in which the idea is clothed.

In this chapter I offer another case study in which an idea, here Nietzsche as pathogen, arises from and influences not merely the world of literature but the total fabric of history. Indeed, the existence of such an idea in daily life does more to focus the implications of that idea than all the pamphlets, plays, and essays that embody it. The view that Nietzsche was a "dangerous" thinker—not merely that he espoused dangerous thoughts, but that he caused dangerous acts—is a leitmotiv of Nietzsche reception from the fin de siècle to Georg Lukács.[5] And yet behind the generality that Nietzsche's works were attractive or destructive because of the sense of danger inherent in them is a specific linkage between the sense of danger and the fin-de-siècle image of humanity. For central to Nietzsche's image at the turn of the century are three qualities: the radical nature of his philosophy, his madness, and their linkage in the sexual pathogenesis of that final break with reality which he experienced in Turin in 1889.[6]

In the earliest discussion of Nietzsche's life, by his friends and contemporaries, emphasis on this triad is always either manifest or implicit. Representative of this discussion is the debate about the etiology of Nietzsche's madness. All three of the positions taken by his contemporaries reflect the debate about the sexual nature of the cause of his madness. One argued that his insanity was the result of his sexual life, that is, the product of his syphilitic infection; the second argued that it was the product of his inheritance, that is, the early death and madness of his father; the third argued that it was the result of social pressures—of overwork and dangerous drugs. The constellation of sexuality, genetic inheritance, and environment is a typical nineteenth-century manner of defining the etiology of one central group of pathologies, those labeled degenerate. Indeed, B.-A. Morel, who more than anyone was responsible for introducing the concept of degeneracy into the medical as well as popular vocabulary of the nineteenth century, in the mid-nineteenth century saw this triad as the cause for all degenerative illnesses.[7] As degeneration came to be regarded as one of the central attributes of the Other during the nineteenth century, it was increasingly invoked to explain psychopathological as well as sociopathic acts. By the turn of the century this manner of viewing deviancy had become a commonplace in both the medical and the popular manner of seeing the Other.

The First Murder Case

In 1901 a court case came before the Higher Regional Court (Oberlandsgerichthof) in Gotha which was a reification of all of the public discussions of Nietzsche's dangerousness. On 4 December 1901 a law student, Walter Fischer, was tried for the murder of his lover, seventeen-year-old Martha Amberg from Eisenach. Fischer, himself only twenty-four at the time of the trial, had admitted his guilt in pretrial hearings, and the state attorney's initial questioning had to do more with the motivation for Fischer's act than with its actual occurrence. After determining Fischer's mental and emotional state when he received a series of anonymous letters about his beloved's fidelity and his feelings during the shooting, the state attorney Blücher turned to the motivation for Fischer's act.

Attorney: How did you come, as a high school student, at such an immature age, to study philosophy?
Accused: I was drawn to it by my natural disposition.
Attorney: What do you mean?
Accused: I am naturally ugly. I have a repulsive nature, and my fellow students and my teacher treated me in a manner that indicated their repulsion.
Attorney: What sort of constitutional error do you have?
Accused: I don't have a normal head, rather a badly formed one.
Attorney: I did not notice that earlier or, for that matter, even now.
Accused: Yes, I felt that people couldn't stand me and I withdrew. Gradually a general disgust for people developed within me.
Attorney: And therefore you withdrew into philosophy.
Accused: Yes.
Attorney: You therefore claim that your abnormally shaped head was the reason that people avoided you. We already have had the testimony of some witnesses that your behavior caused their alienation. One described you as a

"funny sort of fellow," the other as a "tough egg." A third felt that you are an "egotist." It seems that you had few social graces. This was an error in your education. Perhaps you were not taught what is appropriate.

Accused: I am not conscious of that.

Attorney: What did you read?

Accused: Nietzsche and Schopenhauer.

Attorney: Why these two philosophers?

Accused: A postal employee whom I know suggested them.

Attorney: You were then a high school senior.

Accused: Yes.

Attorney: Wouldn't you have done better then to have read Caesar's *Gallic Wars* and Greek history than the work of a man who ended in madness?

The accused is silent.[8]

The attitude of the court is quite clear. Nietzsche is the dangerous philosopher. Indeed, the state attorney, the mouthpiece of the official state view, even elides "Nietzsche and Schopenhauer," two dangerous thinkers, into one, that "man who ended in madness," Nietzsche.

The examination of other witnesses in the trial adds yet more layers of meaning to the reading of dangerous thinkers. The court's examination of one of Fischer's fellow students at the University of Jena, law student Kuhn, follows this line:

Witness: The accused had very perverse ideas and had expressed himself very negatively about law and justice.

Attorney: Did he say to you that he stood above all law?

Witness: Yes. This was evidently the result of his reading, which consisted of Schopenhauer and Nietzsche.[9]

Most important of all of the witnesses called to testify concerning Fischer's mental state, at least of those witnesses who knew him before the murder, was Fischer's father. He testified that his younger son had died in an epileptic fit; that Walter had suffered from epileptic fits from the age of three; and that Walter was obsessed with his physical malformation. He ended his testimony by summarizing his son's belief that all people are basically evil and that it is only through social convention that this evil does not dominate the world:

Attorney: Is that not fruit from the tree of knowledge of a Nietzsche or a Schopenhauer?

Witness: That can be. He also told me how, in Berlin, a mason jumped from his scaffolding, in order to prove his adherence to Nietzsche's teaching. The man stuck a copy of work by Nietzsche in his pocket before committing suicide. This deed seemed to the accused a true ideal.

Attorney: Did you have any knowledge of your son's reading?

Witness: No, no knowledge. I would otherwise have stopped him. His fanaticism went so far that his disgust concerning the female sex affected his relationship with his sister.

Attorney: Do you not see in his disgust that the accused may have had an unpleasant experience with a woman?

Witness: No. I see in it only a result of his reading of Schopenhauer.[10]

Fischer's sexual attitudes are presented as the result of reading. Nietzsche-Schopenhauer, that "dangerous" philosopher, is the reason for his hatred of women, especially those close to him, and therefore, in the mind of father and fellow students, provides an explanation for Fischer's shooting of his beloved.

The final witness in the trial was one of the medical experts called to help determine Fischer's mental status at the time of the murder. He was Otto Binswanger, the Professor of Psychiatry at the University of Jena and the supervising psychiatrist during the period Fischer was under observation in the psychiatric clinic in Jena. Perhaps more important for our reading of his testimony, he had been Nietzsche's psychiatrist of record during Nietzsche's stay in the Jena psychiatric clinic from 18 January 1889 to 13 May 1890.[11] A typical clinical psychiatrist of his generation, Binswanger believed very strongly in somatic causes of mental illness and had as his motto, as did most of the psychiatrists of his generation, Wilhelm Griesinger's aperçu that "mind illness is brain illness." Binswanger's statement to the court moved the trial into a new direction. He characterized the background of the accused—his early childhood illness, his fixation on the works of Nietzsche and Schopenhauer as early as his sixteenth year—as clearly pathological.

From [Nietzsche and Schopenhauer] he developed his pessimistic world view, which saw destruction as the highest value of life, and on the other hand, he found there the unlimited right of the individual to expression, a right greater than that held by the masses. In his immature mental life, a life unprepared for strict logical thought, such concepts overpowered all other spiritual forces, which perhaps without this presence would have enabled him to develop into a harmonious, firm personality. I purposely say "perhaps" because his ego-centric, ruthless attitudes toward the well-being or discomfort of others were already evident in him as a child.[12]

Binswanger sees in the reading of dangerous philosophy a potential cause for Fischer's murderous act, or at least a mitigating circumstance. The power of this view is in no way weakened at the close of his statement, when he says that no judgment about sanity can be made on the basis of an individual's support of a philosophic system. "One cannot conclude from the support of an individual for the philosophy of Nietzsche and Schopenhauer that he is mad."[13]

According to the contemporary record it was Otto Binswanger's statement that finally convinced the jury. They found Walter Fischer, a man who had planned a murder in detail, guilty of manslaughter and sentenced him to ten years in prison. The extenuating circumstance that accounts for the verdict of manslaughter rather than murder seems to have been the baneful influence of that dangerous philosopher, Nietzsche-Schopenhauer.

The editorial reaction to Fischer's sentencing was uniform. The Berlin *Market Courier* on 6 December 1901 noted that "puberty was the time in which he developed his disgust for women. That period was a fruitful basis for the reception of those philosophies, such as Nietzsche's and Schopenhauer's, which preach pessimism, and whose teachings were poison for this young man."[14] The Berlin *Post* wrote on 5 December 1901, the day of the verdict, "that such a young, sensitive individual created the principle of his bitter life out of Schopenhauer and Nietzsche . . . a force which sped his tragic fall."[15] But nowhere was the popular reading of the danger of Nietzsche's philosophy more specifically spelled out than in the conservative *German Guard* which featured an editorial, THE MURDERER OF HIS BELOVED, on the first page of its 6 December 1901 morning edition:

Fischer [as opposed to the Bavarian murderer Kneissl] is not a born murderer—he is not animal-like enough, he is not cold-blooded enough, he is too easily moved by feelings of remorse. He is, however, the born decadent, the individual burdened with moral insanity. He felt that at some time his life would have a tragic end, and this vague feeling drove him as a high school student into the arms of pessimistic philosophy. Schopenhauer taught that this world is the worst of all possible ones, but desired, however, that mankind make this vale of tears tolerable through Buddhist moral pity. Nietzsche, on the other hand, is rather an optimist. He believed in the victory of power, dismissed pity as an acquired

cultural weakness and preached an extravagant self-infatuation, the Morality of
the Strong. Both philosophers together have a horrible, depressing and inhu-
mane deprecation of human nature, especially that of the woman, which
Schopenhauer sees as a completely subordinate, limited, and deceitful being and
which Nietzsche sees able to be held in check like an animal only through
hardness and abuse. "When you go to a woman, don't forget the whip!" taught
Nietzsche. Of course neither one of these thinkers would have sanctioned
Fischer's action. But one can assume that it was their works that supported this
anger as well as the disgust he had directed toward the hotly loved being he
murdered. Both Schopenhauer and Nietzsche show in their attitude toward the
woman an Asiatic turn. Christianity, itself springing from Asia, shows itself
closer to our Germanic sensitivity, since it it shows the woman as the true
companion and helpmate of the man. As a critique of a misunderstood concept of
Christianity, as a counterweight to the pietistic sentimentality and lack of judgment, against the passivity of the will, one can see the justification for Schopenhauer and Nietzsche. It is a dangerous poison for a sickly individual, predisposed
to depression and doubt.[16]

In the popular mind, Fischer's reading of Schopenhauer and Nietzsche
was a crucial catalyst without which the young man, notwithstanding his
predisposition, would not have been moved to murder.

An aside into forensic psychiatry reveals more clearly the implications
of the idea of the dangerous philosopher in late nineteenth-century German thought. German law concerning the criminal responsibility of the
insane rested on the Napoleonic Code's definition of a crime as an action
committed by someone responsible for his own actions. Insanity removes an individual from criminal responsibility, because to be insane is
to be "unconscious" in legal terms. Paragraph 51 of the Criminal Code of
the German Empire declared that "a punishable deed has not taken place if
the accused is, at the time of the commission of his deed, in a state of
unconsciousness or in a state of a morbid disruption of his mental faculties through which free choice is made impossible." The problem of
philosophy as a force dangerous to public order belongs to the latter
category, for someone like Fischer, based on his own testimony and
Binswanger's deposition, is not "unconscious," that is, oblivious to the
world, but rather suffers from a limitation on his "free choice." This
very Protestant formulation is also called, within fin-de-siècle German
law, "moral idiocy," a term closely related to the Anglo-American formulation of "moral insanity." But in Germany a claim that an individual's "free choice" was impaired could not rest simply on evidence

that the individual showed a lack of moral feeling. Some other defect, such as diminished intellectual capacity, had also to be proved before the claim of "moral idiocy" could be brought forward. Of all of the cases cited in standard summaries of German forensic psychiatry, the strongest is for affective pathology based on "epileptic degeneration."[17] This is, of course, the overall thrust of Binswanger's statement. Fischer was impaired because his constitution had limited his "free choice," and this lack of free choice led him to be seduced by a "dangerous" philosophy. The degenerate is particularly apt to succumb to strong systems of thought and thus shows both weakness and madness. Not all who read Nietzsche are driven mad, according to Binswanger, but all who read him and are inherently weak can be driven into madness.

More Murder Cases

Wedekind's Lulu dramas of 1895–1902 expose some further implications of the Fischer case in documenting the perception of Nietzsche as a pathogen. Nietzsche's "influence" on Wedekind has been discussed since the beginning of Wedekind scholarship, but little attention has been given to exactly which "Nietzsche" influenced him.[18] Wedekind's reading of Nietzsche as a "dangerous" thinker figures in very specific aspects of the Lulu dramas, and it is in precisely the same structural continuity that was found in the Fischer trial that Wedekind presents his Lulu. For Lulu is the quintessential degenerate, able through her pathology to seduce and destroy those about her. The triad of heredity, environment, and sexuality determines her nature, as it does that of her sister-in-sin, Nana. Wedekind states quite directly in the introduction that she is not "the primal form of woman," even though she is called Eve; she is rather the product of the new philosophy as found in one without free will, as found in the degenerate. The baneful reading of dangerous philosophy comes in the world of Lulu with the ironic introduction of the mad Nietzsche in the third act of *Earth-Spirit*. Lulu, introduced in the prologue as an animal in need of taming, is juxtaposed with the world of the unreal, the ballet, in which the Dalai Lama, Wedekind's ironic pseudonym for Schopenhauer, is confused with the mad philosopher, Friedrich Nietzsche. This conflation by Dr. Schön is indicative of the medical implications of that duo Schopenhauer-Nietzsche and their or his dangerous influence on the "morally idiotic."

Lulu's sexuality has manifested itself in childhood, perhaps even in her relationship with the beggar Schigolch, a relationship that is a perverse reversal of the relationship in which Wilhelm Meister finds Mignon (a name, like "Eve," which she is given in the course of the plays). Such a pathologically early manifestation of sexuality was for the fin de siècle a clear marker of the individual as the outsider, an outsider either in terms of class or in terms of pathology. Schön, who exploits her sexuality and her pathology, at one point is tauntingly challenged by her to accept a role he has pretended to assume:

Schön: Be silent! You monster!
Lulu: Marry her [Schön's fiancée]—then she'll dance in front of me in her childish misery, instead of my dancing in front of her!
Schön: (raises his fist) God forgive me. . . .
Lulu: Strike me! Where is your whip? Strike me across the legs. . . . (78)

This role, which Schön avoids, is of course the role ascribed to the dangerous philosopher, who when he goes to a woman is to bring his whip along. It is Lulu who dominates and whose pathology, or at least whose function as a pathogen, contaminates and eventually destroys the men in her life in *Earth-Spirit*. The suicides of Goll and Schwarz are directly attributable to her role as a pathogen. Like Fischer, the contaminated becomes the destroyer. Degenerates are portrayed as strong and aggressive only because through weakness they have succumbed to a philosophy of strength. This is the pathology Dostoevsky ascribes to Raskolnikov, at least ironically. He murders because he reads dangerous pamphlets in a debilitated condition!

Wedekind stresses Lulu's role as a disciple of Nietzsche by using Nietzschean metaphors to describe her. Perhaps the most telling is the circus performer Rodrigo's description of her potential as a high-wire artist. Wedekind combines this with a restatement of the male's wish to control the female, a wish that remains unsatisfied until the female as degenerate meets a male of equal pathology:

Rodrigo: I've ordered a rhinoceros-hide whip two inches thick. If that doesn't do the trick with her then I've got potato soup where my brains ought to be. Beating or lovemaking, it's all one to a woman. Keep her amused and she remains firm and fresh. This one is twenty years old, has been three times married, has given satisfaction to an incredible number of lovers, and now at least she's showing signs of having a heart herself. But the fellow will have to have the seven deadly sins written on his forehead or she'll have no respect for him. . . . I'll train her and if she brings off the first "salto" without breaking her neck I'll put on my black frock coat and won't lift a finger the rest of my life. . . . So long as the man takes care of the intellectual side and sees that the sense of family doesn't go down the drain. (122)

Again it is the whip, the instrument demanded by Lulu, which introduces the "Nietzschean" flavor into this passage.[19] But the idea of the female as animal and the use of the circus image also reflect passages in Nietzsche's writing, passages cited by his contemporaries as characteristic of his work.

It is with the final death in *Earth-Spirit,* the murder of Schön, that the second "Nietzsche Murder Case" is introduced and can be seen not as influence but as an extension of the same model of perceiving the world. For Lulu is tried for the murder of Schön and convicted. She is sentenced to jail for her crime and we find her at the beginning of the second play, *Pandora's Box,* escaping from prison. When G. W. Pabst filmed the plays and when Alban Berg set them to music, both found it imperative to present versions of the trial. But what did Wedekind's trial look like? What was Lulu's crime and what was her sentence? None of this is made clear and yet we are given some tantalizing hints.

Perhaps the best point at which to begin to reconstruct Lulu's trial, a trial that takes place between the calling of the police at the end of *Earth-Spirit* and Lulu's imprisonment at the beginning of the second play, is with the final line of *Earth-Spirit.* It is spoken by Lulu's high-school-age admirer Alfred Hugenberg: "I shall be expelled from school." Indeed he is, and in the second play he is lodged in a reformatory because of his fascination for Lulu. In *Pandora's Box,* Alwa, Schön's son and Lulu's future lover, comments on Hugenberg's action during Lulu's trial: "The boy has something our generation lacks. He has the heroic spirit. And of course it will be his undoing. Do you remember how before sentence was passed, he leapt up from the witness bench and called out to the judge, "How can you tell what would have become of you if as a ten-year-old child you'd had to knock about barefoot at night in cafés?'" (121–22). It is for this outburst that he is sentenced to the reformatory and becomes one of the outcasts populating Lulu's world. (Outcasts such as Rodrigo find his sentence quite justified, as he needed to have "respect for the law . . . distilled into him" [122].) The claim that environmental factors excuse Lulu from guilt, that her immoral upbringing led to her crime, is dismissed by court and criminal alike as nonsense. Criminals know that they are part of a world quite different from that of the "normal" world and that this difference is rooted in their manner of perception. This view is seconded by the legal establishment. The followers of Cesare Lombroso, who dominated German forensic psychiatry during the late nineteenth century, demanded some physical sign as well as moral/mental stigmata before the judgment of "insanity" could be made.[20] A deprived childhood would be seen as a mitigating factor only if some inherent anomaly such as a degenerative sign could be adduced.

Alwa claims that Lulu, or at least the heroine of his play *Earth-Spirit*, has already served "a full year behind bars" (113), and Countess Geschwitz tells Lulu that she has "nine years in prison ahead of [her]" (114). It should come as little surprise that Lulu's sentence is the same as Fischer's, a sentence for manslaughter and not for murder. What could the mitigating circumstances have been? The act itself, which the audience is privy to, was not a spontaneous act. Neither was Lulu "unconscious" in the legal sense of the term during its commission. Is she then to be seen as "morally idiotic," and what is the proof?

Here the argument is clouded, as Wedekind provides the audience with no direct information. But this very audience would have brought all the information it needed to the text to explain Lulu's sentence. For Lulu is a sexualized female, a female who is the essence not of the woman but of the prostitute. Like Nana, she belongs to a separate genus, the prostitute (recall the subtitle of Lombroso's definitive work on the subject: *The Prostitute and the Normal Woman*).[21] Lulu shows her degeneracy through the very fact of her seductive beauty. This degeneracy is triggered by her seduction as a child, a literary pattern of the fin de siècle which, we have seen, even confused Freud by the power of its argument. She is a member of a separate species and its signs are the signs of overt sexuality. Zola makes Nana almost grotesquely sexual. Her role as the sexual object in the theater, or the "brothel" as the theater director quite directly labels it, carries through the sense of the sexual outsider inherent in the image of the actress. So too is Lulu a sexual object on the stage. Like Nana she cannot do anything except be admired. It is this seductiveness of the Other which is the stigma of the prostitute as degenerate. Her very beauty is the sexual sign of her degeneracy.

The labeling of beauty as a sign of degeneration is of course an ironic reversal of the standard understanding of the role of beauty in the process of sexual selection as presented in the late nineteenth century. Darwin as well as Darwin's opponents, such as the sociologist Edward Westermarck, see in the physical beauty of the female (as opposed to the strength of the male) the markers of positive sexual selection.[22] The attempt to reverse a hundred-year-old tradition of aesthetic relativism by making beauty a biological mechanism leads Darwin and other thinkers down a path that is almost racist in its implications. And indeed modern biological theory has generally discarded "sexual selection," throwing it on the rubbish heap of "bad" science. For a late nineteenth-century audience, however, Wedekind's emphasis on Lulu's inherent beauty would have sufficed to signal her degeneracy. Her beauty, like that of Dorian Gray, is sensual, contaminated by sexuality—the antithesis of true beauty. This is what accounts for Lulu's reduced sentence. It is not her background alone, but her background in combination with her biology which marks her as a degenerate and therefore as one who is not responsible for her actions.

Two other characters in the Lulu dramas fall into the same pattern. The Countess Geschwitz, Lulu's lesbian friend and potential lover, is also seen as degenerate. Homosexuality was perceived in the late nineteenth century not merely as a sexual deviancy caused by masturbatory excesses, as it had been in the first half of the century, but as the manifestation of an inherent pattern of degeneracy. Here too the degeneracy is presented in an ironic mode, which undercuts the implications of sexual deviation. For Geschwitz is perhaps the only character in the play to evolve, as Wedekind points out in his preface to the plays. The other character who bears the stigma of degeneration appears in the final act of the second play. It is of course Lulu's nemesis, Jack the Ripper, whose physical description, like that of Geschwitz, points to his degeneracy: "He is a square built man, elastic in his movements, with a pale face, inflamed eyes, thick arched eyebrows, drooping moustache, sparse beard, matted sidewhiskers and fiery red hands with gnawed finger nails" (172). This is the description of the degenerate as sociopath found in any number of the classic textbooks of psychiatry of the period. That it is also the description of a lower-class immigrant in Great Britain and that it appeared as one of the many attempts to provide a description of the "real" Jack the Ripper should also not be surprising.[23] For the identity of the Other, whether social outcast, marginal member of society, or sexual degenerate, is carried in his or her appearance. The Other looks different, and that quality is found in the Lulu dramas in Lulu, in the Countess Geschwitz, and, finally, in Jack the Ripper.

Degeneracy, sexuality, and environment all figure importantly in the fin-de-siècle conception of the Other, the Other as mad. For Lombroso and his German followers, prostitution was a mental illness, a form of inherent madness, over which the individual had little control, once the illness was triggered. Madness is thus manifested in sexuality. The case of Walter Fischer as well as the case of Lulu illustrate this conflation of concepts. Fischer's pathological relationship with his girlfriend and Lulu's pathological relationship with an entire world of males prefigured their downfall. For inherent in such sexuality is death. The degenerate is a time bomb who at some moment will explode, destroying those who let themselves be seduced.

Where does Nietzsche as pathogen, as the dangerous philosopher, enter into the picture? For Nietzsche (or Schopenhauer-Nietzsche as he is sometimes called) was read in a very specific manner. His philosophy was distilled into two qualities in its late nineteenth-century reception. First, there was Nietzsche's misogyny. Nietzsche was made the advocate of the whip in dealing with the woman as Other. For the late nineteenth century the woman, both in her new political demands and in her role as the object of sexual control (through the public health laws), had been distanced as a different species, a different form of life. Close to the jungle beast in her sexuality, she could be tamed only through violence. Nietzsche's misogyny was thus seen as the necessary nightside of modern philosophy, needed to deal with a force even more dangerous than his radicalism. Nietzsche was then placed in the role of the dangerous thinker who had a place, but only when used by individuals (read: men) strong enough not to be seduced by his philosophy. Second, there was Nietzsche's pessimism and its resultant madness. The necessary counterbalance to any philosophy of progress was a philosophy of pessimism.[24] It was permitted only as long as its result was madness, placing the pessimist outside the pale of society and within the anti-world of the Other as mad. Wedekind provides his audience with the mirror image, for in his dramas the entire world is an asylum, and Lulu and Jack the Ripper are typical inmates rather than aberrations.

The "Nietzsche Murder Case" illustrates the power of a concept to categorize those forces that were perceived to threaten order, an order built upon the repression of irrationality, sexuality, and deviancy. Nietzsche becomes the code word for those forces both within the individual (sexuality) and in the society (systems of thought) which were perceived as dangerous to order. They are perceived to play themselves out on a very specific stage, that of the court. For the presence of the state within this world was the presence of order. Hegel had seen in the German state of the nineteenth century the ultimate form of human organization. With laws controlling both heterosexuality (under the guise of public health) and homosexuality, this ultimate state had invaded every corner of human activity by the end of the century. In the eyes of this state, the mad, the prostitute, the homosexual, had but one place, and that was in the court, being judged for their crime. This crime was seen as a reflex of their biology, and the only possibility for control and potential rehabilitation was incarceration. Not prison for life, or the ultimate punishment, but limited punishment during which some type of resocialization could perhaps take place. During this period the biological tendencies that had been released through exposure to dangerous thinking could be brought back under control. For the prison, as Michel Foucault has quite correctly observed, became the locus of thought control for nineteenth-century society, and ten years was deemed long enough to reverse the influence of that dangerous thinker, Friedrich Nietzsche.[25]

Echoes

The powerful myth that errors in human biology are connected with antisocial acts in such a way as to mitigate those acts did not play itself out only in Wilhelminian Germany. In 1924 two young Chicago college students, Richard Loeb and Nathan Leopold, Jr., murdered Leopold's young cousin, Bobby Franks. Their lawyer, Clarence Darrow, built the case that his clients were impaired around two central themes: their inherited mental illness and their reading of Friedrich Nietzsche. Several thousand pages of medical testimony were taken which documented the neurological, mental, social, and metabolic anomalies of the two murderers. Dr. H. S. Hulbert, for example, one of the physicians who testified for the defense, stressed that Leopold had "neuro-circulatory-asthenia," a hybrid label which pointed to a physical source for his inherent psychological weakness and his resulting reliance on his more aggressive friend, Richard Loeb. Darrow links this fact with Leopold's mental instability, which Darrow labels "paranoia" and proves by showing his client's identification with Nietzsche's "superman." In his brilliant and oft-quoted summation, Darrow stressed the link between the madness of his clients and their reading of Nietzsche, a reading possible only for them:

Your honor, I have read almost everything that Nietzsche ever wrote. [Darrow implies that his own sanity is beyond question.] He was a man of wonderful intellect; the most original philosopher of the last century. A man who probably has made a deeper imprint on philosophy than any other man within a hundred years, whether right or wrong. More books have been written about him than probably all the rest of the philosophers in a hundred years. More college professors have talked about him. [And they certainly aren't crazy, implies Darrow.] In a way he has reached more people, and still he has been a philosopher of what we might call the intellectual cult. I have just made a few short extracts from Nietzsche to show the things that Nathan read and which no doubt influenced him. . . . It is not how this would affect you. It is not how this would affect me. The question is, how did it affect the impressionable, visionary, dreamy mind of a boy. . . . Here is a boy at sixteen or seventeen becoming obsessed with these doctrines. . . . It was not a casual bit of philosophy with him; it was his life. He believed in a superman. . . . Many of us read this philosophy but know that it has no actual application to life; but not he. He lived it and practiced it; he thought it applied to him, and he could not have believed it excepting that it either caused a diseased mind or was the result of a diseased mind.[26]

Darrow's summation linked the physical state of his clients with the specific nature of their reading of this powerful philosopher. He called attention to certain stigmata: not merely overt signs, though he did draw on the ancient science of physiognomy in his summation, but on the hidden stigmata of the new physiognomy, the science of brain localization. Theodor Meynert's preoccupation with localizing every aspect of the psyche led his best-known student, Sigmund Freud, to wonder whether one could truly accomplish this task. Freud quickly abandoned the "brain mythology" of his early "Project of a Scientific Psychology" when he understood how primitive were the analogies that this approach enabled him to make between brain structures and human behavior and emotion.[27] As brain localization studies became more and more discriminating with Kurt Goldstein's work after World War I, the supposition that a physical process within the brain could be identified which proved the susceptibility of certain individuals to specific readings of powerful texts entered the realm of forensic and literary folklore. If your brain is sick, you read in a crazy manner. The idea of a dynamic psyche with all its abstractions was simply too complex to be reduced to this myth. The idea of a necessary biological source for antisocial acts, an abscess on the soul, captured the fancy of the public. In the case of Leopold and Loeb,

Clarence Darrow achieved his end. He got his clients off with life imprisonment.

The perception of the mad as readers of dangerous texts still lingers in Western consciousness. Nothing illustrates this more clearly than the trial of John W. Hinckley, Jr., who attempted to assassinate Ronald Reagan.[28] Two factors in Hinckley's trial struck the public as unique. First was the demand of Hinckley's attorneys to introduce evidence given by Marjorie Lemay, M.D., a radiologist, that computer-assisted brain scans showed that Hinckley's brain was "shrunken." The debate about introducing this information paralleled the earlier case of the "crocodile man," a young Massachusetts man whose plea in 1974, supported by his endocrinologist father, was that a malfunction of his limbic system led to a sudden outburst of anger during which he attacked two girls.[29] However, the link between Hinckley's "shrunken" brain and the disease he was implied to have was much more subtle. The CAT-scan evidence was introduced to imply, not to prove, that Hinckley was suffering from a somatic disease that caused an irresistible impulse. Throughout the trial this disease was given various names: process schizophrenia, a major affective disorder, pseudoneurotic schizophrenia, paradoxical rage, paranoid personality disorder, borderline personality disorder, and schizophrenia spectrum disorder, among others. Dr. Lemay's evidence was eventually introduced, even though it was accompanied by the witness's statement that the CAT scans could not prove, one way or the other, the existence of any mental disease. The implied argument of the defense contradicted their own witness. The implication made by introducing the "hard" scientific evidence of the CAT scan was that it was "relevant" in determining Hinckley's mental state, and it was on this basis that the judge admitted it as evidence. These CAT scans could be relevant only by supporting the image that Hinckley was suffering from a physical malady that left him unable to resist a strong text. If the argument played out before the jury is to be believed, Hinckley was driven by his shrunken brain to see Jodie Foster in the movie *Taxi Driver* innumerable times and to read the novel upon which the film was based. Thus the Hinckley case is truly an artifact of the 1980s. It is not a strong philosophy but a violent, sexually aggressive film, and not a mad philosopher but a sexualized, preteen actress in the film, that seduce the weak reader/viewer. Hinckley is absolved of his crime, is seen as mad, not because of his insane act, but because of his biological flaw. His madness, like that of the other figures we have discussed, is the living out of his text in the world; this was the substance of the testimony offered by one of the scientific witnesses for the defense, Ernest Prelinger.

Here is, once again, the line that society draws between sanity and insanity, between rationality and susceptibility. Sane readers internalize their reading; the text assumes control of the weak reader. Such views, reflective of society's need for specific signs of illness, are the vestiges of a nineteenth-century brain mythology that made all mind diseases brain diseases and could not conceive of mind diseases independent of this model. This myth is part of a folklore so powerful that we are turned into passive readers of it. We are overwhelmed by it: we believe it and act upon it, robotlike, because of its power and our inherent weakness to resist it. Are we therefore all mad, all weak readers overcome by more powerful systems? Or do we find it necessary to see our own sense of passivity and weakness projected onto the world? And do we not act as if this projection were independent of ourselves, degenerate, weak, crippled, mad, shrunken? But we know better. Do we not, in pardoning the insane, pardon ourselves for fancied transgressions? Are we not in the end all one with the murderer, so different from us, our polar selves, that he or she appears our double? These questions take us far from the text, into the mind of the reader as creator, which may well be the necessary locus for any true understanding of the meeting ground of history and text.

3

The Hottentot and the Prostitute:
Toward an Iconography of
Female Sexuality

Looking at *Olympia* and *Nana*

ONE OF THE classic works of nineteenth-century art records the ideas of both the sexualized woman and the black woman. Edouard Manet's *Olympia,* painted in 1862–63, first shown in the salon of 1865, documents the merger of these two images (see Plate 1). The conventional wisdom concerning Manet's painting states that the model, Victorine Meurend, is "obviously naked rather than conventionally nude,"[1] and that her pose is heavily indebted to such classical models as Titian's 1538 *Venus of Urbino,* Goya's 1800 *Naked Maja,* and Delacroix's 1847 *Odalisque,* as well as to other works by Manet's contemporaries, such as Gustave Courbet.[2] George Needham has shown quite convincingly that Manet was also using a convention of early erotic photography in having the central figure directly confront the observer.[3] The black female attendant, posed by a black model called Laura, has been seen as both a reflex of the classic black servant figure present in the visual arts of the eighteenth century and a representation of Baudelaire's "Vénus noire."[4] Let us juxtapose the *Olympia,* with all its aesthetic and artistic analogies and parallels, to a work by Manet which Georges Bataille, among others, has seen as a modern "genre scene," the *Nana* of 1877 (see Plate 2).[5] Although Nana is unlike Olympia in being modern, a creature of present-day Paris (according to a contemporary),[6] she is like Olympia in having

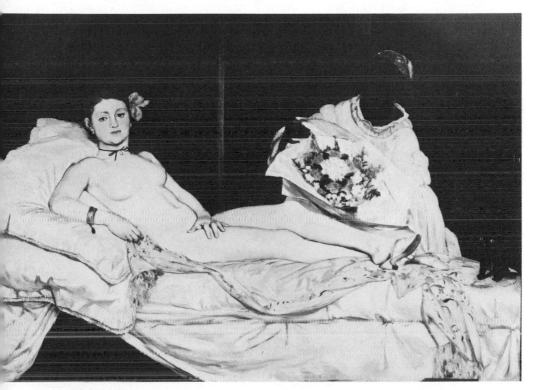

1. Edouard Manet, *Olympia* (1862–63) (Louvre, Paris).

2. Edouard Manet, *Nana* (1877) (Kunsthalle, Hamburg).

been perceived as a sexualized female and is so represented. Yet the move from a work with an evident aesthetic provenance, as understood by Manet's contemporaries, to one that was influenced by the former and yet was seen by its contemporaries as "modern" is attended by major shifts in the iconography of the sexualized woman, not the least of which is the seeming disappearance of the black female.

Black Sexuality and Its Iconography

The figure of the black servant is ubiquitous in European art of the eighteenth and nineteenth centuries. Richard Strauss knew this when he had Hugo von Hofmannsthal conclude their conscious evocation of the eighteenth century, *Der Rosenkavalier* (1911), with the mute return of the little black servant to reclaim the Marschalin's forgotten gloves.[7] But Hofmannsthal was also aware that one of the central functions of the black servant in the visual arts of the eighteenth and nineteenth centuries was as a maker of the sexualization of the society in which he or she was found. For the forgotten gloves mark the end of the opera but also the end of the relationship between Octavian, the Knight of the Rose, and the Marschalin, an illicit sexual relationship that had opened the opera, just as the figure of the black servant closed it. When one turns to the narrative art of the eighteenth century, for example to William Hogarth's two great cycles, *A Rake's Progress* (1733–34) and *A Harlot's Progress* (1731), it is not surprising that, as in the Strauss opera some two centuries later, the figures of the black servants mark the presence of illicit sexual activity (see Plate 3). And, as in Hofmannsthal's libretto, the servants and the central figure are of opposite sex. In the second plate of *A Harlot's Progress,* we are shown Moll Hackabout as the mistress to a Jewish merchant, the first stage of her decline. Present is a young black male servant. In the third stage of Tom Rakewell's collapse, we find him in the notorious brothel, the Rose Tavern in Covent Garden.[8] The entire picture is full of references to illicit sexual activity, all portrayed negatively. Present is a young black female servant.

The association of the black with concupiscence reaches back into the Middle Ages. The twelfth-century Jewish traveler Benjamin of Tudela wrote that "at Seba on the river Pishon . . . is a people . . . who like animals, eat of the herbs that grow on the banks of the Nile and in the fields. They go about naked and have not the intelligence of ordinary

3. William Hogarth, *A Harlot's Progress,* Plate II (1731) (Ithaca, N.Y., private collection).

4. Franz von Bayros, *The Servant* (c. 1890) (Ithaca, N.Y., private collection).

men. They cohabit with their sisters and anyone they can find. . . . And these are the Black slaves, the sons of Ham."[9] The black, both male and female, becomes by the eighteenth century an icon for deviant sexuality in general, almost always, however, paired with a white figure of the opposite sex. By the nineteenth century, as in the *Olympia,* or more crudely in one of a series of Viennese erotic prints by Franz von Bayros entitled *The Servant,* the central white female figure is associated with a black female in such a way as to imply a similarity between the sexuality of the two (see Plate 4). In a contrastive image, Dante Gabriel Rossetti's *The Beloved, or The Bride* (1865) associates the unself-conscious innocence of the half-dressed young black serving girl with the sensuality of the "beloved" (see Plate 5). The association of figures of the same sex

5. Dante Gabriel Rossetti, *The Beloved, or The Bride* (1865) (The Tate Gallery, London).

stresses the special status of female sexuality. In *The Servant* the hypersexuality of the black child signals the hidden sexuality of the white
woman, a sexuality quite manifest in the other plates in the series. The
relationship between the sexuality of the black woman and that of the
sexualized white woman enters a new dimension when the scientific
discourse concerning the nature of black female sexuality is examined.

Buffon, the French naturalist, credited the black with a lascivious,
apelike sexual appetite, introducing a commonplace of early travel literature into a pseudoscientific context.[10] He stated that this animallike
sexual appetite went so far as to encourage black women to copulate with
apes. The black female thus comes to serve as an icon for black sexuality
in general. Buffon's view was based on a confusion of two applications
of the "great chain of being" to the nature of the black. In this view, the
black's position on the scale of humanity was antithetical to the white's.
Such a scale was employed to indicate the innate difference between the
races. This polygenetic view was applied to all human characteristics,
including sexuality and beauty. The antithesis of European sexual mores
and beauty is the black, and the essential black, the lowest exemplum of
mankind on the great chain of being, is the Hottentot. It is indeed in the
physical appearance of the Hottentot that the central icon for sexual
difference between the European and the black was found, a deep physiological difference urged so plausibly on the basis of physical contrast
that it gave pause even to early monogenetic theoreticians such as Johann
Friedrich Blumenbach.[11]

The labeling of the black female as more primitive, and therefore more
sexually intensive, by writers such as Abbé Raynal (1775) would have
been dismissed as unscientific by the radical empiricists of late eigh-
teenth- and early nineteenth-century Europe.[12] They would not have
accepted generalizations but would have demanded the examination of
specific, detailed case studies to evolve a "scientific" paradigm. They
required a case study that placed both the sexuality and the beauty of the
black in a position antithetical to those of the white. The paradigm had to
be rooted in some type of unique and observable physical difference.
Such a criterion was found in the distinction drawn between the pathological and the healthy in the medical model. The absorption into that
model of polygenetic difference between the races bears out William
Bynum's observation that nineteenth-century biology constantly needed
to deal with the polygenetic argument.[13]

The writer in whose work this alteration of the mode of discourse,
though not the underlying ideology concerning the black female, took

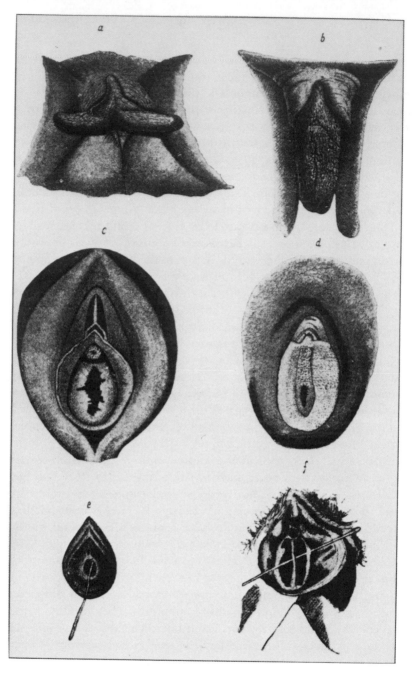

6. "Sexual Anomalies in the Hottentot (a, b) and in the European Woman (c, d, e, f)" (from Cesare Lombroso and Guillaume Ferraro, *La donna deliquente: La prostituta e la donna normale* [Turin: L. Roux, 1893]).

place was J. J. Virey. He was the author of the standard study of race published in the early nineteenth century, *Histoire naturelle du genre humain*. He also contributed a major essay (the only one on a specific racial group) to the widely cited *Dictionary of Medical Sciences* (1819).[14] In this essay Virey summarized his and many of his contemporaries' views on the sexual nature of black females in terms of accepted medical discourse. Their "voluptuousness" is "developed to a degree of lascivity unknown in our climate, for their sexual organs are much more developed than those of whites." Virey elsewhere cites the Hottentot woman as the epitome of this sexual lasciviousness and stresses the consonance between her physiology and her physiognomy (her "hideous form" and her "horribly flattened nose"). His central proof is a discussion of the unique structure of the Hottentot female's sexual parts, the description of which he takes from the anatomical studies of his contemporary Georges Cuvier (see Plate 6).[15]

The black female looks different. Her physiognomy, her skin color, the form of her genitalia mark her as inherently different. The nineteenth century perceived the black female as possessing not only a "primitive" sexual appetite, but also the external signs of this temperament, "primitive" genitalia. Eighteenth century travelers to southern Africa, such as François Levaillant and John Barrow, had described the so-called "Hottentot apron," a hypertrophy of the labia and nymphae caused by manipulation of the genitalia and considered beautiful by the Hottentots and Bushman as well as tribes in Basutoland and Dahomey.[16] In 1815 Saartje Baartman, also called Sarah Bartmann, or Saat-Jee, a twenty-five-year-old Hottentot female who had been exhibited in Europe for over five years as the "Hottentot Venus," died in Paris (see Plate 7). An autopsy that was performed on her was first written up by Henri Ductotay de Blainville in 1816 and then, in its most famous version, by Georges Cuvier in 1817.[17] Reprinted at least twice during the next decade, Cuvier's description reflected de Blainville's two intentions: the likening of a female of the "lowest" human species with the highest ape, the orangutan, and the description of the anomalies of the Hottentot's "organ of generation."

Sarah Bartmann had been exhibited not to show her genitalia, but rather to present to the European audience a different anomaly, one that they (and pathologists such as de Blainville and Cuvier) found riveting: her steatopygia, or protruding buttocks, a physical characteristic of Hottentot females which had captured the eye of early travelers (see Plate 8). For most Europeans who viewed her, Sarah Bartmann existed only as a

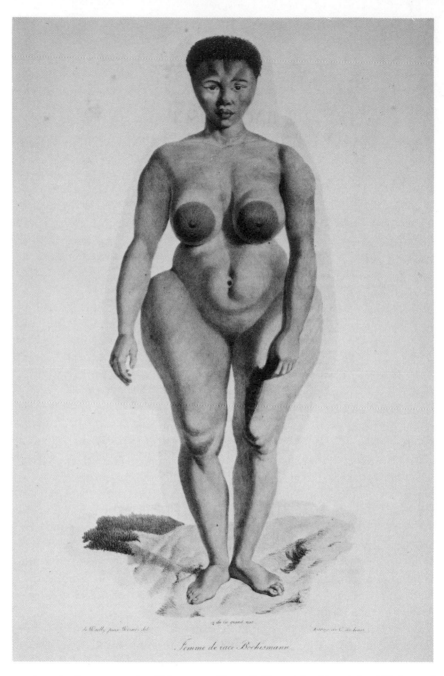

7. Saartje Baartman, the "Hottentot Venus" (from Geoffrey Saint-Hilaire and Frédéric Cuvier, *Histoire naturelle des mammifères avec des figures originales* [Paris: A. Belin, 1824]).

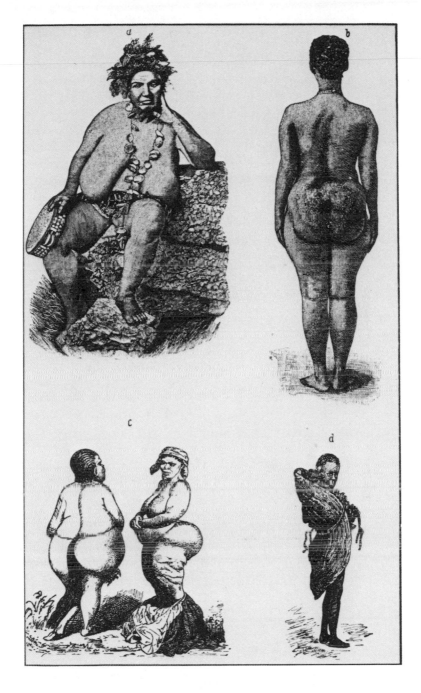

8. Steatopygia in black females (from Cesare Lombroso and Guillaume Ferraro, *La donna deliquente* [1893]).

collection of sexual parts. Her exhibition during 1810 in a London inflamed by the issue of abolition caused a public scandal, since she was
exhibited "to the public in a manner offensive to decency. She . . . does
exhibit all the shape and frame of her body as if naked."[18] The state's
objection was as much to her lewdness as to her status as an indentured
black. In France her presentation was similar. In 1829 a nude Hottentot
woman, also called "the Hottentot Venus," was the prize attraction at a
ball given by the Duchess du Barry in Paris. A contemporary print
emphasized her physical difference from the observers portrayed.

The audience that had paid to see Sarah Bartmann's buttocks and
fantasized about her genitalia could, after her death and dissection, examine both, for Cuvier presented "the Academy the genital organs of this
woman prepared in a way so as to allow one to see the nature of the
labia."[19] And indeed Sarah Bartmann's sexual parts serve as the central
image for the black female throughout the nineteenth century; and the
model of de Blainville's and Cuvier's descriptions, which center on the
detailed presentation of the sexual parts of the black, dominates medical
description of the black during the nineteenth century. To an extent, this
reflects the general nineteenth-century understanding of female sexuality
as pathological. The female genitalia were of interest in examining the
various pathologies that could befall them, but they were also of interest
because they came to define the sum of the female for the nineteenth
century. When a specimen was to be preserved for an anatomical museum, more often than not the specimen was seen as a pathological
summary of the entire individual. Thus, the skeleton of a giant or a
dwarf represented "giantism" or "dwarfism," the head of a criminal, the
act of execution which labeled him as "criminal."[20] Sarah Bartmann's
genitalia and buttocks summarized her essence for the nineteenth-century observer, as indeed they continue to do for twentieth-century observers, since they are still on display at the Musée de l'Homme in Paris.
Thus nineteenth-century autopsies of Hottentot and Bushman females
focus on the sexual parts. The tone set by de Blainville in 1816 and
Cuvier in 1817 was followed by A. W. Otto in 1824, Johannes Müller in
1834, W. H. Flower and James Murie in 1867, and Luschka, Koch, and
Görtz in 1869.[21] Flower, the editor of the *Journal of Anatomy and Physiology,* included his and Murie's "Account of the Dissection of a Bushwoman" in the opening volume of that famed journal. His ideological
intent was clear. He wished to provide data "relating to the unity or
plurality of mankind." His description begins with a detailed presentation of the form and size of the buttocks and concludes with his portrayal

of the "remarkable development of the labia minoria, or nymphae, which is so general a characteristic of the Hottentot and Bushman race." These were "sufficiently well marked to distinguish these parts at once from those of any of the ordinary varieties of the human species." The polygenetic argument is the ideological basis for all the dissections of these women. If their sexual parts could be shown to be inherently different, this would be a sufficient sign that blacks were a separate (and, needless to say, lower) race, as different from the European as the proverbial orangutan. Similar arguments were made about the nature of all blacks' (not just Hottentots') genitalia, but almost always concerning the female. Edward Turnipseed of South Carolina argued in 1868 that the hymen in black women "is not at the entrance to the vagina, as in the white woman, but from one-and-a-half to two inches from its entrance in the interior." From this he concluded that "this may be one of the anatomical marks of the non-unity of the races."[22] His views were seconded in 1877 by C. H. Fort, who presented another six cases of this seeming anomaly.[23] When one turns to autopsies of black males from approximately the same period, what is striking is the absence of any discussion of the male genitalia. For example, in Sir William Turner's three dissections of male blacks in 1878, 1879, and 1896, no mention is made of the genitalia.[24] The genitalia and buttocks of the black female attracted much greater interest in part because they were seen as evidence of an anomalous sexuality not only in black women but in all women.

By mid-century the image of the genitalia of the Hottentot had acquired various important implications. The central view was that these anomalies were inherent, biological variations rather than adaptations. In Theodor Billroth's standard handbook of gynecology, the "Hottentot apron" is presented in detail in the discussion of errors in development of the female genitalia, an association that was commonplace by 1877. The author, H. Hildebrandt, links this malformation with the overdevelopment of the clitoris, which he sees as leading to those "excesses" which "are called 'lesbian love.'" The concupiscence of the black is thus associated with the sexuality of the lesbian.[25] More so, the deformation of the labia in the Hottentot is accounted a congenital error, and thus incorporated into the disease model. For the model of degeneracy presumes some acquired pathology in one generation which is the direct cause of the stigmata of degeneracy in the next. Surely the best example of this is the idea of congenital syphilis, widely accepted in the nineteenth century and vividly expressed in Ibsen's drama of biological decay, *Ghosts*. Thus the congenital error Hildebrandt sees in the "Hottentot apron" is presupposed to have some direct and explicable etiology, as well as a specific manifestation. While Hildebrandt is silent as to the etiology, his presentation clearly links the Hottentot's genitalia with the ill, the bestial, and the freak (medicine, biology, and pathology).

How is it that both the genitalia, a primary sexual characteristic, and the buttocks, a secondary sexual characteristic, function as the semantic signs of "primitive" sexual appetite and activity? A good point of departure for addressing this question is the fourth volume of Havelock Ellis's *Studies in the Psychology of Sex* (1905), which contains a detailed example of the great chain of being as applied to the perception of the sexualized Other.[26] Ellis believed that there is an absolute, totally objective scale of beauty which ranges from the European to the black. Thus men of the lower races, according to Ellis, admire European women more than their own, and women of lower races attempt to whiten themselves with face powder. Ellis lists the secondary sexual characteristics that comprise this ideal of beauty, rejecting "naked sexual organ[s]" as not "aesthetically beautiful" since it is "fundamentally necessary" that they "retain their primitive characteristics." Only people "in a low state of culture" perceive the "naked sexual organs as objects of attraction." The secondary sexual characteristics that Ellis then lists as properly attracting admiration among cultured (i.e., not primitive) peoples, the vocabulary of aesthetically pleasing signs, begins with the buttocks. The nineteenth-century fascination with the buttocks as a displacement for the genitalia is thus reworked by Ellis into a higher regard for the beautiful. His discussion of the buttocks ranks the races by size of the female pelvis, a view that began with Willem Vrolik's 1826 claim that a wide pelvis is a sign of racial superiority and was echoed by R. Verneau's 1875 study of the form of the pelvis among the various races.[27] Verneau cited the narrow pelvis of Sarah Bartmann in arguing that the Hottentot's anatomical structure was primitive. While Ellis accepts this ranking, he sees the steatopygia as "a simulation of the large pelvis of the higher races," having a compensatory function like that of face powder. This view places the pelvis in an intermediary role, as both a secondary and a primary sexual sign. Darwin himself, who held similar views as to the objective nature of human beauty, saw the pelvis as a "primary rather than as a secondary character" and the buttocks of the Hottentot as a somewhat comic sign of the black female's primitive, grotesque nature.[28]

When the nineteenth century saw the black female, it saw her in terms of her buttocks, and saw represented by the buttocks all the anomalies of her genitalia. In a mid-century erotic caricature of the Hottentot Venus, she is observed through a telescope by a white male observer, who can see nothing but her buttocks (see Plate 9).[29] Again, in an 1899 British pornographic novel set in a mythic antebellum southern United States, the male author indulges his flagellistic fantasy on the buttocks of a number of white women. When he describes the one black, a runaway slave, being whipped, the power of the image of the Hottentot's buttocks captures him: "She would have had a good figure, only that her bottom was out of all proportion. It was too big, but nevertheless it was fairly well shaped, with well-rounded cheeks meeting each other closely, her thighs were large, and she had a sturdy pair of legs, her skin was smooth and of a clear yellow tint."[30] The presence of exaggerated buttocks points to other, hidden sexual traits, both physical and temperamental, of the black female. This association is a powerful one. Indeed, Freud, in his *Three Essays on Sexuality* (1905), echoes the view that female genitalia are more primitive than those of the male.[31] Female sexuality is tied to the image of the buttocks, and the quintessential buttocks are those of the Hottentot.

The influence of this vocabulary on nineteenth-century perception of the sexualized woman can be seen in Edwin Long's 1882 painting, *The Babylonian Marriage Market* (see Plate 10). This painting claimed a higher price than any other contemporary work of art sold in nineteenth-century London. It also has a special place in documenting the perception of the sexualized female in terms of the great chain of aesthetic beauty presented by Ellis. For Long's painting is based on a specific text from Herodotus, who described the marriage auction in Babylon in which maidens were sold in order of comeliness. In the painting they are arranged in order of their attractiveness according to Victorian aesthetics. Their physiognomies are clearly portrayed. Their features run from the most European and white (a fact emphasized by the light reflected from the mirror onto the figure at the far left) to the Negroid features (thick lips, broad nose, dark but not black skin) of the figure farthest to the observer's right. The latter figure possesses all of the physical qualities Virey attributes to the black. This is, however, the Victorian scale of acceptable sexualized women within marriage, portrayed from the most to the least attractive, according to contemporary British standards. The only black female present is the servant-slave shown on the auction block, positioned so as to present her buttocks to the viewer. While there are black males in the audience and thus among the bidders, the function of the only black female is to signify the sexual availability of the sexualized white women. Her position is her sign, and her presence in the

9. The Hottentot Venus, a German caricature from the beginning of the nineteenth century (from John Grand-Carteret, *Die Erotik in der französischen Karikatur* [Vienna: C. W. Stern, 1909]).

painting is thus analogous to that of the black servant, Laura, in Manet's
Olympia. In Hogarth, the black servants signify the perversities of human
sexuality in a corrupt society; in Long's work of the late nineteenth
century, on the other hand, the linkage between two female figures, one
black and one white, represents the internalization of this perversity in
one specific aspect of human society, the sexualized female.

10. Edwin Long, *The Babylonian Marriage Market* (1882) (Royal Holloway College Gallery, London).

The Iconography of Prostitution

The prostitute is the essential sexualized female in the perception of the nineteenth century. She is perceived as the embodiment of sexuality and of all that is associated with sexuality, disease as well as passion.[32] Within the large and detailed literature concerning prostitution written during the nineteenth century, most of which is devoted to documenting the need for legal controls and draws on the medical model as perceived by public health officials, there is a detailed analysis of the physiognomy and physiology of the prostitute. We can begin with the most widely read early nineteenth-century work on prostitution, the 1836 anthropological study of prostitution in Paris by A. J. B. Parent-Duchatelet.[33] Alain Corbin has shown how Parent-Duchatelet's use of the public health model reduces the prostitute to a source of pollution in much the same class as the sewers of Paris. Parent-Duchatelet believes himself to be providing objective description as he presents his readers with a statistical profile of the physical types of the prostitutes, the nature of their voices, the color of their hair and eyes, their physical anomalies, their characteristics in childbearing, and their sexually transmitted disease. His descriptions range from the detailed to the anecdotal. A discussion of the "embonpoint" of prostitutes begins the litany of their external signs. Prostitutes have a "peculiar plumpness" owing to "the great number of hot baths that the major part of these women take." Or perhaps to their lassitude, rising at ten or eleven in the morning, "leading an animal life." They are fat as prisoners are fat, from simple confinement. As an English commentator noted, "the grossest and stoutest of these women are to be found amongst the lowest and most disgusting classes of prostitutes."[34] These are the Hottentots on the scale of the sexualized female.

When Parent-Duchatelet turned to the sexual parts of the prostitutes, he provided two sets of information that merged to become part of the myth of the physical anthropology of the prostitute. The prostitute's sexual parts are in no way directly affected by their profession. He contradicts the "general opinion . . . that the genital parts in prostitutes must alter, and assume a particular disposition, as the inevitable consequence of their avocation" (42). He cites one case of a woman of fifty-one "who had prostituted herself thirty-six years, but in whom, notwithstanding, the genital parts might have been mistaken for those of a virgin just arrived at puberty" (43). Parent-Duchatelet thus rejected any Lamarckian adaptation, as well as any indication that the prostitute is physically marked as a prostitute. This follows from his view that prostitution is an illness of a society rather than that of an individual or group of individuals. But while he denies that prostitution per se alters the genitalia, he does observe that prostitutes are subject to specific pathologies of their genitalia. They are especially prone to tumors "of the great labia . . . which commence with a little pus and tumefy at each menstrual period" (49). He identifies the central pathology of the prostitute in the following manner: "Nothing is more frequent in prostitutes than common abscesses in the thickness of the labia majora" (50). In effect, Parent-Duchatelet's view that there is no adaptation of the sexual organ is overridden by his assertion that the sexual organ is especially prone to labial tumors and abscesses: the resultant image is of the prostitute's genitalia developing, through disease, an altered appearance.

From Parent-Duchatelet's description of the physical appearance of the prostitute—a catalogue that reappears in most nineteenth-century studies of prostitutes, such as Josef Schrank's study of the prostitutes of Vienna (see Chapter 1)—it is but a small step to the use of such catalogues of stigmata to identify those women who have, as Freud states, "an aptitude for prostitution."[35] The major work of nineteenth-century physical anthropology, public health, and pathology to undertake this was written by Pauline Tarnowsky. Tarnowsky, one of a number of St. Petersburg female physicians in the late nineteenth century, wrote in the tradition of her eponymous colleague V. M. Tarnowsky, who was the author of the standard study of Russian prostitution, a study that appeared in both Russian and German and assumed a central role in late nineteenth-century discussions of the nature of the prostitute.[36] She followed his more general study with a detailed investigation of the physiognomy of the prostitute (see Plate 11).[37] Her categories remain those of Parent-Duchatelet. She describes the excessive weight of prostitutes and their hair and eye color, provides measurements of skull size and a catalogue of their family background (as with Parent-Duchatelet, most are the children of alcoholics), and discusses their fecundity (extremely low), as well as the signs of their degeneration. These signs are facial abnormalities: asymmetry of the face, misshapen noses, overdevelopment of the parietal region of the skull, and the so-called "Darwin's ear." All of these signs belong to the lower end of the scale of beauty, the end dominated by the Hottentot. All of the signs point to the "primitive" nature of the prostitute's physiognomy; stigmata such as Darwin's ear (the simplification of the convolutions of the ear shell and the absence of a lobe) are a sign of atavism.

In a later paper, Tarnowsky provided a scale of the appearance of the

11. "Anomalies of the face and the ear in prostitutes" (from Pauline Tarnowsky, *Etude anthropométrique sur les prostituées et les voleuses* [Paris: E. Lecrosnier et Bebé, 1889]).

prostitute in an analysis of the "physiognomy of the Russian prostitute" (see Plate 12).[38] The upper end of the scale is the "Russian Helen." Here, classical aesthetics are introduced as the measure of the appearance of the sexualized female. A bit further on is one who is "very handsome in spite of her hard expression." Indeed, the first fifteen on her scale "might pass on the street for beauties." But hidden even within these seeming beauties are the stigmata of criminal degeneration: black, thick hair; a strong jaw; a hard, spent glance. Some show the "wild eyes and perturbed countenance along with facial asymmetry" of the insane. Only the scientific observer can see the hidden faults, and thus identify the true prostitute, for the prostitute uses superficial beauty as the bait for her clients. But when they age, their "strong jaws and cheek-bones, and their masculine aspect . . . hidden by adipose tissue, emerge, salient angles stand out, and the face grows virile, uglier than a man's; wrinkles deepen into the likeness of scars, and the countenance, once attractive, exhibits the full degenerate type which early grace had concealed." Time changes the physiognomy of the prostitute, just as it does her genitalia, which become more and more diseased as she ages. For Pauline Tarnowsky, the appearance of the prostitute and her sexual identity are preestablished in

12. The physiognomy of the Russian prostitute: (25) is the "Russian Helen," (18) the "wild eyes of the insane," (20) "very handsome" (from *Archivio di psichiatria, scienze penali ed antropologia criminale* 14 [1893]).

her heredity. What is most striking is that as she ages, the prostitute begins to appear more and more mannish. Billroth's *Handbook of Gynecological Diseases* links the Hottentot with the lesbian; here the link is between two other models of sexual deviancy, the prostitute and the lesbian. Both are seen as possessing physical signs that set them apart from the normal.

The paper in which Pauline Tarnowsky undertook her documentation of the appearance of the prostitute is repeated word for word in the major late nineteenth-century study of prostitution and female criminality, *La donna deliquente,* written by Cesare Lombroso together with his son-in-law, Guglielmo Ferrero, and published in 1893.[39] Lombroso accepts all of Tarnowsky's perceptions of the prostitute and articulates one further subtext of central importance, a subtext made apparent by the plates in his book. For two of the plates illustrate the Hottentot's "apron" and steatopygia (see Plates 6 and 8). Lombroso accepts Parent-Duchatelet's image of the fat prostitute, and sees her as being similar to Hottentots and women living in asylums. The prostitute's labia are throwbacks to the Hottentot, if not the chimpanzee; the prostitute, in short, is an atavistic subclass of woman. Lombroso uses the power of the polygenetic argument applied to the image of the Hottentot to support his views. His text, in its offhand use of the analogy between the Hottentot and the prostitute, simply articulates in images a view that had been present throughout the late nineteenth century. For example, an essay of 1870 by Adrien Charpy, published in the most distinguished French journal of dermatology and syphilology, presented an analysis of the external form of the genitalia of eight hundred prostitutes examined at Lyons.[40] Charpy merged Parent-Duchatelet's two contradictory categories, seeing all of the alterations as either pathological or adaptive. His first category of anomalies is those of the labia, and he begins by commenting on the elongation of the labia majora in prostitutes, comparing this with the apron of the "disgusting" Hottentots. The image comes as naturally to Charpy as it does to Lombroso two decades later. The prostitute is an atavistic form of humanity whose nature can be observed in the form of her genitalia. What Tarnowsky and Lombroso add to this description is a set of other physical indications that can aid in identifying women, however seemingly beautiful, who possess this atavistic nature. And still other signs were quickly found. The French physician L. Julien in 1896 presented clinical material concerning the foot of the prostitute, which Lombroso in commenting on the paper immediately labeled as "prehensile."[41] (Years later, Havelock Ellis would solemnly declare a long second toe and short fifth toe a "beautiful" secondary sexual characteristic in women—a conclusion consistent with Lombroso's.[42]) Lombroso's coauthor, Guglielmo Ferrero, described prostitution as the rule in primitive societies and placed the Bushman at the extreme end on the scale of primitive lasciviousness. Neither adultery nor virginity has any meaning in such societies, according to Ferrero, and the poverty of their mental universe can be seen in the fact that they have but one word for "girl, woman, or wife."[43] The primitive is the black, and the qualities of blackness, or at least of the black female, are those of the prostitute. The strong currency of this equation is grotesquely evident in a series of case studies on steatopygia in prostitutes by a student of Lombroso's, Abele De Blasio, in which the prostitute is quite literally perceived as the Hottentot (see Plate 13).[44]

The late nineteenth-century perception of the prostitute merged with that of the black. Aside from the fact that prostitutes and blacks were both seen as outsiders, what does this amalgamation imply? It is a commonplace that the primitive was associated with unbridled sexuality. This hypersexuality was either condemned, as in Jefferson's discussions of the nature of the black in Virginia, or praised, as in the fictional supplement written by Diderot to Bougainville's voyages.[45] Historians such as J. J. Bachofen postulated it as the sign of the "Swamp," the earliest stage of human history.[46] Blacks, if both Hegel and Schopenhauer are to be believed, remained at this most primitive stage, and their presence in the contemporary world served as an indicator of how far humanity had come in establishing control over the world and itself. The loss of control was marked by a regression into this dark past, a degeneracy into the primitive expression of emotions, in the form of either madness or unbridled sexuality. Such a loss of control was, of course, viewed as pathological and thus fell into the domain of the medical model.

Medicine, especially as articulated in the public health reforms of the mid- and late nineteenth century, was centrally preoccupied with eliminating sexually transmitted disease through the institution of social controls. This was the intent of such writers as Parent-Duchatelet and Tarnowsky. The social controls they wished to institute were well known in the late eighteenth and early nineteenth centuries but in quite a different context. For the laws applying to the control of slaves (such as the 1685 French *code noir* and its American analogues) had placed great emphasis on the control of the slave as sexual object, in terms of permitted and forbidden sexual contacts as well as documentation as to the legal status

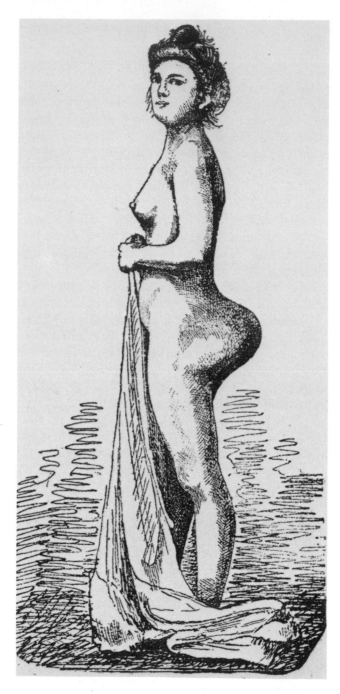

13. Abele De Blasio, "Steatopygia in an Italian prostitute"
(from *Archivio di psichiatria* 26 [1905]).

of the offspring of slaves. The connection made in the late nineteenth century between this earlier model of control and the later model of sexual control advocated by the public health authorities came about through the association of two bits of medical mythology. First, the primary marker of the black is taken to be skin color; second, there is a long history of perceiving this skin color as the result of some pathology. The favorite theory, which reappears with some frequency in the early nineteenth century, is that the skin color and physiognomy of the black are the result of congenital leprosy.[47] It is not very surprising therefore to read in the late nineteenth century (after social conventions surrounding the abolition of slavery in Great Britain and France, as well as the trauma of the American Civil War, forbade the public association of at least skin color with illness) that syphilis was not introduced into Europe by Columbus's sailors but rather was a form of leprosy that had long been present in Africa and spread into Europe in the Middle Ages.[48] The association of the black and syphilophobia is thus manifest. Black females do not merely represent the sexualized female, they also represent the female as the source of corruption and disease. It is the black female as the emblem of illness who haunts the background of Manet's *Olympia*.

Reading *Nana*

Manet's *Olympia* stands exactly midway between the glorification of the sexualized female and her condemnation. She is the antithesis of the fat prostitute. Indeed, she was perceived as "thin" by her contemporaries, much in the style of the actual prostitutes of the 1860s. But Laura, the black servant, is presented as plump—something that can best be seen in Manet's initial oil sketch of her done in 1862–63. In both the sketch and the final painting her face is emphasized, for it is the physiognomy of the black which points to her own sexuality and to that of the white female, who is presented to the viewer unclothed but with her genitalia demurely covered. The hidden genitalia and the face of the black female both point to the potential for corruption of the male viewer by the white female. This potential is even more evident in a work heavily influenced (according to art historians) by Manet's *Olympia,* his portrait *Nana.* In *Nana* the associations would have been quite clear to the contemporary viewer. First, the model for the painting was Henriette

Hauser, called Citron, the mistress of the Prince of Orange. Second, Manet places in the background of the painting a Japanese crane, the French word for which (*grue*) was a slang term for prostitute. The central figure is thus labeled as a sexualized female. Unlike Olympia's classical pose, Nana is not naked but partially clothed, and is shown being admired by a well-dressed man-about-town (a flaneur). Manet draws further upon the vocabulary of signs associated by the late nineteenth century with the sexualized female. Fatness is one stigma of the prostitute, and Nana is fulsome rather than thin. This convention became part of the popular image of the sexualized female even while the idealized sexualized female was "thin." Constantin Guys presents an engraving of a fat, reclining prostitute in 1860, and Edgar Degas's *The Madam's Birthday* (1879) shows an entire brothel of fat prostitutes. At the same time, Napoleon III's mistress, Marguerite Bellanger, set a vogue for slenderness.[49] She was described as "below average in size, slight, thin, almost skinny." This is certainly not Nana. Manet places her in a position vis-à-vis the viewer (but not the male observer in the painting) which emphasizes the line of her buttocks, the steatopygia of the prostitute. Second, Nana is placed in such a way that the viewer (but again not the flaneur) can observe her ear. It is, to no one's surprise, Darwin's ear, a sign of the atavistic female. Thus we know where the black servant is hidden in *Nana*. She is hidden within Nana. For even her seeming beauty is but a sign of the black hidden within. All her external stigmata point to the pathology within the sexualized female.

Manet's *Nana* thus provides a further reading of his *Olympia,* a reading that underlines Manet's debt to the pathological model of sexuality present during the late nineteenth century. The black hidden within *Olympia* bursts forth in Pablo Picasso's 1901 version of the painting, in which Olympia is presented as a sexualized black, with broad hips and revealed genitalia, gazing at the nude flaneur bearing her a gift of fruit, much as Laura bears a gift of flowers in Manet's original (see Plate 14). But the artist, unlike in the works of Manet, is himself present in the work as a sexualized observer of the sexualized female. Picasso owes part of his reading of *Olympia* to the image of the primitive female as sexual object, as found in the lower-class prostitutes painted by van Gogh and the Tahitian maidens à la Diderot painted by Gauguin. Picasso saw the sexualized female as the visual analogue of the black. Indeed, in his most radical break with the Impressionist tradition, *Les demoiselles d'Avignon* (1907), he linked the inmates of a brothel in Barcelona with the black by using the theme of African masks to characterize their appearance. The

14. Pablo Picasso, *Olympia* (1901) (New York, private collection).

figure of the male holding a skull in the early version of the painting is the artist as victim. Picasso's parody points toward the importance of seeing Manet's *Nana* in the context of the prevalent medical discourse concerning the sexualized female in the late nineteenth century. For the portrait of Nana is embedded in a complex literary matrix with many signs linking the sexualized female to disease. The figure of Nana first appeared in Emile Zola's 1877 novel *L'assommoir,* in which she is presented as the offspring of the alcoholic couple who are the central figures of the novel.[50] Her heredity assures the reader that she will eventually become a sexualized female, a prostitute, and indeed that identity is inaugurated at the close of the novel when she runs off with an older man, the owner of a button factory. Manet was taken by the figure of Nana (as was the French reading public), and his portrait of her symbolically reflected her sexual encounters presented in the novel.

Zola then decided to build the next novel in his Rougon-Macquart cycle on the figure of Nana as a sexualized female. Thus in Zola's *Nana* the reader is presented with Zola's reading of Manet's portrait of Nana. Indeed, Zola uses the portrait of the flaneur observing the half-dressed Nana as the centerpiece for a scene in the theater in which Nana seduces the simple Count Muffet. Immediately before this scene, Zola presents Nana's first success in the theater (or, as the theater director calls it, his "brothel"). She appears in a review, unable to sing or dance, and becomes the butt of laughter until in the second act of the review she appears unclothed on stage: "Nana was in the nude: naked with a quiet audacity, certain of the omnipotence of her flesh. She was wrapped in a simple piece of gauze: her rounded shoulders, her Amazon's breasts of which the pink tips stood up rigidly like lances, her broad buttocks which rolled in a voluptuous swaying motion, and her fair, fat hips: her whole body was in evidence, and could be seen under the light tissue with its foamy whiteness."[51] What Zola describes is the sexualized woman, the "primitive" hidden beneath the surface: "All of a sudden in the comely child the woman arose, disturbing, bringing the mad surge of her sex, inviting the unknown element of desire. Nana was still smiling: but it was the smile of a man-eater." Nana's atavistic sexuality, the sexuality of the Amazon, is destructive. The sign of this, her voluptuousness, reappears when she is observed by Muffet in her dressing room, in the scene that Zola found in Manet's painting: "Then calmly, to reach her dressing-table, she walked in her drawers through that group of gentlemen, who made way for her. She had large buttocks, her drawers ballooned, and with breast well forward she bowed to them, giving

her delicate smile" (135). Nana's childlike face is but a mask concealing a
disease buried within, the corruption of sexuality. Thus Zola concludes
the novel by revealing the horror beneath the mask. Nana dies of the
pox. (This is a pun that works in French as well as in English, and that
was needed because of the rapidity of decay demanded by the moral
implication of Zola's portrait. It would not do to have Nana die slowly
over thirty years of tertiary syphilis. Smallpox, with its play on the pox,
works quickly and gives the same visual icon of decay.) Nana's death
reveals her true nature:

Nana remained alone, her face looking up in the light from the candle. It was a
charnel-house scene, a mass of tissue-fluids and blood, a shovelful of putrid flesh
thrown there on a cushion. The pustules had invaded the entire face with the
pocks touching each other; and, dissolving and subsiding with the greyish look
of mud, there seemed to be already an earthy mouldiness on the shapeless mus-
cosity, in which the features were no longer discernible. An eye, the left one, had
completely subsided in a soft mass of purulence; the other, half-open, was sink-
ing like a collapsing hole. The nose was still suppurating. A whole reddish crust
was peeling off one cheek and invaded the mouth, distorting it into a loathsome
grimace. And on that horrible and grotesque mask, the hair, that beautiful head
of hair still preserving its blaze of sunlight, flowed down in a golden trickle.
Venus was decomposing. It seems as though the virus she had absorbed from the
gutters and from the tacitly permitted carrion of humanity, that baneful ferment
with which she had poisoned a people, had now risen to her face and putrefied it.
(464–65)

The decaying visage is the visible sign of the diseased genitalia through
which the sexualized female corrupts an entire nation of warriors and
leads them to the collapse at Sedan. The image is an old one; it is *Frau
Welt*, Madam World, who masks her corruption, the disease of being a
woman, with her beauty. It reappears in the vignette on the title page of
the French translation (1840) of the Renaissance poem *Syphilis* (see Plate
15).[52] But it is yet more, for Nana begins in death to revert to the
blackness of the earth, to assume the horrible grotesque countenance
perceived as belonging to the world of the black, the word of the "primitive," the world of disease. Nana is, like Olympia, in the words of Paul
Valéry, "pre-eminently unclean."[53] And it is this uncleanness, this disease, which forms the final link between two images of the woman, the
black and the prostitute. For, just as the genitalia of the Hottentot were
perceived as parallel to the diseased genitalia of the prostitute, so too the

15. Frontispiece to the August Barthelemy translation of Fracastorius's Renaissance poem on syphilis (from August Barthelemy, trans., *Syphilis: Poème en deux chants* [Paris: Béchet junior et Labé & Bohaire, 1840]).

powerful idea of corruption links both images. Nana is corrupted and corrupts through sexuality.

Miscegenation is a word from the late nineteenth-century vocabulary of sexuality. It embodies a fear not merely of interracial sexuality, but of its supposed result, the decline of the population. For interracial marriages were seen as exactly parallel to prostitution in their barrenness. If they produced children at all, these children were weak and doomed. Thus Havelock Ellis, enlarging on his view of the objective nature of the beauty of humanity, states that "it is difficult to be sexually attracted to persons who are fundamentally unlike ourselves in racial constitution"[54] and approvingly quotes Abel Hermant:

Differences of race are irreducible and between two beings who love each other they cannot fail to produce exceptional and instructive reactions. In the first superficial ebullition of love, indeed, nothing notable may be manifested, but in a fairly short time the two lovers, innately hostile, in striving to approach each other strike against an invisible partition which separates them. Their sensibilities are divergent; everything in each shocks the other; even their anatomical conformation, even the language of their gestures; all is foreign.[55]

It is thus the innate fear of the Other's different anatomy which lies behind the synthesis of images. The Other's pathology is revealed in her anatomy, and the black and the prostitute are both bearers of the stigmata of sexual difference and thus pathology. Zola sees in the sexual corruption of the male the source of political impotence and provides a projection of what is basically a personal fear, the fear of loss of power, onto the world.[56] The "white man's burden," his sexuality and its control, is displaced into the need to control the sexuality of the Other, the Other as sexualized female. For the colonial mentality that sees "natives" as needing control easily shifts that concern to the woman, in particular the prostitute caste. Because the need for control was a projection of inner fears, its articulation in visual images was in terms which were the polar opposite of the European male. The progenitors of the vocabulary of images of the sexualized female believed that they were capturing the essence of the Other. Thus when Sigmund Freud, in his essay on lay analysis (1926), discussed the ignorance of contemporary psychology concerning adult female sexuality, he referred to this lack of knowledge as the "dark continent" of psychology, an English phrase with which he tied female sexuality to the image of contemporary colonialism and thus to the exoticism and pathology of the Other.[57] It was Freud's intent to explore this hidden "dark continent" to reveal the hidden truths about female sexuality, just as the anthropologist-explorers, such as Lombroso, were revealing further hidden truths about the nature of the black. Freud continues a discourse that relates images of male discovery to images of the female as the object of discovery. The line from the secrets possessed by the Hottentot Venus to those of twentieth-century psychoanalysis runs reasonably straight.

4

Black Sexuality and
Modern Consciousness

Fantasy and Representation

AMOS OZ, one of the most insightful of contemporary Hebrew novelists, paints an extraordinary portrait of the *yeke,* the German Jew in Israel, in his epistolary novella "Longing." In this tale Dr. Emanuel Nussbaum remembers a moment in prewar Vienna, "a summer's day," while, when walking through the city, he saw "a pair of Negro beggars": "I stop and linger, watching them from a short distance away. Not long ago I took a course in anthropology, yet I believe that these are the first Negroes I have ever seen. Outside the circus, of course. Yes, they are woolly-haired. Coffee-skinned, not cocoa-colored. A slight shudder ripples through me. I brush aside a fleeting mental image of the shape of their sexual organs."[1] This epiphany associates the German image of the black with the fantasy of black sexuality. But even more directly it associates the act of seeing the black with a fantasy of the genitalia: seeing the black evokes the genitalia in a direct and unmitigated manner. For Oz this association reveals the attitude of German Jews to the sexuality of that exotic which they will become once transplanted into the Near East. German Jews become the object of their own sexual fantasy. Amos Oz's literary portrayal of this association enables me to state my own thesis most directly. During the rise of modernism, from the fin de siècle to the collapse of the Nazi state (and beyond), the black, whether male or female, came to represent the genitalia through a series of analogies. It is this series of mental associations which must be un-raveled in order to understand Amos Oz's epiphany of the Viennese view of black sexuality.

To begin, let us remove ourselves to a pre–World War I German or Austrian zoological garden. If we cast our eye back into time, to turn-of-the-century Vienna, to see with the eye of the Viennese of the period, we will be seeing a zoological garden quite different from our contemporary "zoo." We will be struck by the fact that among the animals on display are specimens of the genus *Homo sapiens*. Indeed, the European zoo-logical garden of the late nineteenth century provided "ethnological" exhibitions, representations of "exotic" cultures, eating what were viewed as appropriate foods, living in appropriate housing, and under-taking appropriate tasks for "primitives." Replaced in the 1920s by the film travelogue, the "ethnological" exhibition was a natural extension of the ethnological museum, placing living "exotics" within the daily expe-rience of the European. As we have seen, Vienna was no exception to this. In the Prater, the major city park, imported exotics were viewed with fascination by the masses. Here were "noble" exotics whose pres-ence countered the malignant "ignobility" of the local exotics, Eastern Jews; but as we shall see, they were credited with many of the same stereotyped sexual characteristics.

The Jews, especially the Eastern Jews, represented a specific type of perverse sexuality within the stereotypes of fin-de-siècle perception (in their case, incest); and the black represented another. The black's sexu-ality, like that of the Jew, was classed as a disease. In both cases the pathology was one that articulated many of the publicly repressed sexual fantasies of the turn of the century. In the case of blacks, their sexual pathology was tied to the form of their genitalia.

This is not to deny that the black was perceived as an attractive sexual object in fin-de-siècle Vienna. Magnus Hirschfeld reported in a rather jaundiced tone (quite unusual for this great sexual liberal) a "queer pre-dilection for Ashantis that for a while raged in Vienna" among the wom-en of that city, who would "approach these negroes under different pretexts" for sexual encounters.[2] The Ashantis exhibited in Budapest as well as Vienna became the sexual icon for the "royal and imperial" monarchy. But it is important to understand that the Ashantis were simply substitutes for a mythic image of the black, just as such "blacks" in turn signified the diseased yet attractive Other. The attraction of the black was coupled with the sense of danger, as we shall see.

Vienna

After an exhibition of a group of Ashantis in 1896, Peter Altenberg published his *Ashantee* (1897), a work that was then anthologized, but always in extract, in his later collections.[3] Altenberg was a master of the sketch, the creation of an intense, evocative literary image; in *Ashantee* he provided an interlocking series of such sketches with an overall literary structure lacking in his other works. *Ashantee* is a record of Altenberg's fascination with the young Ashanti women and girls exhibited in the Prater. On the surface the book is a liberal protest against the exploitation of the blacks by a European public with a taste for the exotic. But a powerful subtext betrays a habit of mind that the author shares with the guilty public of reflexively fantasizing about human genitalia when he "sees" the black.

The work opens with a long quotation from *Meyer's Encyclopedia*, placing the Ashantis ethnologically (3–4). Following the general view of the most influential geographer of the late nineteenth century, Friedrich Ratzel, the unsigned author of the encyclopedia article, observes that the Ashantis are "true, woolly-headed blacks," whose priests have the function of exorcising evil spirits through "hysterical" dances.[4] These two qualities, the "true" nature of the Ashantis as a race and the "hysterical" quality of their religion, begin Altenberg's text. By opening with hallowed words from an encyclopedia, a textual ethnological museum that exhibits the black within the context of scientific discourse, Altenberg attempts to counter or undermine the popular tone of Prater's exhibition of the black. Yet the citation also begins to document, no matter how subtly, an association between the black and the genitalia.

Altenberg's opening vignette provides the expected liberal condemnation of the Ashanti exhibition in the Prater (5–13). In the zoological garden there stands a cage inhabited by exotic beasts from the Amazon, two pampas hares, sitting quite humanlike on their haunches nibbling the sweets tossed to them by the crowd. Next to this cage are the Ashantis, seen performing a native dance. We, the readers, find ourselves viewing the scene in the company of two employees of the zoo, who discuss one of the young Ashanti women in much the same tone as that with which they had spoken about the pampas hares. The ideological message—how horrible it is to have human beings exhibited and gawked at like pampas hares!—is completed in the closing sketch. One of the employees comments to the director of the zoo about someone who has just left the abandoned huts of the Ashantis in tears. The director's response is: "By the way, these huts have to be demolished tomorrow to make way for the tightrope walkers and a tethered balloon ride" (72). Thus, on its surface, Altenberg's most sustained message is a condemnation of Viennese society for having turned the Ashantis into an amusement. This overtly ideological frame, however, contains within it a complex set of textual references to the sexual nature of the black, references embedded in the observations of the narrative I/eye, "Peter A." These references are a hidden code that, once deciphered, reveals to us the function of the black not only within the fantasy world of Peter Altenberg, but also within the world of the modernist text.

Our first introduction to the consciousness of this "eye" is in the second vignette. The structure of this vignette is shared by those that follow—a dialogue (with or without Peter A.'s interlocutor actually being present and responding) with one of the young females in the ersatz village of the Ashantis. The vignette, programmatically titled "Dialogue," begins with a discourse by "Peter A." on the nakedness of the young girls: "It is cold and very damp, Tioko. There are puddles everywhere. You all are naked. What are these thin linen things? You have cold hands, Tioko. I will warm them. You need at least cotton flannel, not this smooth cloth" (14). Tioko responds by stressing the fact that it is the exhibitioners who demand that the Ashantis appear "naked." She observes that the Ashantis would never dress this way in Africa, nor would they live in huts fit only for dogs. "They want us to represent animals," she comments. The organizer of the exhibition has told her that there are enough clothed females in Europe, and what they need is for the Ashantis to be "naked." *Naked* is Altenberg's word in this context; it is clear that the Ashanti women are dressed in the fashion customary for exhibitions of blacks in Europe from the beginning of the nineteenth century, in a garment thin enough to be quite revealing. But exactly what was the signification of the nakedness of the black female, a nakedness Peter Altenberg deplores?

The "Hottentot Venus," as has been shown, served as the emblem of black sexuality during the entire nineteenth century, a sexuality inherently different from that of the European. An attempt to establish that the races were inherently different rested to no little extent on the sexual difference of the black. When, in the late nineteenth century, medical literature likened the genitalia of the black female to those of the infected prostitute, the fear (and fascination) accompanying the one became associated with the other. Thus by the time Peter Altenberg began to write

Ashantee the idea of black sexuality as pathological was well implanted in European consciousness. The black woman had become doubly unapproachable: unapproachable both because of her difference as a member of an inherently different race and because of her pathological character. As we shall see, this stereotype assumed a most surprising dimension in literary discourse.

The sketch following "Dialogue" in Peter Altenberg's *Ashantee,* "Culture," presents the reader with an account of a dinner party in Vienna to which two of the Ashanti women were invited (28–29). The dinner party chitchat revolves about the guests' perception of a difference between the "childlike" nature of the black woman and (although the word never falls) the "adult" nature of Western women. Our eye in the tale, Peter A., comments quite directly that "blacks are children." Here is a further marker of difference, the roots of which can be found in classical antiquity. The Other is like the child, different from the mature and sensible adult. But we have seen that in the fin de siècle "adult" sexuality was commonly imputed to the female "child." Indeed, when Josephine Baker appeared in Vienna in 1929, or at least tried to appear— for the city council found her costumes much too lascivious—she was glorified, totally without irony, by her supporters in Vienna as "that beautiful black child."[5] In Altenberg's dinner party sketch, the implications of the child as sexual object become evident when the younger of the two Ashantis is given a "wonderful French doll," to which she begins to sing. The older of the two "suddenly bared her perfect upper body and began to nurse the doll from her magnificent breasts." The audience to this spectacle is awed by the naturalness of her action, and one of the guests is moved to say that this is one of the "holiest" moments in her life. The bared breast has a function as a sexual sign of physical maturity, but is given here a clearly contradictory association with "childishness." Its signification is quite different from (to take a well-known example) the iconography of the breasts in Theodor de Bry's illustrations of the early reports of the explorers of North America, where, as Bernadette Bucher has shown, the shift from "classic" (firm) breasts to sagging breasts has major structural significance in representing the general shift in attitude toward the "exotic."[6] Here the sign of the breast is that of the "girl-woman": the child with the physical characteristics of the adult.

The power of this association within the world of Peter Altenberg can be judged by the central sexually referential vignette, "A Letter from Africa" (32–35). This, the eleventh vignette in the book, begins on a somber note. The brother of one of the young women has died in Accra, and this news is received by all with an act of communal mourning. This opening leads, however, to a further moment in this natural history of Altenberg's perception of the black. Suddenly it is nine at night: "I enter the hut. On the ground lie Monabo, Akole, the wonderful one, and Akoschia. Not a pillow, not a blanket. Their perfect upper bodies are naked. The air is filled with the odor of pure, noble young bodies. I lightly touch the wonderful Akole." The sexual overtones to this passage are unmistakable. What is striking is the association of the concept of racial purity, such as is mentioned in the selection from *Meyer's Encyclopedia,* and the "purity" ascribed to the "odor" of the black. Olfactory qualities had long been used to label the Other as different. Indeed, in the biology of race in late nineteenth-century Germany, a mephitic odor was one of the central markers of difference imputed to Jews.[7] The apparent function of the "pure" odor of the "noble young bodies" of the black women is to reverse the valence of difference. Yet difference and odor are both associated with sexuality in late nineteenth-century discourse. I have already remarked on Altenberg's use of the absence of shame as an indicator of the childlike nobility of the Ashanti. Lombroso provided a reading of the origin of this sense of shame in the "primitive." He remarked that in the Romance languages the term for shame is taken from the root *putere,* which he interprets as indicating that the origin of the sense of shame lies in the disgust for body smells. This he "proves" by observing that prostitutes show a "primitive pseudo-shame," a fear of being repulsive to the male, since they are loath to have their genitalia inspected when they are menstruating. The "pure odor" and absence of shame of the Ashantis (their exposed upper bodies serving as an icon of their unself-consciousness) are signs of their sexual availability.[8] But the association between odor and difference also points quite directly to the image of the source of pollution. The smell of the menses is equated with the stench of ordure, both human and animal, in the public health model of disease of the late nineteenth century. Edwin Chadwick, the greatest of the early Victorian crusaders for public sanitation (who built upon the theoretical work of German writers such as E. B. C. Heberstreit), perceived disease as the result of putrefaction of effluvia. For Chadwick "all smell is disease." Public sanitation and the image of the corrupting female (and her excreta) are linked through the agency of smell.[9]

The next moment in the vignette makes the covert reference to the sexuality of the black overt. Monambo, awakened, turns to him and asks: "Sir, tomorrow can you bring us a 'piss-pot'? It is too cold to leave the hut at night. It must be blue outside and white inside. We will pay you what it costs. You could give Tioko one! What might it cost?!" Peter A. replies: "Monambo, I have never bought a 'piss-pot.' I don't know how much it will cost. Between 50 Kreuzer and 500 Gulden. Queens use golden ones." Monambo then repeats her first speech to him and the vignette has Peter A. leaving the hut as dawn comes.

Altenberg's fantasy of consummation with the black is cast in a literary mold. His seduction takes place within the safe confines of the text. But it is a fantasy of seduction which equates the black woman with her genitalia, which makes her into the representation of sexuality per se. Altenberg's literary encoding of this is uncomplicated. Without a doubt the most blatant sign is the conclusion of the vignette, the lover departing at the crack of dawn. This theme, that of the *aube,* is part of the standard literary repertoire of seduction. It is an image whose associations are self-evident. Consummation has been accomplished and the male leaves, walking into the new day. The act of coitus is part of the nightside of fantasy. The dawn song serves as an extended metaphor for the postcoital depression of the male. But Altenberg has peppered his text with further sexual associations that make the final "dawn song" unstartling. Central to them is Monambo's request for a "piss-pot."

The sexual association of the female genitalia with urination has a long textual history. In fact, the first major text in the Western literary tradition which associates these two images relates them also to the figure of the black. The Song of Songs (7:2) sings of the "navel [that] is like a round goblet, which wanteth not liquor." But it is with the further, post-Enlightenment association of urination and shame within a literary context that the fascination of the nineteenth-century male for the genitalia of the female is made overt. Goethe's *Wilhelm Meister's Apprenticeship* describes Wilhelm's seduction by the actress Marianne: "It seemed to him when he had here to remove her stays in order to reach the harpsicord, there to lay her skirt on the bed before he could set himself, when she herself with unembarrassed frankness would make no attempt to conceal from him many natural acts which people are accustomed to hide from others out of decency—it seemed to him, I say, that he became bound to her by invisible bonds."[10] The act of observing excretion destroys the power of "shame," just as the nakedness of the Ashantis and their request for a "piss-pot" remove the veil of social practices and bind the Western observer to them. The power of this passage from *Wilhelm Meister's Apprenticeship* can be judged by a report of William Wordsworth's response. Wordsworth read the novel until "he came to the scene where the hero, in his mistress's bedroom, becomes sentimental over her dirty towels, etc., which struck him with such disgust that he flung the book out of his hand, would never look at it again, and declared that surely no English lady would ever read such a work."[11] It was clearly the "etc." that caused Wordsworth's agitation. For the observing of Marianne's act of exposure revealed the power that the perception of sexuality has on the male. The observation of a woman urinating stresses both the difference and the similarity of the Other. The act is one associated by the male with the phallus, but as undertaken by a woman it calls attention to the absence of the phallus. This image of the "damaged" (and "damaging") genitalia of the female becomes associated with the black as the antithesis of self. The black becomes the genitalia as the sign of pathological difference. And at this level of analogy it is quite unimportant whether the genitalia are male or female.

Altenberg picks up this theme and links it to the fantasy of "seeing" the black, a black of "pure" race and "pure" sexuality. It results, however, in a seduction that takes place only within the text, only through the association of perceiving blacks and fantasizing about their genitalia. The movement from talking about the act of urination to the fantasy of coitus is buried in a nest of ellipses in the text, ellipses that herald the trope of the parting lovers. Again, Altenberg uses a "liberal" overlay to rationalize his projection concerning the sexuality and genitalia of the black. His use of the English term "piss-pot" leads the reader back to a colonial world where, according to the women, "piss-pots" would not be used by blacks. The blacks need the "piss-pot" because they are being housed in kennels and clothed in thin, revealing garments that make it uncomfortable to leave their huts at night. The covert association comes about through speaking about urination, for urination in the late nineteenth-century mind leads to a fantasy of the buttocks.

Among Havelock Ellis's case studies—which, as Phyllis Grosskurth has shown, are themselves fantasies on sexual themes—is one "firsthand" account of this association between the act of urination and the buttocks:

Florrie herself, who became so acute an analyst of her own experiences, pointed out the significant fact that in a woman there is invariably a mental association,—an association which has no existence in a man's mind,—between the nates and the act of urination. The little girl's drawers must be unfastened behind to permit of the act being accomplished and the grown woman must raise her clothes behind for the same act; even when, as is now so often the custom, she adopts the standing attitude in private, she usually raises the clothes behind, though, as the stream tends to take a forward direction, it would be more convenient to raise them in front. Thus, throughout life, in a woman's mind there is an association between urination and bared prominent nates. Custom, as Florrie emphasizes, compels a woman to bare and protrude the nates and sit for the purpose of urination, and when there is nothing to sit upon to squat, although, she adds, "as far as decency goes, it might be much more modest to turn one's back to any stray passerby, and raise the skirts in front, towards a protective bush; but this would be contrary to habit—and savour of a man!" Even when, as we have seen to be the case with Florrie, the practice of urination in the open without raising of the skirts is adopted, the prominence of the nates may still be asserted, for, as Florrie discovered, the act is best performed in this attitude when bending forward slightly and so protruding the nates.[12]

Present in Ellis's text are the associations of childhood and of exhibitionism with the act of urination and the baring of the buttocks. The powerful association of the buttocks with the primitive, with the buttocks of the black in the nineteenth century, thus leads the reader back to Altenberg and the bodies of the young Ashanti women on display in the Prater.

Havelock Ellis's case study of Florrie is a tale of the growth of a perversion. Florrie's association of the buttocks and the act of urination, which is strongly connected with the development of her flagellist fetish, is representative of the fin-de-siècle perception of the sexual act. The effect of presenting this association as the central focus for the image of the black is to link the black with the pathological, especially the sexually pathological. The fascination of fin-de-siècle writers such as Altenberg with the sexually pathological mirrors the Victorian image of the sexualized being found in works such as George Gissing's *The Whirlpool* (1897). "When one of the characters is killed off by bad street drains," comments Bernard Meyer, "it is tempting to suspect that this annihilating instrument of public plumbing was a symbolic representation of the devouring female genital, an awful image of that cloacal anatomy that appears to have become for Gissing an emblem of all ugliness. The very streets of London appear to partake in the mephitic attributes of the women who roam them."[13] Meyer quite correctly associates pathology and excretion with the image of the genitals. (Later in the twentieth century the excretory act and the genitals are linked; both remain associated with pathology.)

In Altenberg's text the "piss-pot" serves as a marker of a shift from the accepted exoticism of the breasts of the black to the hidden sexuality of the black female. The "scientific" passage from *Meyer's Encyclopedia* cited at the beginning of *Ashantee,* by laying emphasis on the fetishistic nature of the Ashantis' religion and the "hysterical" dances of their priests, evokes a complementary idea. For by 1896 the term *hysterical* had a specific female context and was used in analogy to the repressed sexuality of the clergy;[14] so that to describe the priests of the Ashanti as "hysterical" meant to classify them with the Bacchanti and other groups of "hysterical" females. The German makes this overt, since the masculine form of *priest (Priester)* is used, excluding the female from this now feminized category, the fetishistic priest. The Ashanti females are thus portrayed as the antithesis of the hysteric. They are not hysterical *even in their shared grief.* They are users of objects in their nonfetishistic function; the "piss-pot" is to be used as a "piss-pot." Altenberg has confused two categories that can quite easily be unraveled. The first is that of the adult, sexualized exotic, whether male or female. In this category are the priests, the male blacks who are banished to the margins of the text, appearing only in the opening passage. The second is that of the child, the unconsciously sexualized exotic, the black as child, which Altenberg can approach in his fantasy.

Monambo is conscious of Altenberg's fantasy when she asks him to buy her a "piss-pot" and says that she would most probably give one to Tioko. Altenberg approaches a fantasy of physical intimacy only hinted at in Baudelaire's description of "Vénus noire." It is indeed a detailed fantasy of the difference of the black based on ethnologists' discussions of the inherent difference between black female sexual structure and that of the nonblack. Again, it is in Friedrich Ratzel's ethnology that this sexual difference, perceived in the structure of the "Hottentot apron," is invoked as an important exhibit in the case for the polygenetic difference of the races. Ratzel sees this sexual anomaly as present in many of the African races; it makes the woman into a "perfect monster."[15] For Altenberg, the difference between the clothed, demure prepubescent Austrian "Mädel" such as the thirteen-year-old Bertha Lecker, whose photograph he ornamented with a lover's heart, and the bare-breasted "young Egyptian" whose photograph he described in a letter to Arthur Schnitzler as "my black friend Nahbaduh, . . . the last madness of my soul," is approachability.[16] It is the difference between health and pathology. When Altenberg sees the black, it is as the approachable exotic, the bared breast functioning as a signifier analogous to beckoning genitalia.

Earlier I discussed how the image of the child-woman in fin-de-siècle Vienna became closely linked with sexual license through the distancing effects of projection (Chapter 1). It is indeed the pure child as sexual object, the child free from the curse of adult sexuality (with all of its pathological associations for the nineteenth century), which is projected onto the exotic as sexual object. I have stressed the importance of class as well as age as the matrix into which the projection of sexuality, the creation of the permissible object of desire, is made. With Altenberg the exotic is not merely class- and age-determined, she is also race-determined. In part this reflects the patriarchal attitude of the West toward the black, which is as much in evidence in the liberalism of "Peter A." as in the conservatism of the entrepreneur in the Prater. But there is a hidden agenda in Altenberg's projection. For there is yet another group viewed as a "pure" race, speaking a different tongue, whose males are portrayed as possessing feminine characteristics. It is, of course, the Jews. At the same time that Altenberg was publishing *Ashantee* (1897), Walter Rathenau published his "Hear, O Israel," which was one of the most widely discussed self-critical texts of the day.[17] In it Rathenau described the Jews as a tribe much like the Ashantis, but stressed the negative aspects of such attitudes and behavior in the context of Western culture. Rathenau's views, which included the description of the male Jew as possessing all of the qualities usually ascribed to the woman (or indeed the homosexual), were part of the discourse on race which dominated the nineteenth century. The two major examples for theories of race in the nineteenth century were the blacks and the Jews. Altenberg, who would convert to Catholicism three years after *Ashantee* was published, identifies with the Ashanti as part of his distancing and projection of the conflicts arising from his own Jewish identity. He sees the young black female as the antithesis of the racial stereotype of the Jew. The Jew is a male who acts like a female, one who belongs to the category of the "hysteric" like the Ashanti male priests. The Jew belongs to a "pure" race, the sign of which is degenerative sexual selectivity. The Ashantis are females who act like children, who do not belong to the category of the "hysteric." The Ashantis are a "pure" race who, however, permit the sexual attention of the outsider. This is Altenberg's reaction to the criticism of Jewish sexual selectivity. For nineteenth-century psychiatry saw *all* blacks, male and female, as especially prone to hysteria.[18] Like the

Jews, the blacks were at risk because of the racial association. Altenberg has created an acceptable projection of his own internalization of the charges brought against the Jews because of their sexual selectivity. He has incorporated this into his fantasy about the sexuality of the child and has thus created his own image of the accessible black child.

Altenberg's fin-de-siècle fantasy of the black is not unique. His mentor, Karl Kraus, makes numerous references to the prejudiced attitudes of German and Austrian society toward the black, but refers only to incidents concerning the depiction of black sexuality.[19] Kraus's focus is on the German and Austrian interest in black sexuality, but this focus reveals his own fascination with black sexuality. Fin-de-siècle Austrian liberalism trained its attention on the black as possessing an alternative, perhaps even utopian, human sexuality. The sense of difference dominates this discourse, as it does the discourse of other writers, writers whose view of human nature stresses biology and downplays culture.

Paris

The role of the black as the icon of sexuality, a source of fascination that Kraus shares with conservative critics whom he rebuts, permeates the entire liberal discussion of the black during the early twentieth century. The blacks' identity is as surrogate genitals, often but not always of the other sex. As we move from Vienna to Paris, what is striking is that even though the ideology of the writers we examine is diametrically opposed to the "liberal" ideology of Altenberg and Kraus, they share the same perception of the black. If Viennese modernism condemned the exploitation of the black as sexual object and used this condemnation to veil the authors' fascination with the sexual difference of the black, authors in Paris during the 1930s required no such ruse. For them blacks represented sexual expression untrammeled by the repressive conventions of European society, or so it was supposed to appear.

The complexity of a conservative, vitalistic image of the black as sexual object can be judged by an aside Mellors makes to Connie in D. H. Lawrence's *Lady Chatterley's Lover:* "I was really getting bitter. I thought there was no sex left: never a woman who'd really 'come' naturally with a man: except black women, and somehow, well, we're white men: and they're a bit like mud."[20] This analogy between blacks and the earth, not the fecund earth but the earth associated with death, is reminiscent of the image of Nana at the conclusion of Zola's novel. Fantasies of black sexuality are usually linked, as in Lawrence, to some negative qualification of black sexuality as pathological. Henry Miller in his *Tropic of Capricorn* (1938) presented a world that, like Lawrence's, centers around the sexual act as the image of natural force.[21] His black figure, Valeska, had one "sad thing about" her. "She had nigger blood in her veins. It was depressing for everybody around her" (57). She also possessed the mephitic odor still associated in the 1930s with blacks and Jews (113). These flawed black sexual objects evoke the association of the black as the image of human sexuality, but only as peripheral figures (or metaphoric asides) in modernist literary works.

Henry Miller's novel was part of the inspiration for the first major work by one of modernism's most widely read authors, Lawrence Durrell. His novel *The Black Book,* while not his first work of fiction, was viewed by the author as well as his readers as his first "original" work. Published in 1938 under Henry Miller's influence (and in a series edited by him), the novel is a sexual adventure tale drawing heavily on Miller and James Joyce for its inspiration. It is a *Bildungsroman,* a tale of the education of an author in the complexities of the world. This world is represented by the womb (as it is in Miller's *Tropic of Capricorn*), and the novel uses the image of the womb as one of its central metaphors. None of these images is more revealing, because of its high modernist language, than the evocation of the black by the protagonist, Lawrence Lucifer. His interior monologue functions as an aside in the novel, presenting a contrast to the image of the central female figure, Hilda, who, following Otto Weininger's precept, is both mother and whore, and whose presence, while dying of venereal disease, links fecundity and Thanatos. At the close of the novel, Hilda is sterile, her ovaries having been removed, and yet she remains the womb incarnate, a diseased, nonproductive womb, but a womb nevertheless. In contrast to her accessibility is the figure of the black: "Miss Smith's red coon slit, her conk, her poll, her carnivorous ant-eating laughter, her Chaucerian Africa with Freudian fauna and flora . . . more coon slits and coon slatted laughter."[22] So ran Henry Miller's response to the manuscript of Durrell's novel. Here the circle is closed and the black female literally becomes her genitalia.

Lawrence Durrell introduces the black "Miss Smith" as a student of Lawrence Lucifer, a student to whom he is to teach Chaucer's language and with whom he is warned not to "muck about." Miss Smith is inarticulate, responding to all questions with "a snigger, laughing behind her hand." Lawrence Lucifer looks at her, seeing her as a work of art, as an aesthetic object:

She will laugh in her sleeves. Her eyeballs will incandesce. Her red Euro-African mouth will begin to laugh again. It becomes impossible to walk hand in hand with Chaucer on the first Monday morning of the world. The laughter penetrates us, soaks us, winds us in spools of damp humorous macaroni. Beads of Nubian sweat break from the chocolate skin, powdered into a matt surface. Miss Smith sits forever at the centre of a laughing universe, her large languid tits rotating on their own axes—the whizzing omphaloi of locomotion. African worlds of totem and trauma. The shingle deserts, the animals, the arks, the floods, carved in a fanatical rictus of the dark face, bent hair, and the long steady pissing noise under the lid of teeth.[23]

In beginning with the laughter of the black and the author's perception of the black as aesthetic object, Lawrence Lucifer's interior monologue has much in common with Peter Altenberg's *Ashantee*. As in Altenberg, the image contains hidden contamination, the breath of sexual pathology. For as Lucifer listens to Miss Smith's laughter, the sound of laughter reverberates: "All she can do is laugh in her sleeve and powder that black conk of hers jutting from the heavy helmet of her head; when she pisses, pressed down, squashed over the sound-box, from the laughter spurt jets of hideous darkness, a storm of Zanzibar, like black treacle."[24] What begins as the hidden laughter of the black ends with the equation of laughter and "pissing." Urination becomes the focus of the image of the black; unlike in Altenberg's fantasy, however, the focus does not remain on urination. Lawrence moves from urination to sexuality as the all-consuming force:

That focus which attracts us all so much is centred, like a cyclone, over sex. You may think you are looking at her, looking at the idea of her, but really, seeking under her cheap European dress, you are looking at her fertility. The potential stirring of something alive, palpitating, under her dress. The strange stream of sex which beats in the heavy arteries, faster and faster, until the world is shaken to pieces about one's ears, and you are left with an indeterminate vision of the warm African fissure, opened as tenderly as surgery, a red-lipped coon grin . . . to swallow all the white races and their enervate creeds, their arks, their olive branches.[25]

All the world is the womb, according to Lawrence, Miller, and Durrell, but the black womb is quite different. In Miller's *Tropic of Capricorn* the reader is given the fantasy of the womb as the microcosm, the womb belonging to a languageless, mute woman; Durrell's image is quite directly parallel. Miss Smith's inarticulateness is paralleled by the extraordinary nature of her sexual parts, which contain, not the world, but the blackness of the world, Africa, the essence of Thanatos:

Always I find myself turning from the pages of Geography, of flora and fauna, of geological surveys, to these studies in ethos. The creeds and mores of a continent, clothed in an iridescent tunic of oil. I turn always to those rivers running between black thighs for ever and for ever. A cathartic Zambesi which never freezes over, fighting its way through, but flowing as chastely as if it were clothed in an iridescent tunic of oil. I turn always to those exquisite horrors, the mutilations and deformations, which cobble the history of the dark continent in little ulcers of madness. Strange streaks here and there you will find: hair-trigger insanities, barely showing, like flaws in ice, but running in a steady, heavy river, the endless tributary of sex. They feed those fecundating rivers of seed which flow between the cool thighs of the Nubian, stiffen in his arteries, and escape in steaming laughter down his sleeve. Look, if you dare, and see the plate-mouthed women of the Congo Basin, more delectable than the pelican. Vaginas turning blue and exploding in dark flowers. The penis slit like a ripe banana. Seed spurting like a million comets. The menstrual catharsis swerving down from the loins, dyeing the black carpets of flesh in the sweet smell, the rich urao of blood. The world of sensation that hums, dynamically, behind the walls of the belly. The slit lips of the vagina opening like a whale for the Jonahs of civilization. The vegetable rites. The prepucophagous family man: the foreskin eater. All this lives in the wool of Miss Smith, plainly visible, but dying.[26]

The black womb becomes the world of blackness, in which the black becomes the genitalia. But the black womb encompasses not only the "vagina" but also the "penis." What was a gender-specific image equating "blackness" with female sexuality becomes, through its assimilation of the rites of circumcision, an image of the power of sexuality in general—but a damaged, corrupted, and corrupting sexuality.

James Joyce had introduced the association of urination, sexuality, and stream-of-consciousness discourse in Molly Bloom's closing monologue.[27] Her sole act during this monologue so redolent with the fantasies and memories of her own sexuality is to urinate. Joyce's cloacal obsession is but a variation on the biblical association of the sexual object's genitalia with the act of urination. These images haunt his work, from the chamberpot fantasies of *Chamber Music* to the "potting the po to shambe" of *Finnegans Wake*.[28] Joyce's use of the positive associations of sexuality, fantasy, and the act of writing reflects the modernist association of the female with creative (but also potentially destructive) sexuality. Durrell is quite unique in his presentation of "Miss Smith." His vocabulary is that of pathology as well as geography. Henry Miller was struck by the exoticism of this vocabulary, and even supposed that Durrell had invented the medical vocabulary he uses in this passage. Later critics have seen in this passage Durrell's flirtation with the study of medicine.[29] What Durrell is undertaking, in fact, is to further the associations found in the fin de siècle between black sexuality and the pathological. For Miss Smith's genitalia represent Thanatos. Beginning with his evocation of her urination, an act he associates with her laughter, Durrell presents a fantasy of corruption and death. As in the dinner party in *Ashantee,* the laughter of the black evokes the unself-consciousness attributed to black sexuality by writers such as Lawrence. But it is a corrupted and corrupting sexuality. Like *Ashantee,* Durrell's British, colonial fantasy (parallel to Miller's racist American one) places the black and her genitalia in the world of the pathological and unapproachable. Blackness evokes sexuality, and sexuality (*pace* the late Freud) evokes death:

It is this aura of death which seems exciting to experience, to speculate on, as I watch her sitting in this attic room, surrounded by charts of the prehistoric world in which Chaucer still farts and micturates debonairly. The black and the white latitudes gathered together in one septic focus. Hush! She has no idea of the disease of which she is the victim. Her face is so beautiful among the medieval castles, the hunchbacks, the swans, that even Tarquin is dimly affected by her. From his diary he read me the immortal phrase in which he put down (in clean light Chinese brush strokes) the essence of her. *"Like a black saucer her mind is, shattered among a million white saucers."* And reading it, walked gravely up and down, fingering his temporal lobes. "Hum. Hum. Yes. To judge by the shape of the cranium I am a man of sudden terrible rages. Hum. Hum. I think," he said at last, "I would marry her perhaps, what? Do you know anything about her? Would she marry an Englishman of good family? It would be decorative even if I never fucked her, what?"[30]

Durrell presents a fantasy of the black as the literal representation of the genitalia. This extraordinary passage reflects precisely the same fear and fascination as is found in Altenberg's *Ashantee.* The black is the embodiment of sexuality, her genitalia are the sign of decay and destruction, a marker against which the Western world can judge its own degeneracy and decline. Durrell loads this interior monologue, the monologue of the white male observing the black female, with a level of medical discourse which was evidently confusing even to sympathetic readers. The overtly medical vocabulary, with its images of ripening and decay, points toward the same pathological image as underlies Altenberg's text. Altenberg used a literary topos to carry his approach to the fantasy of fulfillment. He consummated his fantasy within the world of the text through the use of a literary topos. Durrell, in a novel saturated with sexual encounters, a novel built upon the sexuality of its central character, has this character make his fantasy explicit only within an interior monologue. The very use of the interior monologue is a sign of the protagonist's inaction. The reason for this difference may lie in the difference between Altenberg's Vienna and Durrell's background in India and colonialist Britain. For Altenberg the black was the exotic, polluted in many ways, but still the exotic; for Durrell, stemming from a colonial tradition which viewed sexual contact with the "native" as debasing, the very idea of the black, as mirrored in D. H. Lawrence's aside, is linked to the untouchable. Both use the idea of blackness with its link to pathology as a means of exploring the idea of difference. The genitalia, complete yet damaged, diseased yet attractive, poisoning yet potent, become the confused double of the black.

Eternal Return

The association of the black with sexuality can be one of the touchstones to any examination of the problem of consciousness among the moderns. The Viennese fin-de-siècle writer, such as Peter Altenberg, shares his overtly literary patterning of such awareness with vitalist writers such as Lawrence Durrell. More than merely the "substit[ution] for the mouldering and overstuffed capitalism of late Victorian life the mystique and promise of some intense and heightened, more authentic existence" (Fredric Jameson on Wyndham Lewis), the "liberal" as well as the "conservative" writers, in theme as well as form, deeply infuse their texts with the myth of black difference.[31] For both Altenberg's and Durrell's images of the black are embedded in a story of the education of a fictional author who uses the sexualized figure of the black, the outsider, as an alter ego. As an alter ego for Altenberg and Durrell themselves, it is of course crude, for the sexual pathology ascribed to the black, the reduction of the black to the genitalia, is a great exaggeration of the feeling of isolation from society personally suffered by these authors. Altenberg may have been labeled as an outsider because of his Jewish identity, but he had to create a persona for himself, that of the mad poet, to see himself truly as the outsider. Durrell, removed to Greece from Britain, educated in the finer points of British colonial attitudes toward the natives (attitudes that reappear with variation in *The Alexandria Quartet*), under Henry Miller's tutelage styles himself as a writer manqué. Both use the image of the genitalia of the black as markers for difference, but a difference more profound than that which they perceive in themselves.

The best psychological analogy to these authors manqué and their fascination with the sexuality of difference can be found in the borderline syndrome. As Otto Kernberg has pointed out, the sexual fantasies of patients in this category parallel those of patients with sexual perversions.[32] Their fantasies are aggressive. Sexual contact becomes the equivalent of filling the body cavities with excrement. Oral, anal, and genital fantasies merge and are condensed, simultaneously expressing impulses and threats from all levels of psychosexual development, not merely the urethral stage. The characteristic dedifferentiation of sexual characteristics in such patients mingles homosexual and heterosexual impulses chaotically. All external objects merge. The consciousness of the writer-characters created by Altenberg and Durrell stands at this confused and undifferentiated stage. Not that this is necessarily the consciousness of the living authors, but it mirrors their real confusions. The image of the black thus serves a number of functions for the modernist author. First, it is an adaptable embodiment of the idea of difference. Second, it mirrors the confusions associated with the developmental structures that the authors project onto protagonists in search of themselves. The association of the black with an undifferentiated sexual drive and with the incomplete internalization of the object points toward the necessary association of the black (as a surrogate for the self) with the sense of incompleteness, of the undifferentiated world of power and sexuality perceived as separate from the self. While this pattern has a basis in the creation of a sense of consciousness in the writer-figure, it incorporates the black as the best analogy to this sense of incompleteness, of undifferentiated, pure sexuality, because of the ideological implications of the image of the black in the late nineteenth and early twentieth centuries.

Any number of literary works from either end of the political spectrum could have made this point as well as those by Altenberg and Durrell. George Bernard Shaw's agnostic broadside *The Adventures of the Black Girl in Her Search for God* (1932) concludes with the "black girl" married and the mother of a number of "coffee-colored piccaninnies." John Farleigh's illustrations for the volume stress precisely the iconography of sexual difference associated with the "Hottentot Venus." Klaus Mann's image of his protagonist's black mistress in his *Mephisto* (1936) reflects much the same preoccupation with the black as the object and source of sexual perversity. The fascist science-fiction novel *Patrol against Death* (1939) by Rudolf Heinrich Daumann plays with the image of the black as sexual object while embedding this concept in an Africa of the future racked with plague.[33] Saul Bellow's evocation of the corruption and pathology of upper Broadway in his *Mr. Sammler's Planet* (1970) uses the exposed member of the black pickpocket as a sign for the potency of those pathological forces that claim the city for themselves. In all of these cases, the image of the sexuality of the black becomes key in the search for the "authentic." Giacomo Leopardi stated it quite correctly in 1832:

In the present century, black people are believed to be totally different from whites in race and origin, yet totally equal to them with regard to human rights. In the sixteenth century, when blacks were thought to come from the same roots and to be of the same family as whites, it was held, most of all by Spanish theologians, that with regard to rights blacks were by nature and Divine Will greatly inferior to us. In both centuries, blacks have been bought and sold and made to work in chains under the whip. Such is ethics; and such is the extent to which moral beliefs have anything to do with actions.[34]

Writers, both liberal and conservative, employed the image of the black as a reflex of difference within their texts. Political ideology can thus be formed by stereotypes as much as it forms them.

PART II

STEREOTYPES
OF RACE

CERTAINLY NO stereotypes have had more horrifying translations into social policy than those of "race." Tied to the prestige of nineteenth-century science, the idea of racial difference in the twentieth century became the means for manipulating and eventually destroying entire groups. The following essays document how easily racial stereotypes have been linked with images of pathology, especially psychopathology. In this case the need to create the sense of difference between the self and the Other builds upon the xenophobia inherent in all groups. That which defines one's group is "good," everything else is frighteningly "bad." The cohesiveness of any group depends on a mutually defined sense of identity, usually articulated in categories that reflect the group's history.

Categories such as linguistic unity, perceived identity of skin color, and geographic cohesion have all played their role in defining larger groups ("races") within the Western tradition. But even more brutally simple categories underlie these. For language implies the correct and meaningful use of language. Any other use is "crazy." Thus one of the inherent definitions of any linguistic group is that it is the norm of sanity. The Other is always "mad." Insanity is not merely a label (any more than is geography or skin color). It exists in reality. But the Other's "madness" is what defines the sanity of the defining group.

The group is embodied with all of the positive associations of the self. The Other is the antithesis of the self and is thus that which defines the group (that which has robbed the self of power but in exchange provided it with protection). The Other is therefore both ill and infectious, both damaged and damaging. As the essays in this section show, the image of the dangerous Other serves both as the focus for the projection of anxiety concerning the self and as the means by which the Other defines itself.

The first two essays look at the association of the black and the Jew with the "myth of mental illness," to use Thomas Szasz's term. It is not necessary to create a Gobineau-like hierarchy of races as victims to see that, of the many groups that have served the function of the Other in the West, these two have been singled out with uncommon frequency. The Western definition of the "racial" Other has indeed been so conditioned by images of the black and the Jew that many of the other "races" (gypsies, for example) have been defined within the categories first applied to them.

Two other essays deal with textual representations of this myth of difference in the work of I. J. Singer and Sigmund Freud, two Jewish writers of quite different backgrounds who both dealt with the image of the damaged (and damaging) Jew. This theme is carried forward into a detailed study of the development of one of the basic nineteenth-century labels for difference, degeneration, and the implications of Freud's revision of this concept. The volume closes with a study of the tradition that linked labels of difference within the broader category of "degeneration." Taking as its theme the idea of madness and its place in the discourse about creativity in the late nineteenth century, the essay points toward the real political horrors that resulted in Germany from labeling of groups as pathologically different.

Throughout the six essays, the question of the pathological remains central. The Other is labeled as ill and must come to terms with that designation. The creative refunctioning of this label, as well as the function of the idea of pathology as a means of dealing with shifting historical patterns, remains constantly in the background of these individual cases, cases that run the historical range from the association of the concepts of blackness and madness in medieval biblical exegesis to the literary representation of the "madness" of the Jews in one of the major works of twentieth-century Yiddish fiction.

5

On the Nexus of
Blackness and Madness

Paranoid Delusions

THE COMPLICATED uses to which culturally engendered stereotypes can be put for individual adaptation are nowhere more clearly
illustrated than in Arrah B. Evarts's 1919 case study of a patient at St.
Elizabeth's, a psychiatric institution in Washington, D.C. This patient
had evolved her own color symbolism with extremely private connota-
tions. For her, blackness signified pederasty: "To her the whole African
or black race was originally conceived by pederasty, and is so perpetuated."[1] The private significance of such an equation demands further
analytic interpretation, as Evarts observed: "There is much that is individual, much that is determined by her own life and experience, and
much that she has absorbed from the current symbolism about us all, yet
the archaic roots are quite faithfully adhered to, and do not need more
than a recapitulation; black, the color of evil . . ." (157). The patient
clothes her anxiety both in the imagery present in early twentieth-century Western society, including what Frantz Fanon has described as the
satanic image of the black in the West,[2] and in images that would have
had specific implications for her own time and place. Her linking of
"blackness" with "illness," here sexual deviation as it was understood by
medicine and society in 1919, plays upon an age-old association. The
focus of anxiety shifts from era to era, but is always an entity that is
labeled as potentially corrupting the body politic. The Communists were

the focus for paranoid delusions in the 1950s; the Mafia, in the 1960s; Richard Nixon, in the 1970s. The color symbolism of Evarts's patient links the daily reality of early twentieth-century Washington, D.C.—its "Jim Crow" laws and its heightened awareness of the black as a growing and repressed force in the city—with the age-old associations of the black with corruption and disease. The stereotype of the black from which this private code draws associates blackness not merely with pathology, but with one very specific category of disease, psychopathology.

The Black as Mad

Following the abortive third performance of their obscene farce, the duke and the king successfully escape the wrath of the inhabitants of an Arkansas river town and, accompanying Huck and Jim, float inexorably down the river ever deeper into the slave-holding South. By this point *The Adventures of Huckleberry Finn* has assumed all the trappings of a fugitive slave narrative.[3] For while Huck's central problem is his moral dilemma concerning Jim's escape to freedom, Jim's focus remains on his escape from slavery. When the two confidence men stop a bit farther down the river to plan their next "sting," the problem of preserving Jim's freedom and thus his ability to continue his escape must be faced: "You see, when we left him all alone we had to tie him, because if anybody happened on him by himself and not tied, it wouldn't look much like he was a runaway nigger, you know. So the duke said it *was* kind of hard to have to lay roped all day, and he'd cipher out some way to get around it" (see Plate 16).[4] The duke's ingenious solution provides a good test case for examining the historical relationship between madness and blackness in Western culture:

He was uncommon bright, the duke was, and he soon struck it. He dressed Jim up in King Lear's outfit—it was a long curtain-calico gown, and a white horsehair wig and whiskers; and then he took his theatre-paint and painted Jim's face and hands and ears and neck all over a dead dull solid blue, like a man that's been drownded nine days. Blamed if he warn't the horriblest looking outrage I ever see. Then the duke took and wrote out a sign on a shingle so—
SICK ARAB—BUT HARMLESS WHEN NOT OUT OF HIS HEAD.
And he nailed that shingle to a lath, and stood the lath up four or five foot in front of the wigwam. Jim was satisfied. He said it was a sight better than laying

THE MURDERER, WILLIAM FREEMAN.

16. The black as insane murderer. A portrait of the murderer William Freeman shackled in the position assumed by Jim (from *Cayuga Tocsin*, 9 April 1846).

tied a couple of years every day and trembling all over every time there was a sound. The duke told him to make himself free and easy, and if anybody ever come meddling around, he must hop out of the wigwam, and carry on a little, and fetch a howl or two like a wild beast, and he reckoned they would light out and leave him alone. Which was sound enough judgment; but you take the average man, and he wouldn't wait for him to howl. Why, he didn't only look like he was dead, he looked considerable more than that. (126–27)

Twain, who had a specialist's interest in Shakespeare, provided the duke with a mangled Shakespearean vocabulary.[5] Earlier in the novel the parodied soliloquy from the third act of Hamlet, with its heavy dose of everybody's favorite quotes from Shakespeare, had preceded the playbill announcing scenes from *Romeo and Juliet* and *Richard III* to be performed by the duke and the king in the guise of David Garrick and Edmund Kean. Yet with all the references to Shakespeare there is never any mention of *King Lear* until this passage.

Lear is Shakespeare's quintessential madman; as Mark Van Doren observes, it is "madness of which he becomes the pattern in all poetry."[6] But it is a very specific manifestation of madness, the visual appearance of the madman, which Twain borrows from Lear. Lear, after the storm scene in the third act, begins to look more and more like the madman as wild man "fantastically dressed with wild flowers." He rages against his daughters: "Through tatter'd clothes small vices do appear; / Robes and furr'd gowns hide all. . . ." (4.6.168). Here the reverse is true. Jim is hidden by the tattered cloak of the madman and not the cloak alone. For the duke also covers Jim with "a white horsehair wig and whiskers." Hairiness is the icon of the madman as wild man, having its roots in the biblical description of the madness of Nebuchadnezzar, who, in Daniel 4:33, "was driven from men and did eat grass as oxen, and his body was wet with the dew of heaven, till his hairs were grown like eagles' feathers, and his nails like birds' claws."[7] The traditional iconography of Nebuchadnezzar, as late as William Blake's image of 1795, portrays the monarch as a wild man with flowing beard and hair.[8]

The duke finishes Jim's disguise by covering all his visible skin with makeup of a "dead dull solid blue" hue. In another context in the novel Twain uses blue as the color of death. Aunt Sally describes the victim of a steamboat explosion as having "turned blue all over, and died in the hope of a glorious resurrection" (175). The color also appears in a slightly altered context in the deleted raft episode when the rivermen discover the naked Huck on their raft and threaten to "paint him a sky-blue all over from head to heel" (240). Huck escapes punishment by assuming the identity of a dead child about whom the rivermen had just heard a tale. Here death and deceit are associated with blueness. These are not random associations. Blue is the traditional color of the fool, stemming from its association with deceit and madness:

> Love lies in that, not in wearing blue.
> But it may be that many think
> To cover the offence of falsehood under a tombstone,
> By wearing blue . . .[9]

Jim's disguise gives him the protective coloration of both death and insanity, the fears of which are parallel. This disguise is an example of "flying under false colors," but to the best of all possible goals, the preservation of freedom. Only in the mask of the ultimate lack of freedom, madness and death, can Jim be assured of freedom.

Jim's comic opera camouflage seems not to be sufficient for the duke, for he knows his audience all too well. Hence the sign: SICK ARAB—BUT HARMLESS WHEN NOT OUT OF HIS HEAD. The blue Arab is a portmanteau irony. For Twain, an amateur folklorist, it may have referred to the indigo-dyed Tuaregs of North Africa with their system of black slavery. The slave becomes the slaver. But Twain is also pointing at the traditional Western confusion between the Arab and the black embodied in the ambiguous use of the word *Moor* in English (or *Mohr* in German).[10] Here the conflation of Arab and black replicates the history of the image of the black in the West. Jim becomes the mythic black in order to escape the realities of blackness. The use of the figure of the Arab as black in this context is in no way accidental. It refers the reader back to the very beginning of the novel, where Huck Finn rejects the civilized adventures of Tom Sawyer's world of "Spaniards and A-rabs" as "just one of Tom Sawyer's lies. I reckoned he believed in the A-rabs and the elephants, but for me I think different. It had all the marks of a Sunday school" (17). By the time Jim assumes his disguise, Huck has come to see the pragmatic value of myth, which can be used to manipulate those who believe in it.

It is, however, the second half of the duke's sign which focuses on the central implication of Jim's disguise. Jim is the black man as madman and both are the equivalent of the wild man: "if anybody ever come meddling around, he must hop out of the wigwam, and carry on a little, and fetch a howl or two like a wild beast." Huck is sensitive to the likely reaction of the white Southerners. He knows that "you take the average man, and he wouldn't wait for him to howl. Why, he didn't only look like he was dead, he looked considerable more than that." The mad black is the nexus at which all fears coalesce. But these fears are felt only by the perceiver, the Arkansas (read Western) community. In a superb chapter on Twain's use of superstition in *Huckleberry Finn,* Daniel Hoffman observes that "only Negroes, children, and riffraff [are] . . . the bearers of folk superstitions in the re-created world of [Twain's] childhood."[11] Yet here it is the entire world of the whites (excluding those liminal figures on the raft with Jim) that responds to this figure of the mad black with fear and horror. The successful use of a universal Western stereotype preserves Jim's freedom, at least for the moment.

At the conclusion of *The Adventures of Huckleberry Finn* Twain returns to the theme of madness and blackness for the final time. Huck capitulates to Tom Sawyer's convoluted, romantic plan for Jim's final escape. Straight from the world of "Spaniards and A-rabs" which Huck had earlier rejected, Tom's elaborate escape plan with its series of *Man in the Iron Mask* graffiti causes wonderment in the local population. Typical of the reactions is that of "Old Mrs. Hotchkiss," who said, "her tongue . . . agoing all the time":

"Well, Sister Phelps, I've ransacked that-air cabin over an' I b'lieve the nigger was crazy. I says so to Sister Damrell—didn't I, Sister Damrell?—s'I, he's crazy, s'I—them's the very words I said. You all hearn me: he's crazy, s'I; everything shows it, s'I. Look at that-air grindstone, s'I; want to tell *me*'t any cretur 'ts in his right mind 's agoin' to scrabble all them crazy things onto a grindstone, s'I? Here sich 'n' sich a person busted his heart; 'n' here so 'n' so pegged along for thirty-seven year, 'n' all that—natcherl son o' Louis somebody, 'n' sich everlast'n rubbage. He's plumb crazy, s'I; it's what I says in the fust place, it's what I says in the middle, 'n it's what I says last 'n' all the time—the nigger's crazy—crazy's Nebokoodneezer, s'I." (218)

The confusion wrought by Tom and Huck leads to the inescapable conclusion that Jim is crazy, crazy like Nebuchadnezzar, a wild man outside the pale of humanity. The fear of the Other's wildness and potential destructiveness is a common feature of the nexus of blackness and madness. Twain uses it for comment on a very specific contemporary issue.

The Historical Context

Twain's rationale for incorporating the seemingly arcane stereotypical myth of the black madman in *Huckleberry Finn* was based on the power of that myth in his time—the time recreated by the novel (the 1840s) as much as the time of writing. The major moral and political issue of the 1840s in the United States was the debate about abolition. One of the interesting sidelights of that debate was triggered by the sixth national census of 1840.[12] When the results were published in 1841, it was for the first time possible to obtain data concerning mental illness in the United States. The total number of those reported to be insane and feeble-minded in the United States was over 17,000, of which nearly 3,000 were black. If these staggering census statistics were to be believed, free blacks had an incidence of mental illness eleven times higher than slaves and six times higher than the white population. The antiabolitionist forces were thus provided with major scientific evidence that blacks were congenitally unfit for freedom. John C. Calhoun, the U.S. vice president and perhaps the most vocal spokesman for the slaveholding states during the 1840s, incorporated this argument as his mainstay in a letter to the British ambassador defending the "peculiar institution":

The census and other authentic documents show that, in all instances in which the States have changed the former relation between the two races, the condition of the African, instead of being improved, has become worse. They have been invariably sunk into vice and pauperism, accompanied by the bodily and mental inflictions incident thereto—deafness, blindness, insanity, and idiocy—to a degree without example; while, in all other States which have retained the ancient relation between them, they have improved greatly in every respect—in number, comfort, intelligence, and morals. . . .

In addition, it deserves to be remarked, that in Massachusetts, where the change in the ancient relation of the two races was first made (now more than sixty years since), where the greatest zeal has been exhibited in their behalf, and where their number is comparatively few (but little more than 8000 in a population of upwards of 730,000), the condition of the African is amongst the most wretched. By the latest authentic accounts, there was one out of every twenty-one of the black population in jails or houses of correction; and one out of every thirteen was either deaf and dumb, blind, idiot, insane, or in prison. On the other hand, the census and other authentic sources of information establish the fact that the condition of the African race throughout all the States, where the ancient relation between the two has been retained, enjoys a degree of health and comfort which may well compare with that of the laboring population of any country in Christendom; and it may be added, that in no other condition, or in any other age or country, has the negro race ever attained so high an elevation in morals, intelligence, or civilization.[13]

Calhoun's political rhetoric was not the only justification of slavery based on the 1840 census. Even more interesting than the political use of the data associating blackness and madness was the medical literature the census spawned.[14] Even though Edward Jarvis cogently rebutted the faulty statistics of the census of 1840 as early as 1842 by showing that there were gross errors in its compilation (for example, there were 133 black, insane paupers listed in the town of Worcester, Massachusetts, which had a total black population of 151), the association of blackness and madness remained in currency throughout the rest of the century.[15]

As late as 1851 an essay in the *American Journal of Insanity* cited the 1840 census as proof of the inferiority of the blacks: "It is obvious, however . . . that there is an awful prevalence of idiocy and insanity among the free blacks over the whites, and especially over the slaves. Who would believe, without the fact, in black and white, before his eyes, that *every fourteenth colored person in the State of Maine is an idiot or lunatic?* And though there is a gradual improvement in their condition, as we proceed west and south, yet it is evident that the free States are the principal abodes of idiocy and lunacy among the colored race."[16] In that same year Samuel Cartwright published a paper in the *New Orleans Medical and Surgical Journal* in which he attempted to substantiate the association of blackness and madness by specifically identifying psychopathologies to which blacks alone were prey.[17] Among the classes of illness he pinpointed were "Drapetomania, or the diseases causing slaves to run away" and "dysaesthesia aethiopis or hebetude of mind and obtuse sensibility of body—a disease peculiar to negroes—called by overseers, "rascality.'" In both instances, manifestations of the blacks' rejection of the institution of slavery were fitted into the medical model of insanity. Cartwright's views had fairly wide dissemination and were the subject of attack as well as defense. His rhetoric was couched in a medical vocabulary but had a clearly political thrust, as is obvious in his description of the etiology of "dysaesthesia aethiopis":

According to unalterable physiological laws, negroes, as a general rule, to which there are but few exceptions, can only have their intellectual faculties awakened in a sufficient degree to receive moral culture, and to profit by religious or other instruction, when under the compulsory authority of the white man; because, as a general rule, to which there are but few exceptions, they will not take sufficient exercise, when removed from the white man's authority, to vitalize and decarbonize their blood by the process of full and free respiration, that active exercise of some kind alone can effect. A northern climate remedies, in a considerable degree, their naturally indolent disposition; but the dense atmosphere of Boston or Canada can scarcely produce sufficient hematosis and vigor of mind to induce them to labor. From their natural indolence, unless under the stimulus of compulsion, they doze away their lives with the capacity of their lungs for atmospheric air only half expanded, from the want of exercise to superinduce full and deep respiration. The inevitable effect is, to prevent a sufficient atmospherization or vitalization of the blood, so essential to the expansion and the freedom of action of the intellectual faculties. The black blood distributed to the brain chains the mind to ignorance, superstition and barbarism, and bolts the door against civilization, moral culture and religious truth. The compulsory power of the white man, by making the slothful negro take active exercise, puts into active play the lungs, through whose agency the vitalized blood is sent to the brain to give liberty to the mind, and to open the door to intellectual improvement. The very exercise, so beneficial to the negro, is expended in cultivating those burning fields in cotton, sugar, rice and tobacco, which, but for his labor, would, from the heat of the climate, go uncultivated, and their products lost to the world. Both parties are benefitted—the negro as well as his master—even more. But there is a third party benefitted—the world at large. The three millions of bales of cotton, made by negro labor, afford a cheap clothing for the civilized world. The laboring classes of all mankind, having less to pay for clothing, have more money to spend in educating their children, and intellectual, moral and religious progress.

The wisdom, mercy and justice of the decree, that Canaan shall serve Japheth, is proved by the disease that we have been considering, because it proves that his physical organization, and the laws of his nature, are in perfect unison with slavery, and in entire discordance with liberty—a discordance so great as to produce the loathsome disease that we have been considering, as one of its inevitable effects—a disease that locks up the understanding, blunts the sensations and chains the mind to superstition, ignorance and barbarism. Slaves are not subject to this disease, unless they are permitted to live like free negroes, in idleness and filth—to eat improper food, or to indulge in spirituous liquors.[18]

It is specifically the physiology of the blacks which predisposes them to mental illness. Here the association of blackness and madness is made incontrovertible. An uncommon potential for madness is inherent in the nature of the black.

In his presentation of the image of the insane black, Twain was obliquely referring back to the debate concerning the nature of the black which raged in antebellum America. The political argument associating madness and blackness had its roots in the faulty statistics of the 1840 census; however, this argument did not vanish with the resolution of the question of abolition after the Civil War. The special relationship between the black and insanity became a theme throughout the following decades, even into the time Twain wrote *Huckleberry Finn*.

In 1887 J. B. Andrews noted a disproportionate increase of mental illness among blacks:

In the Negro race the proportionate increase of insanity is far greater than in any other division of the population. From 1870 to 1880 there was an increase in the census of the coloured race of 34–85 per cent, while for the same period there was an increase of 285 per cent of the insane. This large multiplication has occurred since emancipation from slavery and the consequent changes in conditions and life. The causes are briefly told: enlarged freedom, too often ending in licence; excessive use of stimulants; excitement of the emotions, already unduly developed; the unaccustomed strife for means of subsistence; educational strain and poverty. The total census of the other coloured races is 172,000 with 105 insane, or one insane person to every 1,638. The small percentage of insane among the aborigines and Chinese is fully in accord with the observations of writers upon the causes productive of mental disease. There is much less of the refinement of civilization; less competition and struggle for place, power or wealth, and as a consequence, less tendency to mental deterioration.[19]

In 1896 J. F. Miller attributed a radical increase in the number of blacks in lunatic asylums since emancipation to the nature of the black, who could live in comfort "under less favorable circumstances than the white man, having a nervous organization less sensitive to his environments; yet it is true that he has less mental equipoise, and may suffer mental alienation from influences and agencies which would not affect a race mentally stronger."[20] In 1908 William F. Drewry, in a paper presented to the thirty-fifth National Conference of Charities and Correction, used the more modern scientific vocabulary of eugenics when he attributed "the causation of insanity" among the blacks to their "hereditary deficiencies and unchecked constitutional diseases and defects."[21] And four years later a scholarly presentation of the relationship between madness and blackness argued that it was the "simple nature" of the blacks, their childlike essence, which did not permit them to function well in the complexities of the modern world and predisposed them to insanity.[22]

The commonplace nineteenth-century association of blackness and madness reflects the negative image of the black as "the ignoble savage," a counterweight to the disease-free Noble Savage. But the strength of this association was not spent by the early twentieth century. In 1964

Benjamin Pasamanick felt called on to refute "Myths Regarding Prevalence of Mental Disease in the American Negro" (as he entitled his
essay). His conclusion was that if all data were taken into consideration
"the total Negro mental disorder rate would not exceed that of the
whites."[23] Pasamanick attempted to pinpoint the historical origin of the
association of blackness and madness in the Enlightenment:

The dogma of the inferiority of the Negro begins largely with the beginnings of
the Age of Reason in the eighteenth century and has been reinforced from all
sources since. A corollary dogma which arose almost simultaneously stated that
slavery was the ideal state for such inferior and inadequate persons and indeed
that freedom resulted in their decay and degradation. The nineteenth century
political, sociological and anthropological literature is filled with the demonstration of these allegations. During our century, the scientific evidence and tools
have been sharpened and these dogmas fiercely applied.[24]

Pasamanick sees the myth of a special relationship between blackness and
madness as reflecting the growing politicization of the concept of blackness in the late eighteenth and nineteenth centuries. For as the concepts of
"black" and "slave" merged, abolitionists and antiabolitionists viewed
the black man/slave as, respectively, the noble enslaved prince and the
marginal man saved from barbarity by civilization. This alteration in
perspective incorporated the existing model of the nexus between madness and blackness to achieve its varied ends.

Pasamanick is not the only scholar to localize the nexus of blackness
and madness in the Age of Reason. Peter Thorslev, Jr., observed:

Rousseau was the first to "internalize" the Wild Man, to suggest that he lives on
in all of us, that when we strip ourselves of the evils as well as of the refinements
of civilization, we find naked savages. So long as this naked savage is also noble,
the prospect is not unpleasant. This is not to say that Rousseau suggested that we
should or even that we could so divest ourselves—although this was most often
what he was interpreted to have said—but at least he did not suggest that the soul
of this primeval savage was tainted with original sin or possessed of dark and
mysterious powers. In the nineteenth century, however, when the civilized man
looked within to discover his primitive unconscious, ever more frequently it was
not the brave and open face of the Noble Savage which greeted him, but the dark
face of Dionysus.

I believe this must be accounted for in the first place by the fact that the Wild
Man came to be thought of increasingly as black, and the black man was in the

white man's chains. Of course, there is a very long Christian tradition which associates black hearts and black skins with evil and the ways of Satan, and there must surely have been some unconscious vindication of slavery in this association. On the other hand, antislavery literature has existed almost as long as has slavery, in English-speaking countries at least, and a constant theme of this literature was the brotherhood of black and white, and the concomitant theme, in view of the black's less advanced civilization, of the black man's being a child, especially a Child of Nature—affectionate, spontaneous, with sometimes the capricious and somehow innocent cruelty of children.[25]

This view is only partially correct. The identification of blackness with slavery does arise in the eighteenth century, but the structural relationship between madness and blackness is of much greater antiquity.

The Mad as Black

In the Ywain legend, part of the medieval matter of Brittany, a pivotal incident is Ywain's betrayal of his promise to his wife Alundyne to return to her after a year. After the year has passed, Ywain is confronted by his wife's handmaiden, who seizes a ring given him by Alundyne. This gesture drives Ywain into madness. In Hartmann von Aue's German version of this legend, written about 1200, Iwein wanders the forest as a madman, creating fear wherever he appears: "What shall the madman do?"[26] In appearance he becomes more and more the image of the madman as wild man: "Thus the madman returned to the forest with his food and his entire body was like that of a Moor" (3345–49). But it is not only the mad Iwein who is described as a black. In Wirnt von Grafensberg's *Wigalois*, written about a decade after Hartmann's *Iwein*, the hero is confronted with a monster: "Soon the Knight of the Wheel saw floating on the water a small raft which was tied to a post at the bank by a large willow twig. He squeezed through the dense underbrush, took the raft, and pulled it back to where he had left his horse. In a nearby rock was a cave from which he saw running toward him a woman *who was all black* and shaggy as a bear. She had neither great beauty nor good manners; indeed she was a monster."[27] Here the wild woman is described as both black and hairy (see Plate 17). This same tradition is incorporated in the anonymous *Wolfdietrich* of the mid-thirteenth century: "A monstrous woman, born from the wild, came toward him through the trees. There

17. The mad black woman confronting Attila. Her pendulous breasts, like her skin color, are a sign of her difference (from Valentier Alberti, *Dissertatio academica* [Leipzig: Christoph Fleischer, 1690]).

was never any bigger woman. The noble knight thought to himself: 'O dear Christ, protect me!' Two monstrous breasts hung from her body. 'Whoever gets you,' the wise knight spoke, 'gets the devil's mother, I do believe.' Her body was created blacker than coal. Her nose hung over her chin; stringy, black was her hair.''[28]

The association of blackness and wildness or madness seems a commonplace, at least of the German romance.[29] Richard Bernheimer, in his standard study of the wild man, has observed: "It must be added in parenthesis, that the writers of the romances do not regard hairiness as a necessary symptom of wildness induced by insanity; they are satisfied with describing the victim's total disarray, or with letting him turn all black as a sign of his demoniac state."[30] The association of madness with hairiness has a clear biblical parallel in the story of Nebuchadnezzar. Yet Bernheimer argues that the association of blackness and madness, both acquired (as in *Iwein*) and inherent (as in *Wigalois* and *Wolfdietrich*), is the simple equation of demonic possession with madness. A better understanding can be gleaned by examining the biblical presentation of blackness as aesthetic form.

The Historical Context

Such simple examples as Duarte Pacheo Pereira's 1505 labeling of the natives of West Africa as wild do no more than illustrate how African cultures were invidiously contrasted with Western civilization;[31] the association of the abstractions of madness and blackness has a more complicated nexus.

When the biblical discussions of blackness and their exegesis in the Middle Ages are examined, one text assumes a central position.[32] It is the passage from the beginning of the Song of Songs, "Nigra sum, sed formosa" ("I am black but beautiful"). This passage, even more than the discussion of the origin of the races from among the sons of Noah,[33] was heavily played upon in discussions of the nature of blackness.

The most cursory survey to the end of the Middle Ages would take into consideration at least thirty major commentaries on this passage. A chronological examination of these interpretations reveals a pattern of development.[34] An early exegete, St. Hippolytus (ca. 170–ca. 236), one of the early theologians of the Roman Church, in an Armenian fragment of his lost commentary on the Song of Songs simply and directly equates the blackness of the speaker, the Shulamite, with a fall from grace.[35] Hippolytus—and all of the early commentators, both Jewish and Christian—read this first dialogue of the Song of Songs as an allegorical portrayal of the relationship of God to the individual soul. The figure of the black woman becomes an allegory for the soul that has fallen from grace but still contains the potential for salvation ("I am black *but* beautiful").

Such an uncomplicated interpretation provided the allegorical groundwork for a more involved presentation of why the soul is blackened in the fall. St. Ambrose (ca. 399–97), both in his commentary on the *Song of Songs* and, even more pointedly, in his discourse *On Isaac, or the Soul*, refers to the concept of blackness as a means of elucidating the post-Edenic state of the soul:

And yet the selfsame soul, knowing that she has been darkened by her union with the body, says to other souls or to those powers of heaven that have charge of the holy ministry, "Look not on me, because I am of a dark complexion, because the sun has not looked upon me. The sons of my mother have fought against me"; that is, the passions of the body have attacked me and the allurements of the flesh have given me my color; therefore the sun of justice has not shone on me.[36]

Ambrose interprets the figure of the black in the Song of Songs as allegorically representing the dominance of the physical over the spiritual. In doing so he invokes the Greek medical model, speaking of the passions as the determiners of human temperament. After the fall the soul is under constant attack by the forces that dominate the body.

These forces are the humors. They color the nature of the soul through their presence. How all-pervasive this manner of seeing black in the abstract was can be judged at least in part by the most famous reading of the Song of Songs, that of St. Bernard of Clairvaux (1090–1153) In the third sermon St. Bernard refers to the passage "Nigra sum, sed formosa":

Or, blinded by the unparalleled splendours of the Divine Majesty, they may be overcast with a cloud of denser darkness than belonged to their former state. O whosoever thou be that art such a soul, do not, I implore thee, do not regard as mean or contemptible that place where the holy Penitent laid aside her sins and clothed herself in the garment of sanctity! There the Ethiopian woman changed her colour, being restored to the whiteness of her long-lost innocence. Then, indeed, she was able to answer those who addressed her in words of reproach, "I am black but beautiful, O daughters of Jerusalem." Do you wonder, my brethren, by what art she effected such a change, or by what merits she obtained it? I will tell you in a few words. She "wept bitterly," she heaved deep sighs from her inmost heart, she was agitated interiorly with salutary sobbings, and thus she spat out the venomous humour. The heavenly Physician came speedily to her aid, because His "word runneth quickly." Is not the word of God a spiritual medicine? Yes, truly, and a medicine that is "strong and active, searching the heart and the veins."[37]

St. Bernard sees the affliction of blackness as directly caused by the humors. Christ is cast in his traditional role as the heavenly physician to cure the Shulamite since she is suffering from an illness. But the illness of the Shulamite, which comes from the humors and affects her color, is not somatic. It is an emotional illness, an illness typified by blackness and despair, two of the qualities characterizing the speaker in the Song of Songs. Now to return to the Ywain legend, Penelope Doob describes the madness of Ywain as the direct result of his grief at having violated his word to his wife: " 'For wa he wex al wilde and wode' (l. 1650). Considered medically, this passion produces excess melancholy and deprives Ywain of reason, after which—like other melancholy madmen—he wishes to shun men's sight by flight into the forest."[38] Grief, despair, madness, and blackness seemed inextricably linked in the Middle Ages. Here there is the allegorical merger of blackness as a racial characteristic with the concept of melancholy, the excess of black bile.

The amalgamation of blackness and madness has its roots in classical medicine. The melancholic was understood to have a black countenance: "Facies nigra propter melancholiam," according to ibn Ezra.[39] In the classical work of Greek physiognomy, long ascribed to Aristotle, the image of the melancholic seems to be that of the black:

Why is it that some people are amiable and laugh and jest, others are peevish, sullen and depressed, some again are irritable, violent and given to rages, while others are indolent, irresolute and timid? The cause lies in the four humours. For those governed by the purest blood are agreeable, laugh, joke and have rosy, well-coloured bodies; those governed by yellow bile are irritable, violent, bold, and have fair, yellowish bodies; those governed by black bile are indolent, timid, ailing and, with regard to body, swarthy and black-haired; but those governed by phlegm are sad, forgetful, and with regard to the body, very pale.[40]

However, an important distinction must be made. In this same text there are two parallel passages describing the Ethiopian: "Those who are too swarthy are cowardly; this applies to Egyptians and Ethiopians. . . . Those with very wooly hair are cowardly; this applies to the Ethiopians."[41] While blackness here is given a quality, it is an attribute that relates directly to individuals. The classical physiognomies had their own negative stereotypes in regard to the Ethiopian, but the confusion between two types of blackness, the racial and the humoral, does not occur. Racial difference may stem from climate or any number of other causes,[42] but not from the humors.[43]

The actual amalgamation of the stereotypes of blackness and madness could not take place in Greek medicine; such a telescoping could not occur for the reason that blacks were present in the daily experience of the Greeks.[44] The presence of real individuals, not abstractions of blackness, worked as a check on faulty generalizations. Because of the later disassociation of the black in the interpretations of the Song of Songs from any relationship to actual individuals, in the Middle Ages the abstraction of the black replaced the reality. Blacks were no longer within the daily experience of Europeans except through the world of myth.[45] The power of this mythic association between pathology and racial identity was so great, based to no little degree on the need to distance the Other as dangerous, that the linkage of the two images was maintained even under radically different social conditions. For the world of the antebellum South, both in its reality and in Mark Twain's retrospective representation, needed to perpetuate a model for the difference of the black, one which would locate (and thus isolate) the fear and anxiety caused by the black in a source other than the institution of slavery. Thus blacks were labeled as "mad" or at least as less rational than their white owners. The fear engendered by the political reality of slavery in the antebellum South was localized in the myth of a specifically black "madness" which drew on the older association between skin color and pathology. The anxiety felt by the white had its locus in the perceived "madness" of the slave, not in the social institution of slavery. The daily experience of the antebellum southern white, who saw the black exclusively within the structure of slavery, reified this view. White southerners needed to project the anxieties felt about the potential violence engendered by slavery onto the black. They focused these anxieties through the myth of illness rather than understanding them as stemming from the brutal reality of slavery. In this shadow world the association of the concepts of blackness and madness occurs on the level of mythic abstraction. Once this merger is accomplished, once visible blackness is identified with the medical model of melancholy, the two become indelibly linked.

Summary

The association of blackness and madness is clearly a product of the mythologizing of both the black and the mad. It is the union of two abstractions of the Other. Both are focuses for the projection of Western culture's anxieties. That these anxieties could be projected onto both the mad and the black is a comment on their lack of differentiation. In his brilliant essay on *Huckleberry Finn*, Leslie Fiedler sees Jim's disguise as an example of the archetype of the Other as the attractive exotic:

Our dark-skinned beloved will take us in, we assure ourselves, when we have been cut off, or have cut ourselves off, from all others, without rancor or the insult of forgiveness. He will fold us in his arms saying, "Honey" or "Aikane"; he will comfort us, as if our offense against him were long ago remitted, were never truly *real*. And yet we cannot ever really forget our guilt; the stories that embody the myth dramatize as if compulsively the role of the colored man as the victim. Dana's Hope is shown dying of the white man's syphilis; Queequeg is portrayed as racked by fever, a pointless episode except in the light of this necessity; Crane's Negro is disfigured to the point of monstrosity; Cooper's Indian smolders to a hopeless old age conscious of the imminent disappearance of his race; Jim is shown loaded down with chains, weakened by the hundred torments dreamed up by Tom in the name of bulliness. The immense gulf of guilt must not be mitigated any more than the disparity of color (Queequeg is not merely brown but monstrously tattooed; Chingachgook is horrid with paint; Jim is portrayed as the sick A-rab dyed blue), so that the final reconciliation may seem more unbelievable and tender. The archetype makes no attempt to deny our outrage as fact; it portrays it as meaningless in the face of love.[46]

This special subset of the exotic also includes Joseph Conrad's Jimmy Wait (*The Nigger of the Narcissus*). Wait, like Jim in the passage discussed earlier, combines antithetical aspects of the Other, the repulsiveness and the attractiveness of the exotic. For the ill, as well as the black, have a fascination for Western culture.[47] In observing the former, as in the absolute dichotomy perceived between black and white,[48] observers create an abyss between themselves and the sufferer. They project their own frailty onto the one observed. The frailty thus seen makes the ill at one and the same time the servants and the masters of the observer. Their need to be succored (a reflection of the need of the observer) provides a focus for either Samaritan feelings or fear and repulsion. Compassion prevails in Hartmann's *Iwein,* where the women who recognize Iwein in spite of his blackness and nakedness are overcome by tears (l. 3390) and undertake to cure him. Iwein's rescue from madness, like Jim's rescue from slavery, is accomplished through the use of aspects of the model of the Other as diseased. Jim's disguise as the mad black works because of the fear Twain attributes to the Western mind (not unlike the superstition Hank Morgan exploits in *A Connecticut Yankee in King Arthur's Court*), while Hartmann von Aue has the black madman become the object of saving concern by courtly society. Different "archetypes" (to employ Fiedler's term) are present in the two cases, but both variations draw on the same tradition. The merging of the concepts of blackness and madness, even though it arose from a historically understandable confusion of abstractions, reflects the protean nature of the Other.

6

The Madness of the Jews

HEINE SAID IT BEST. He introduced his poem on the endowment of the Jewish hospital in Hamburg with the verses:

> A hospital for poor, sick Jews,
> for people afflicted with threefold misery,
> with three evil maladies
> poverty, physical pain, and Jewishness.
>
> The last-named is the worst of all the three:
> that thousand-year-old family complaint,
> the plague they dragged with them from the Nile valley,
> the unhealthy faith from ancient Egypt.
>
> Incurable, profound suffering. No help can be looked for
> from steam-baths, shower-baths, or all the implements
> of surgery, or all the medicines
> which this house offers its sick inmates.[1]

Heine saw being Jewish as an illness, an illness equal to if not greater than physical illness, and medically untreatable. The idea of the Jew suffering from (as well as for) Jewishness, an ironic one in the light of Heine's later illness, reflects Heine's use of anti-Semitic rhetoric in his characterization of the Jew. Heine used set tropes for his Jewishness taken from the vocabulary of anti-Semitic discourse, and shaped them to his own ends.[2]

Heine's use of the motif of the diseased Jew acquires an altered function as the discourse concerning the Jew moves from a theological to a pseudoscientific paradigm during the course of the nineteenth century. Medieval thought had long before associated Jews with disease. Jews assumed the status of the proverbial leper during the Middle Ages. Like lepers, they were marked with inherent signs of their difference as well as those signs (such as the Jew's hat) imposed by the state; they were confined in closed places; and they were associated with the transmission of illness—they caused the plague by poisoning wells. Through their close association with illness they were also perceived as the best healers. For healing was magic, and the Jews, since they could cause illness, must also be able to effect cures. But Renaissance thought found all such associations much too primitive. Lepers simply did not exist in any numbers in Renaissance Europe, so the role formerly filled by the leper was assigned to the mad. Poisoning wells was not the Jews' sole means of polluting the Christian world; they also gave off poisonous fluids. Jewish men menstruated and thus shared with women the ability to contaminate through the menses.[3] Jewish doctors trained in the Arabic tradition healed all too well, so that limits were placed on their numbers and their ability to carry out their profession. By the time Heine penned his lines on the founding of the Jewish hospital in 1842 the association of the Jew with illness had become a complex anti-Semitic commonplace.

In F. L. de La Fontaine's medical survey of Poland (1792), the Polish Jew, the reification of anti-Semitic caricatures of the Jew in Germany, is the subject of an entire essay.[4] The author blames the filthy environment of the Jews, their food, and their sexual practices for a catalogue of illnesses ranging from syphilis to conjunctivitis. In short, the Jews are ill, more diseased than their contemporaries even though they have greater "public freedom and security" (147). Charging the Jews with a special tendency to contract specific illnesses is an effective means of differentiating them from their Christian neighbors. Particularly important, according to de La Fontaine, their "all too early marriage in their thirteenth, fourteenth or fifteenth year with their weak bodies takes from them the necessary fluid of life (Lebenssaft) of lasting health; therefore a Jew here at forty looks much older than a healthy peasant or citizen at sixty or seventy" (151–52). The importance attached to conservation of semen echoes much of the late eighteenth-century discussion of the evils of masturbation and other sexual excesses.[5] Here it is early marriage that saps the individual's stamina, and the resulting catalogue of diseases is similar to that blamed on "the heinous sin of self-pollution."

What is of interest in de La Fontaine's presentation is that, even though it seems to be phrased entirely within the medical discourse of its time, it has a specific political overtone. For in 1788, in a widely circulated paper presented to the Royal Society in Metz concerning the status of the Jews, the Abbé Grégoire discussed the "physical [as well as the] moral and political regeneration of the Jews."[6] This document, more than any other, was responsible for all the later images of the Jews as "diseased"— images that influenced revolutionaries and counter-revolutionaries alike. It lists five causes of the physical decay of the Jews, all of which are based on the social inequality imposed upon the Jews or their religious practices (such as early marriage). De La Fontaine's views echo Grégoire's observations and their underlying ideological belief that if the Jews were given social equality and if they altered their particularly Jewish practices they would be freed from illness. In the eyes of many Germans, such as the philosopher Johann Fichte, no such alteration could take place. Jews remained Jews no matter what changes were made in their status, their religion, or their physical well-being.

Fichte's views were paralleled by other calls for the "physiological transformation" of the Jews, to use Jakob Katz's felicitous phrase.[7] Karl Wilhelm Friedrich Grattenauer, in a pamphlet entitled *Concerning the Physical and Moral Characteristics of Contemporary Jews* (1791), argued that the mentality of the Jew was unalterable, even through the act of baptism.[8] Grattenauer and many other contemporary anti-Jewish pamphleteers saw in the movement toward Jewish emancipation a threat to their means of keeping themselves distanced from the Jews. For with emancipation came the Jews' claim on German, the language of the anti-Semites' own polemics. Thus Grattenauer was forced to argue for the immutability of the Jews' hidden discourse as the reason for their inability to learn German (2). But he was also reacting to the claims by proponents of emancipation, such as Abbé Grégoire, that the negative aspects of Jewish life, language, and mentality were merely artifacts of the repression of the Jews. Grattenauer reverses this. He labels the advocates of Jewish emancipation as ill, consumed by the disease of equality (131)! Both views, however, relate the Jews' special nature to their sexuality. Grégoire sees the sexual selectivity of the Jews as one of the reasons for their illness; Grattenauer sees their "whoredom and shamelessness" (3) as a sign of their moral corruption. Both relate sexuality to disease and disease to the special nature of the Jews and their corrupt discourse.

Even though the Jews of Europe followed the guidelines set out for them by the Enlightenment, even though they began to integrate themselves into the body politic, the idea of the illness of the Jews did not vanish. A half-century after the Revolution, within the confines of the Parisian Anthropological Society, the question of specifically Jewish tendencies toward illness, their form and frequency, was again raised. It was the time of the most vocal demands of French Jewry for a share in the power of the bourgeoisie, from which attempts had been made to exclude them during the Third Republic.[9] In the *Bulletin* of the Anthropological Society, M. Boudin, writing from Vichy, commented on "idiocy and mental illness among German Jews" based on census statistics. The focus of this short paper was on the much higher frequency of psychopathologies among Jews in Germany than among Catholics and Protestants in the same population. For example, the incidence of mental illness in Bavaria was found to be 1:908 for Catholics and 1:967 for Protestants, but 1:514 for Jews. From the census figures Boudin concluded that psychopathologies were "twice as frequent among the Jewish population as among the German population." He attributed this to "the frequency of marriage between blood relatives."[10] We have seen that statistics had been used as a means of quantifying insanity as a sign of Otherness following the 1840 American census (Chapter 5). In the interpretation of that data the antiabolitionist forces, headed by John C. Calhoun, argued that blacks suffered more frequently from mental illness when free than when enslaved: freedom, in other words, promoted psychopathology. In the case of the German Jews, Boudin argued that their inbreeding—their racial exclusivity—accounted for their higher rate of psychopathology. Given the degree of acculturation of French and German Jews by the middle of the nineteenth century, Boudin's comment about German Jewry was a critique of the Jews' claim for further political emancipation. For the Jews, it is implied, have isolated themselves from the European body politic. They are now showing the results of their self-imposed isolation in their greater predisposition for insanity. And one sign of their insanity, it is implied, is their demand for political equality. The ability of the Jews to alter their pathological state is placed, if it is seen as at all possible, in the distant future. The immediate demands for the political equality of the Jews in the Third Republic are thus demands made by a group that is tainted with madness. The contemporary demand for legal equality is translated into its antithesis, madness and its resultant dependency. He concluded his paper with a critique of the view that psychopathology among the Jews could be traced to their "cosmopolitanism"—their association with modern civilization and the decadence of city life. What de La Fontaine in the late eighteenth century had seen as a general predisposition to illness had thus become by the mid-nineteenth century a predisposition specifically to mental illness. The Jews were seen as covertly ill, ill in a manner that provided observers with proof of their own emotional and intellectual superiority.

The statistics cited by Boudin and other nineteenth- (and indeed twentieth-) century writers on the topic of the mental instability of the Jews do not, of course, reflect any true predisposition of the European Jewish community. Indeed, this view has been recently labeled one of the "misconceptions" about genetic disorders among Jews.[11] The statistics, cited over and over by mental health practitioners during this period, most probably reflect the higher incidence of hospitalization of Jews for mental illness due to their concentration in urban areas, which are less tolerant of the presence of the mentally ill than are rural areas. Also urban Jews had developed a superior network, as represented by the Jewish Hospital in Hamburg, for the identification and treatment of illness, including mental illness. A strong sense of community coupled with the impression that the mentally ill were unable to function within urban society may have led to more frequent hospitalization, and thus to the higher statistical incidence of psychopathology among the Jews.

By the 1880s the linkage of the Jew with psychopathology was a given in anthropological circles. In the Parisian Anthropological Society the Prussian census of 1880 was the point of departure for a quite detailed debate on the psychopathologies of the Jews. Again statistics were used to stress the greater occurrence of mental illness among the Jews. The comments on the etiology of the mental illness were more diffuse. M. Zabrowski blamed a preoccupation with mysticism and the supernatural, a clear reference to the Eastern Jews, whose presence was being felt in Paris more than ever following the assassination of Alexander II in 1881 and the resulting forced immigration.[12] Zabrowski and M. Sanson also stressed the curative role of agricultural employment and the absence of Jews in this field. The "cosmopolitanism" of the Jews, the pressure of the fields in which they were occupied, was part of the reason for this. But M. Blanchard simply stated that "hysteria and neurasthenia are more frequent among the Jewish race than all other races." Thus Jews tended to be not simply ill, not simply mentally ill, but specifically hysterical and neurasthenic. The reason? According to Sanson, endogamous marriage.

The view that Jews are especially prone to hysteria and neurasthenia because of a weakening of the nervous system due to inbreeding appeared in canonical form in Jean Martin Charcot's *Tuesday Lesson* for 23 October 1888.[13] Charcot described "a case of hysterical dyspnie. I already mentioned that this twenty-year-old patient is a Jewess. I will use this occasion to stress that nervous illnesses of all types are innumerably more frequent among Jews than among other groups." Charcot attributed this fact to inbreeding.[14]

By 1890 Charcot's view had become a commonplace in European psychiatry, accepted in such standard German textbooks of psychiatry as those by Emil Kraepelin, Theodor Kirchhoff, and Richard Krafft-Ebing. Krafft-Ebing is typical for the general tenor of his discussion:

Statistics have been collected with great care to show the percentage of insanity in the various religious sects, and it has been shown that among the Jews and certain sects the percentage is decidedly higher. This fact stands in relation with religion only in so far as it constitutes a hindrance to marriage among those professing it; the more when its adherents are small in number, and there is consequent insufficient crossing of the race and increased inbreeding.

This is a phenomenon similar to that observed in certain highly aristocratic and wealthy families, whose members, whether from motives of honor or money, constantly intermarry, and thus have many insane relatives. In such cases the cause is not moral, but anthropologic.[15]

The "anthropological" cause of the greater incidence of insanity among the Jews is their endogamous marriages, which Krafft-Ebing, as a liberal, compares to the degeneracy found in the inbred upper class. But he goes on to contrast mysticism, inherent in the image of the Eastern Jew, with the rationality of Christianity. Here he stands in a long tradition of "liberal" anti-Semitism. David Friedrich Strauss, for example, labeled biblical miracles, such as the resurrection, as the product of a hysterical fantasy, the fantasy of the Jews.

The result of Krafft-Ebing's stress on inbreeding and mysticism is a focus on the exclusivity of the Jews. The form of their insanity has sexual implications: "Very often excessive religious inclination is itself a symptom of an originally abnormal character or actual disease, and, not infrequently, concealed under a veil of religious enthusiasm there is abnormally intensified sensuality and sexual excitement that lead to sexual errors that are of etiological significance."[16] The disease of the central nervous system to which Jews are most prey is neurasthenia, and it is in Krafft-Ebing's description of neurasthenia that his (by no means original) image of the Jewish male appears. The Jewish male is "an over-achiever in the arena of commerce or politics" who "reads reports, business correspondence, stock market notations during meals, for whom 'time is money.'"[17] The association of the Jew with the "American Illness" through the use of the English phrase "time is money" presents the cosmopolitan Jew as the quintessential American. This conflation of two personifications of Otherness underlines the political implications of seeing in the "cosmopolitanism" of the Jews, in their function in the modern city, the source, on one level, of their neurasthenia. Yet this integration of the Jews into the negative image of modern civilization is contradicted by the view of the Jews' sexual exclusivity in Western society.

The interchangeability of the image of the neurasthenic and the Jew is, however, not found only within Krafft-Ebing's text (even though he elsewhere in the same text does stress the special proclivity of the Jews for neurasthenia) (54). It also occurs in a discussion of the psychopathology of the Jews written from the Jewish point of view. The quote from Krafft-Ebing on the overachieving neurasthenic reappears in Martin Engländer's essay on *The Evident Most Frequent Appearances of Illness in the Jewish Race* (1902). Engländer was one of the early Viennese supporters of Theodor Herzl and the Zionist movement. In his pamphlet he discussed the cultural predisposition of the Jews to neurasthenia as a result of the "over-exertion and exhaustion of the brain . . . among Jews as opposed to the non-Jewish population."[18] "The struggle, haste and drive, the hunt for happiness" have caused a "reaction in their central nervous system" (17). Neurasthenia is the result of the Jewish brain's inability to compete after "a 2000 year diaspora" and "a struggle for mere existence up to emancipation." To refute the argument that neurasthenia was a result of inbreeding, Engländer cited the Americans as an example of a "race" in which neurasthenia predominates and in which exogamous marriages are common. The cause of the Jews' illnesses is their confinement in the city, the source of all degeneracy; the cure is "land, air, light" (46).

Engländer's view that the madness of the Jews was a direct result of their political and social position in the West is not idiosyncratic. Cesare Lombroso, whose name is linked with the concept of "degeneration" which he helped forge, was also a Jew. After authoring a number of studies on the degeneracy of the prostitute and the criminal, Lombroso was confronted with the charge that Jews too were examples of a degenerate subclass of human being, a class determined by their biology. Lombroso's answer to this charge, *Anti-Semitism and the Jews in the Light of Modern Science* (1893), attempted to counter the use of medical or pseudoscientific discourse to characterize the nature of the Jew. Lombroso accepted the basic view that the Jew was more highly prone to specific forms of mental illness, quoting Charcot to this effect. But like Engländer, Lombroso saw the reason for this tendency as not the physical nature of the Jew but the "residual effect of persecution."[19] Both Engländer and Lombroso accepted the view that some type of degenerative process, causing a disproportionate incidence of specific forms of mental illness, existed among all Jews. They only differed about the cause of this process. In rejecting the charge of inbreeding, Jews such as Engländer and Lombroso were also rejecting the implication that they indulged in primitive sexual practices, practices in violation of a basic human taboo against incest. The confusion of endogamous marriage with incestuous inbreeding was a result both of the level of late nineteenth-century science and of the desire for categories with which to define the explicit nature of the Other. Thus the Jews are mentally ill, they manifest this illness in the forms of hysteria and neurasthenia, and the cause is their sexual practice or their mystical religion or their Western cosmopolitanism. All of this is betrayed by their corrupt discourse.

The belief in a relationship between mental illness and the disruption of discourse has its roots in late nineteenth-century medicine. The neurologist who listened to his hysterical patient and diagnosed "general paralysis of the insane" from the patient's monomaniacal tirades, as well as the psychiatrist who characterized the discourse of the patient suffering from "dementia praecox" as "word salad," centered their perception of illness on the nature of the patient's language. Indeed, by the closing decades of the nineteenth century abnormal discourse was deemed to be one of the primary signs of psychopathology. How a patient spoke was important.

It is in this medical context that Max Nordau's often-cited call for the Jews to become "muscle Jews," published in 1900, must be read.[20] Nordau's title recalls the "Muscular Christianity" of the late nineteenth century, with its advocacy of regular exercise to improve the body and to control "lascivious thinking." The emphasis on the body was an attempt to link spiritual and physical well-being. The futher connection of Jewish nationalism in the form of Zionism with German nationalism through the code of *mens sana in corpore sano* is evident. But the earlier call by the father of German nationalism, Friedrich "Turnvater" Jahn, had of course been heavily overladen with anti-Semitic rhetoric. Nordau's essay is yet another attempt by a Jew to adapt the underlying structure of anti-Semitic rhetoric and use its strong political message for the Jewish community's own ends. Nordau's call for a "new muscle Jew" is premised on the belief that the Jew had degenerated "in the narrow confines of the ghetto." But it was not merely the muscles of the Jews but also their minds that had atrophied in the ghetto. It is clear that Nordau was alluding to the "old Jews" and their attitude toward life. Zionism demands that the new muscle Jew have a healthy body and a healthy mind. Thus Nordau condemns his critics as having not only weak bodies but weak minds! This charge must be read within the inner circles of the Zionist movement, in which the Jewish opponents of Zionism were viewed as possessing all of the qualities (including madness) ascribed to them by the anti-Semites.

Neurasthenia, the American disease, the disease of modern life, was also the disease of the Jews, modern humans incarnate. Degeneration was the result of faulty breeding and was symptomatized by deviant sexuality. If the best authorities were to be believed—and at least in Germany the best authorities argued that inbreeding was the cause of the neurasthenia of the Jews—there was more than a hint of incest. Indeed, Engländer expressly defends the Jews against the charge of "racial inbreeding" while condemning the provisions of Mosaic law which do permit marriage between uncle and niece. He thus gives evidence for the implicit charge that runs through all the literature on the insanity of the Jews—that they are themselves the cause of their own downfall through their perverse sexuality. The lack of redemption of the Jews is made manifest by their perverse sexuality. The sexuality of the Other is always threatening. The implicit charge against the Jews invokes one of the ultimate cultural taboos of nineteenth-century thought. Inbreeding is incestuous and is a sign of the Jews' "primitive" nature, their existence outside of the bounds of acceptable, Western sexual practice.[21]

The decadence of civilization, of the city, is inextricably linked with the sexual exclusivity of the Jew. Nowhere is this more evident than in the first (and unpublished) version of Thomas Mann's novella "The Blood of the Walsungen" (1905), a tale of brother-sister incest. The Jewish identity of the siblings is made plain when, after the brother consummates their relationship, his sister ponders the fate of her German fiancé: "We robbed (beganeft) the non-Jew (goy)." Mann's father-in-law, Alfred Pringsheim, so objected to the inclusion of these Yiddishisms that Mann suppressed the planned publication of the story.[22] The novella, which Mann reedited in 1921 to eliminate the Yiddishisms, affirmed the corruption of both "modern life," as typified by the Wagner cult, and the Jews. The Jews, through their lack of redemption, are morally weak, and this manifests itself in the most primitive manner, through incest. Indeed, Adolf Hitler, never the most original of thinkers, summarized "Jewish religious doctrine" as simply "prescriptions for keeping the blood of Jewry pure."[23] The view that within the Jews' sexuality is hidden the wellspring of their own degeneration is the message of the overtly sexual imagery of anti-Semitic writings from the end of the nineteenth century. The Jew, the most visible Other in late nineteenth-century Europe, is also the bearer of the most devastating sexual stigma, incest.

As the model of biologically determined psychopathology gradually gave place to a psychodynamically oriented model during the opening decades of the twentieth century, one might have expected the image of the madness of the Jew to have vanished. With Freud's reorientation of psychopathology, any particularistic attribution of a specific pattern of mental disease to any group, especially on the basis of a presumed group-specific sexual aberration, should have been impossible. But Freud's view of the universality of patterns of human sexuality, especially in regard to fantasies of incest, could not destroy the image of the Jew as one predisposed to mental illness. This view continued not only in the conservative bastions of German clinical psychiatry but in that clinic where the most radical rethinking of the etiology of mental illness was being undertaken. In Eugen Bleuler's Burghölzli, the clinic in which Freud's dynamic psychopathology was being applied in a hospital setting, Rafael Becker, a young Jewish doctor, was given the assignment of comparing Jewish and non-Jewish patients to determine whether the work done by earlier investigators could be validated through the new psychoanalytic approach. Becker first presented his findings before a Zionist organization in Zurich in March 1918.[24] He began with those statistics upon which everyone else had based their assumptions and thus predetermined his own basic finding: Jews do indeed suffer from a higher rate of mental illness than does the non-Jewish population. The higher frequency is not, however, owing to inbreeding. Indeed inbreeding has led to the Jews becoming less frequently infected by various illnesses, such as smallpox and cholera, since they "acquire immunizing force through inbreeding and the purity of the race" (6). Becker also denies any specific "psychosis judäica," any specific form of mental illness affecting only the Jews, as well as any specific anthropological signs demonstrating the inferiority of the Jews (8). Becker (like Bleuler) sees mental illness as not brain illness but psychic illness. He dismisses the Jews' apparently in-creased rates of syphilitic infection and senile dementia as merely social artifacts—the result of the *general* spread of syphilis in the one case, and the *general* increased life expectancy provided by better social conditions in the other. While denying that the Jews have a special proclivity for any specific kind of mental illness, he explains the increase in the rate of other forms of psychopathology among Jews as the direct result of their West-ern acculturation. Even though Jews before emancipation suffered more greatly from oppression, their sanity was preserved by a strong faith. Only with the decline of Jewish identity in the nineteenth century was there an increase in mental illness. Becker picks up a thread in late nine-teenth-century antiassimilationist Jewish thought which blames Jewish emancipation and acculturation for the moral decline of the Jew. Franz Wittels in 1904 wrote a study of the psychopathology of baptized Jews.[25] Becker renews this image and introduces Alfred Adler's newly coined concept of the "inferiority complex" to give a dynamic dimension to his assumption that Jews were more frequently driven into madness than their non-Jewish persecutors (49). It is the "assimilated Jew" who is diseased, who is self-hating and thus self-destructive.

Becker outlines the etiology of Jewish psychopathology. Because Jews are forbidden *de facto* from practicing certain occupations, many Jews marry very late. As a result they have fewer and fewer children. (This is a substantial change from the charge made in the eighteenth century that the Jews' illnesses come from their early marriage and their large number of children!) The normal sexual development of the Jew is consequently stunted for lack of an appropriate sexual outlet. Becker provides his readers with a solution, one they would have immediately accepted as correct. He sees as the appropriate "therapy" for such illness an alteration of the social structure that caused it. Provide appropriate occupations, dispel the sense of inferiority which results from being unable to enter the profession one desires, and earlier marriages will occur, which will remove the direct cause of the psychopathologies. In the meantime Jews can avoid sexual overstimulation by shunning alcohol and sharp spices ("so beloved in the Jewish cuisine") and by exercising, following Nor-dau's prescription. This was Becker's presentation before a Jewish lay audience in 1918; a book he published the next year, presenting the results of his scholarly research in the Burghölzli, repeated many of these earlier views.[26] At least one element in the book, however, is worth a look: a case study of the inferiority complex of one of Becker's patients, a thirty-eight-year-old merchant. Again, Becker sees this not as a case of "psychosis judäica" but rather, in the new rhetoric of psychoanalysis, of the "Jewish Complex," a result of the position of the Jew in Western society. The Jewish Complex in this patient, illustrated by long passages from the patient's own biographical account, is marked by the sense of inferiority brought about by his treatment in society from the age of four, when "at the market day in Altstätten I alone of all the children was mocked. . . . I felt the humiliation which the Jew as a human being must feel in society."[27] Inasmuch as, for Becker, madness was self-hatred, the internalization of European anti-Semitism, it was still specifically Jewish.

This view that mental illness in Jews has a specifically Jewish etiology was not limited to Germany. In 1920 A. Myerson at the Boston State Hospital attributed the psychopathology of the Jew to "social" causes rather than "biological heredity."[28] Like Becker, he sees the Jews' isolation from appropriate forms of work as one of the major causes of their psychopathology. He also blames the Jews' rejection of "sports and play." Calling up the image of the "muscle Jew," here referred to as the "all American athlete," Myerson provides yet another formulation of the myth popularized by Nordau:

Sports and play . . . form an incomparable avenue of discharge for nervous tension. They breed confidence in oneself. Being extenser in their character, they allow for the rise of pride and courage. Circumstances excluded the Jew from their wholesome influence, and the children of the race grew up to be very serious, very earnest, too early devoted to mature efforts, excessively cerebral in their activities, and not sufficiently strenuous physically. *In other words, the Jew, through his restrictions, was cheated out of his childhood.* (96)

Myerson, like Becker, needs to localize the baneful influence on the Jews outside of the Jews themselves. He locates it in European society (America, the melting pot from which the slag of foreign values is removed, gets a clean bill of health). Just how strained his evocation of the sober, inactive Jewish child is can be reckoned by the fact that a large number of Eastern European Jews were manual laborers, working under the most primitive conditions.

In the course of the nineteenth and early twentieth centuries various approaches were made to the myth of the mental illness of the Jews. European biology, especially biology in Germany and France, served to reify accepted attitudes toward all marginal groups, especially the Jews. Once the supposition that the Jew was predisposed to madness was established as scientific "fact," society, acting as the legal arm of science, could deal with Jews as it dealt with the insane. However, the reality was quite different. While the privileged group might have wanted to banish the Jews out of sight, into the asylum, the best it could do was to institutionalize the idea of the madness of the Jews. Jews, like women, possessed a basic biological predisposition to specific forms of mental illness. Like women, who were also making specific political demands on the privileged group at the same moment in history, Jews could be dismissed as unworthy of becoming part of the privileged group because of their aberration. Like the American slaves who were labeled as mad because they desired to escape from slavery, Jews, by acting on the promise made to them through the granting of political emancipation in the eighteenth century, proved their madness.[29] Jewish doctors, who were not admitted to medical schools in Germany and Austria in any numbers until very late in the nineteenth century, were as close as any group to being permitted into the limited world of privilege.[30] These Jewish doctors, who were under some constraint to accept the rhetoric of nineteenth-century medicine, needed to limit the applicability of that rhetoric concerning themselves. They accordingly identified various subgroups of Jews (the merchant Jew, the Eastern Jew, the disenfranchised Jew, the immigrant Jew) as those at greatest risk, scrupulously exempting themselves. By differentiating themselves from the Jew as mad, they strengthened their tenuous position in the power structure of medicine. The doctor and the patient, after all, are not to be confused, least of all by the doctor.

The history of the myth of the mad Jew is a good case study for exploring how groups react to rhetoric aimed at them from their primary reference group. It is a striking example both of unquestioning acceptance of medical dogma and of the convoluted manner in which those labeled at risk must sometimes deal with being so labeled. But perhaps most vividly, it illustrates how hardy a myth can be—surviving even a paradigmatic shift in the perception of illness. For the ideological demands for the Jew to be different (from both non-Jews and Jews) were great. Zionists and anti-Semites make strange companions, but both used and needed the image of the Jew as mad for their own ends, as did, of course, the American Jews, who saw their acculturation as the cure for the madness of the Jew.

7

Race and Madness in I. J. Singer's *The Family Carnovsky*

OF ALL YIDDISH prose fiction dealing with the Nazi horror, none seems, in retrospect, quite as flawed as Israel Joshua Singer's *The Family Carnovsky*.[1] Written in the United States in 1943, it appears to suffer even more than most novels of the early forties about contemporary events from a myopia imposed upon it by its place and time of creation. Read superficially, the work seems to be an attack on the German Jews for having brought the Holocaust upon their own heads through their apostasy. Is this novel, given its date of composition and the bias of its author in favor of traditional Eastern European values, merely a crude tractate against assimilation and intermarriage? Is it the vengeance of the Eastern European Jew against the *yeke*, the German Jew, for real or imagined slights?

The Family Carnovsky is a much more complicated text than such a superficial reading suggests. However, much of its complexity lies in I. J. Singer's adaptation of two paradigms, one literary and the other quasi-scientific, filtered through the prism of contemporary racial theories. Ignoring this aspect of the novel reduces it to a work of questionable value. Taken in its context, the novel proves to be one of the major Yiddish attempts to deal with the entire myth of race and its application to the stereotype of the Jew.

Singer chose to recount the history not of an indigenous family of German Jews, but rather of a family of Eastern Jews who emigrate to Germany in search of the ideals of the Jewish enlightenment, the *Haska-*

lah. David Carnovsky is a Lithuanian Jew, the stereotypical *Litvak,* the doubter of traditional values, who seeks the idealized world of Moses Mendelssohn at the center of the *Haskalah,* Berlin. But this is Berlin of the 1920s, a city in moral collapse, a city of political street riots as well as the rising power of the NSDAP.[2] David attempts to raise his son Moishe Georg, called Georg in German as well as Jewish society, as "a Jew in the house . . . in the street a German" (24). This model of the individual as German and Jew, to paraphrase the title of Jakob Wassermann's autobiography of 1921, is indeed the model for the idealized image of the enlightened Jew, publicly the involved nationalist, privately the religious head of the family. The separation of state and religion, an Enlightenment myth, never instituted in Europe, became part of the required model for the German Jew. Parallel to this model Singer introduces the family of Solomon Burak, a man with the same roots as David Carnovsky but with an abiding sense of his own identity quite separate from that assumed by the German Jews.

So apparently successful is the Carnovsky family's acculturation that Georg, in spite of his racial stigma, becomes accepted into German-Jewish society—both because of his new social position and because of his abandonment of his Eastern European identity:

Although David Carnovsky was Polish-born, which was a definite drawback, the long-settled Jews of West Berlin wanted to marry their daughters to his son who was a native German and a rising associate of the famous Dr. Halevy. They were prepared to give sizable dowries, to provide a fully furnished office on the Kurfürstendamm, and to completely forgive the young man's unfortunate Eastern origins. And because he had risen to the rank of captain, had a good bearing, and was a proper German officer and gentleman, the haughty young Jewish ladies of West Berlin were even willing to forgive his Semitic features, black eyes, and black hair, attributes they normally disdained.[3]

Singer has introduced an equation that will assume ever greater importance as a subtext in the novel, that of the Jew as possessing the blackness of the Other. Georg is seen as a racial inferior by those German Jews who have accepted the racial standards of the majority.

Georg's assimilation eventually leads to his marriage to Teresa, a member of the German middle class. His father perceives this as a step toward apostasy:

When he reached Grosse Hamburger Strasse he stopped to look at the sculptured features of his idol, Moses Mendelssohn. "Rabbi Moshe," he said to him silently, "our children are going away from us . . . and their way leads to apostasy. . . ."

The philosopher looked back at him with a wise, mournful face while drops of rain ran like tears down his chin and stooped shoulders. (122)

For their part, the German Protestant family of Georg's fiancée perceive Georg as a member of a different and lesser race, a black race:

To [Frau Holbeck], he represented the whole species: dark, nervous, talkative, clever, and sinister. One night, when the young doctor unexpectedly brought Teresa home, Frau Holbeck's first glance bore out her preconceived impression of him and his kind. The thing that struck her light blue eyes first was an overpowering blackness. The hair, the brows, the lashes, the mustache, above all, the large and burning eyes, introduced an exotic kind of swarthiness into a house accustomed to pallid people. (122 23)

The offspring of the marriage between Georg and Teresa, Joachim Georg, called Jegor, represents the final break with the tradition of the Eastern European Jew. Jegor's existence on earth begins with his father ambivalent about circumcising him. Georg moves from opposing the act of circumcision to performing it himself. Circumcision is not only the external sign of the traditional bond of the Jews, but it is perceived by the Germans as a physical sign of the unique sexuality of the Jews. Georg's son seems the perfect mix of both parents' traditions: "To compensate Teresa for having made a Jew of her son, Georg named the boy Joachim, after her father. Teresa added the middle name of Georg, and, just like his names, the boy seemed a mixture of his two strains. His eyes were blue and his complexion fair like the Holbecks, but his brows and hair were raven black and the nose prominent and stubborn like a true Car-novsky" (134). The idea of the genetic mix, of an individual falling between the races, is inherent in the image of Jegor. It is the division of the two races which is emphasized, rather than their amalgamation.

Jegor's Christian uncle, the former *Oberleutnant* Hugo Holbeck, is both attracted and repelled by his half-Jewish nephew. An advocate of the *Dolchstosslegende,* which argued that German defeat in World War I was the result of Jewish betrayal on the home front, Hugo fills Jegor's head with tales of battle:

"Good night, Mutti," Jegorchen said, watching the last rays of light vanish. As soon as they faded, the terrible figures came back. The shapes on the carved ceiling came to life and began to dance. Although the lamp had been turned off, it continued to give off fiery rays of light. Circles whirled in front of his eyes—big circles, small circles, tiny ones. They spun so fast that they seemed to be playing tag. Jegor was ashamed to call his mother again but he was terrified of the darkness that was so full of sounds and movement. His fear finally put him to sleep curled up in a ball and with the blankets drawn over his head. But even in his sleep the figures kept coming from every corner of the room, every crack in the door. All the dead soldiers about whom Uncle Hugo talked came together with torn, bloody bodies, without heads or legs. They swarmed around his bed. Now he was fully grown, like his Uncle Hugo. He wore high boots, a spiked helmet, and carried a sword. He was taller than everybody else and a lieutenant. The goddamn Frenchmen charged him, each of them a freak, a monster. He led his company in an attack and wreaked terrible havoc with his sword. They fell, one by one. But suddenly one leaped at him, a black man from Africa, the kind Uncle Hugo had described to him. He rolled the whites of his eyes, held a giant knife between his teeth, and leaped at him. Jegorchen held up his sword but the Negro caught the blade in his bare hands and snapped it. He took the knife from between his teeth and tore at Jegorchen's throat. "Yay!" he screamed like the wind whistling through the chimney. (149)

Jegor's dream, the attack of the black, fits in well with the general fear of the black prevalent in Germany after World War I. The "Black Terror on the Rhine," the stationing of French colonial troops on the Rhine as part of the army of occupation, turned a German colonialist myth into a reality.[4]

Part of the myth and thus part of the stereotype of the blacks is their hypersexuality. Indeed the French colonial troops, only a small segment of whom were black, were primarily accused of sexual misdeeds. In Jegor's dream the real political myths about the black, which centered about sexuality, appear in the context of normal childhood fears of castration and dismemberment. For Jegor, the idea of being incomplete, of being black, is contrasted with the image of completeness offered by his qualified acceptance by his uncircumcised, blond uncle. Childhood sexual competitiveness, which rejects the father as the potential castrator, seems justified as the father has permitted a type of dismemberment in allowing the child to be circumcised. The proven castrating power of the father, at least as perceived by the child, is contrasted with the protectiveness of the uncle and mother. The confusions of evolving sexuality are thus given a locus in the blackness and Jewishness of the father, and in the understanding that these forces are also present within the self. I. J. Singer's use of the literary nightmare, the dream as the icon of the subconscious, stresses the inner life of the child. The reader observes those conflicts which would normally be played out within the psyche, hidden from all consciousness, including that of the character. As the reader sees, the fears of the child are articulated through images and stereotypes existing within the real world. These images are reinterpreted to give form to the child's anxieties. The sense of Jewish self-hatred found in Jegor's image of himself is but a reflection of the normal competitiveness existing between father and son. In this case, however, an added dimension is the inherent polarity between darkness and light, Jewish and non-Jewish, which exists through the presence of Jegor's uncle and his racial theories. Within his fantasy Jegor can flee into a world antipodal to that of his father, a world in which he becomes the epitome of light. In the real world there is no such escape.

Jegor's, as well as the reader's, introduction to the political implications of racial theories espoused by the "New Order" comes through the presentation of Dr. Kirchenmeier, one of Jegor's teachers and a crass opportunist. He takes the lead in introducing Jegor's school to the physical signs of the "degenerate," using Jegor as his unwilling model:

Then Dr. Kirchenmeier delivered a long and impassioned dissertation. "The audience will see from the figures on the blackboard the difference between the structure of the Nordic dolichocephalic skull—the long and handsome head that projects racial beauty and superiority—and that of the Negroid-Semitic, brachycephalic skull—the stubby and blunted head that resembles that of an ape and typifies racial deformity and inferiority. But in the case of our subject, it is particularly interesting to note the influence of the Negroid-Semitic strain on the Nordic. As you can clearly observe, the mixture has created a kind of freak. It may occur at first glance that the subject resembles the Nordic type, but this impression is strictly illusory. From the anthropological viewpoint one soon realizes that the Negroid-Semitic strain, which is always predominant in cases of mongrelization, has very subtly allowed the Nordic strain to dominate the external appearance in order to mask its own insidious influences. But this can be ascertained from the subject's eyes, which, although they may appear blue, lack the purity and clarity of classic Nordic eyes and are full of the nigrification and obfuscation of the African jungle and the Asiatic desert. You will also note that the hair, which may seem straight, contains Negro blackness and a hint of inherent woolliness. The prominence of the ears, nose, and lips clearly demonstrates the inferior racial strain." (194–95)

When Jegor is forcibly stripped by his teacher and his body is exposed in order to exhibit his "Jewish" characteristics to his classmates, his ambivalence concerning himself is underscored:

Jegor kept on struggling. He had already begun to mature and this made him especially bashful about his body, as boys usually are during the period of puberty. The thought of revealing his nudity terrified him. Besides, he was very sensitive about being circumcised. The mark of inferiority that his father had imposed upon him had always revolted him. When he was small, children had twitted him about it and nicknamed him "Damaged Goods." Since then he had always avoided undressing in front of others. (195)

By now the linkage of blackness, Jewishness, and sexuality has been made, at least through Jegor's perception of his world. His reaction to his degradation, to the exposure of his Jewishness and blackness, prefigures his attempted suicide at the end of the novel:

In Dr. Carnovsky's house his son lay on his bed with his face toward the wall and flatly refused to tell his parents what had happened. "Don't come near me!" he shrieked hysterically.

Late that night he developed a fever. Dr. Carnovsky applied ice packs to his son's burning brow and checked his pulse and heart.

"What happened, son?" he pleaded with the boy.

"I want to die," Jegor said. He had suddenly developed a stammer.

Dr. Carnovsky was terribly concerned about this development, as he was about the boy's high fever. But what was most frightening was the madness that now emanated from his son's eyes. (197)

But Singer does not permit the confusion of stereotypical perceptions of the Jew to rest here. He has stressed that this confusion, while present in the dominant society, is perceived through the adolescent mind of Jegor. Jegor's confusion concerning his own identity is compounded by the normal sexual competitiveness he senses between himself and his father. However, this sexual competitiveness is articulated by Jegor in terms of the stereotypical structures of blackness and Jewishness, as well as the hypersexuality of the Jew:

He was also terribly jealous of his mother, who each night was taken from him by this dark and malevolent Jew. He couldn't stand it when his father turned out the light in the dining room and retired to the bedroom with her, slamming the door in his face. She would then comb out her long flaxen hair and put it up in braids. In her clinging nightgown she seemed to Jegor a vision, a divine yet voluptuous idealization of the perfect Aryan woman, the symbol of the New Order. He couldn't stand the lustful and rapacious way his father looked at her. Jegor used every excuse to disturb his parents in their bedroom and to keep them from being together. The women in his sexual dreams always resembled his mother and he often stayed in bed late to hide his shame from her when she came in to change his sheets. His father's medical library contained many volumes describing in clinical detail the sexual experience. There were books there on anatomy, on venereal disease, on pathology, and on sexual aberration. Jegor studied these books for hours, lying in his pajamas in his bedroom. The books aroused such emotions in him that he often didn't hear his mother call him to the table. His eyes shone with an unhealthy glow, his cheeks broke out in blotches. He made copies of the forbidden pictures as well as all kinds of fantastic drawings of naked female bodies. He also copied drawings from newspapers and magazines that ridiculed the Jews.

He hid these drawings carefully, but one day his father caught him at it. Jegor had drawn a blonde angel being raped by a fat curly-haired *Itzik*. (205)

Even after the family Carnovsky is forced to leave Germany for America, the equation of sexuality, blackness, and Jewishness continues: "Like most boys, he resented it when his father acted without dignity, nor did he like to see him kiss his mother, least of all in public. He certainly could not understand why his father was so excited over a country that seemed hot, dirty, noisy, and full of all kinds of blacks and other racial inferiors" (228). Indeed in America the inferiors, such as his Jewish cousins, seem to have become his superiors: "Their every gesture was vulgar and uncouth. They reminded him of the caricatures drawn of the Jew on the other side; the dark, big-nosed, pushy degenerate. But what was perplexing was that these people seemed none the worse for belonging to an inferior race. They were strong and rough; they boxed, wrestled, swam, and ran like athletes" (235). Being German, at least German with the racial attitude of Jegor, is perceived in this new world as negative (255). Jegor's values are confronted with a truly "new world," one in which he cannot function. He thus flees ever deeper into his "German" identity, for in Yorkville he seems more German than the Germans (274). His ultimate attempt to identify with the German side of his divided self is seen in his letter to the Nazi officials in New York, in which he asks to be "allowed to return to his homeland where he was prepared to lay down his life for the Third Reich" (282). The letter reaches the desk of Dr. Siegfried Zerbe, an amalgam of Goebbels and Mephistopheles, who sees in the boy a potentially usable tool. Jegor drifts into the fringes of Yorkville society, then strikes out across the country with his German friends, in search of work. Unlike his Jewish cousins and the Buraks, Jegor is unable to function in the competitiveness of the new world. He returns to Zerbe, filthy, hungry, a failure, and Zerbe attempts to seduce him:

Jegor only stared at him through clouded eyes and Dr. Zerbe considered the matter closed. He poured two glasses of wine. "Here, let us drink to our new existence," he said, quaffed the wine in one swallow, and kissed Jegor full on the mouth.

Jegor felt so revolted by the wet slime that he recoiled. Dr. Zerbe moved after him. "*Bube!*" he panted through drooling lips. His gnarled face had turned an unhealthy blue. His eyes were like tarnished pieces of dirty glass. His weak, eager hands clawed at Jegor's garments.

Jegor's eyes opened wider and wider and suddenly saw double—two faces at once. One moment it was Dr. Zerbe's; the next, Dr. Kirchenmeier's. The wrinkles, the murky eyes and naked skulls, even the rasping voices seemed one and the same. He felt the tremendous surge of revulsion, hate, and strength that possesses one when facing a particularly loathsome reptile. From the bookshelf against which he cowered, an ebony statue of an African goddess with exaggerated breasts looked down on him. He gripped it in his hand and drove it with all his strength into the naked, sweating skull of the frantic little man before him. (331–32)

Mephistopheles' attempt to seduce the chorus of angelic boys at the close of *Faust II* is echoed here. But even more strongly evoked is the author of Jegor's first major confrontation with his own sexuality and distorted self-image, his teacher Kirchenmeier. Jegor stumbles out of Zerbe's apartment and returns to his father's building, where he shoots himself. The novel closes with the family reassembled, the father attempting to save the life of his son, and the sun beginning to dawn.

On one level, in *The Family Carnovsky* Singer attempts to restructure the story of a family's decay into a moral as well as a social document. The most evident model for such a novel is Thomas Mann's *Buddenbrooks,* subtitled *The Decay of a Family*.[5] Like the Buddenbrooks, as the Carnovskys become more and more alienated from their origins, they become more and more sensitive to their ambiguous place in the world. In the world of Lübeck, the Buddenbrooks, decaying patricians, are contrasted with the Hagenströms, the rising bourgeoisie. Singer, too, uses contrast (with the Buraks) to emphasize the decay of the Carnovskys. And both novels center about the question of intermarriage. For Thomas Buddenbrook's marriage to his Dutch wife results in the birth of Hanno, the ultimate artist unable to function in the world, just as Georg's marriage results in Jegor, in whom, as in Mann's *Tonio Kröger,* "two hearts beat in one breast."

One message of the family novel in modern European letters (and here one can include other novels by I. J. Singer, including *The Brothers Ashkenazi*) is that alienation from shared community values can foster a greater sense of the self. This illusion of heightened self-awareness is the direct result of the ambiguity of decaying family structures within a world in which the family remains the paradigm of interpersonal relationships. The decaying family belongs neither to the traditional world of its own past nor to the world of the present. Stranded between value systems that seem absolute, individuals perceive themselves (whether rightly or wrongly) as belonging to neither world. They feel themselves to be beyond normal moral codes, and yet long for acceptance. Among the tasks performed by the family novel in this century has been to articulate the search for individual identity within a world in which the family's role is being altered. The family novel becomes the tale not only of a family's fate but of individual education. The position and the self-definition of the individual are determined, in such fictions, by society as recreated by the author. Education is acquired and character shaped as the protagonist comes into repeated collision with the artificially rigid structures of this recreated society.

One further quality is introduced into the negative hero of this negative novel of education. Jegor, like Hanno, as a product of a vision of collapse, acquires a picaresque quality. His rootlessness means, however, that he is constantly at the mercy of society, rather than, like the true picaro, its master. Jegor's wanderings through the American landscape are more than slightly picaresque, but rather than being able to manipulate this rigid world for his own ends he is almost overwhelmed by it. Like Hanno Buddenbrook, he is able to function only in the world of his own fantasy. He is the final link in the degenerate family, the artist of life, whose sensitivity to the world precludes his functioning creatively within its confines.

But Singer's adaptation of the story of a family at once decaying and gaining in sensitivity and sensibility is rooted in yet another paradigm. For the late nineteenth century saw the degeneracy of the Jew in a very special light. As has been discussed, the Jew, more than any other outsider in the West, was thought to have a special tendency toward insanity. And the reason commonly given for the prevalence of insanity among the Jews was their inbreeding. Through inbreeding, the Jews became ever more degenerate over the centuries. Singer argues quite the opposite. In *The Family Carnovsky* the inbreeding of the Jew results in strength being built upon strength. It is only when an exotic strain is introduced that the problem of degeneracy becomes evident.

Singer did not originate such views of the social and physical decay of the family, Jewish racial identity, and the effect of inbreeding. Adolf Hitler's stereotype of the Jew used some of these arguments.[6] It is the Jews who, in spite of their own exclusivity, wish to bastardize the pure German race:

> With satanic joy in his face, the black-haired Jewish youth lurks in wait for the unsuspecting girl whom he defiles with his blood, thus stealing her from her people. With every means he tries to destroy the racial foundations of the people he has set out to subjugate. Just as he himself systematically ruins women and girls, he does not shrink back from pulling down the blood barriers for others, even on a large scale. It was and it is Jews who bring the Negroes into the Rhineland, always with the same secret thought and clear aim of ruining the hated white race by the necessarily resulting bastardization, throwing it down from its cultural and political height, and himself rising to be its master. (325)

The Jew and the black are equivalent in their hypersexuality. They wish to destroy the Germans' purity while preserving their own.

I. J. Singer's image of race in *The Family Carnovsky* questions this entire equation. Singer stresses the complex mix in Jegor of confused self-perception, family ambivalence, and normal human sexuality. Jegor selects racial metaphors to express his inner conflicts not because the Jews are degenerate but because he confuses aspects of Otherness. He identifies his father with all negative facets of the Other, seeing as darkness against light Georg's blackness and aggressive sexuality against the blondness and passive acceptance of Teresa (and, by extension, her family). The confusion arises when authority figures other than the father disrupt the normal triad. Kirchenmeier, Jegor's teacher in the *Gymnasium,* and Zerbe, the representative of the "New Order" in New York, both manipulate the boy for their own ends. Jegor, who has identified with the values of his mother and her brother, with their blondness and *Kultur,* is almost destroyed by Kirchenmeier's use of him as the example of the prototypical Jew. Jegor still manages to identify his negative feelings toward Kirchenmeier with those directed against his father. It is only with Zerbe's attempted seduction at the close of the novel, an act that in medico-legal terms after 1905 would be viewed as degenerate, that Jegor is able to direct his negative feelings away from those elements in his own self-image which he has long associated with his father. Suddenly racial metaphors are no longer appropriate.

The child's association of his father with fearful, punishing images of

blackness is finally dissipated when Jegor, using an artifact associated
with blackness, kills Zerbe. Jegor's reflexive identification of Zerbe with
Kirchenmeier in this crisis, by bringing the forces of evil into association,
removes them from any relationship to the father. Thus after Jegor's
attempted suicide, the novel closes with "the first light of dawn" enter-
ing the room where Georg is laboring to save his son's life. The father,
who before was a stereotype of darkness, has become a figure of light in
the reader's eye.

Jegor's attempted suicide at his father's doorstep is not an act of madness. It is the ultimate acknowledgment of his abandonment of his own
self-hatred and his expiation for it. For the destruction of the idols he had
created to establish an identity separate from that of his father leaves a
vacuum. As Nietzsche said at the conclusion of the *Genealogy of Morals,*
the collapse of these idols results in "a will to nothingness, an aversion to
life, a rebellion against the most fundamental presuppositions of life. . . .
man would rather will nothingness than not will."[7] Jegor is not mad,
quite the contrary. His act is the final acknowledgment of his own lack of
identity and his abandonment of his earlier "madness." It is his will to
nothingness. It is not a comment on his genetic background but on his
psychological structure.

I. J. Singer's novel is a successful attempt to abandon the association of
Jews with degeneracy and madness. Indeed it is an effective repudiation
of racial stereotypes and racial explanation per se. Singer is criticizing
assimilationism not for its racial consequences but for the loss of identity
in which it eventuates and the effect that such a loss has upon the personality. Singer's message is thus strikingly similar to that of Bruno Bettelheim, who wrote concerning the German-Jewish bourgeoisie in the
camps:

Their behavior showed how little the apolitical German middle class was able to
hold its own against National Socialism. No consistent philosophy, either moral,
political, or social, protected their integrity or gave them strength for an inner
stand against Nazism. They had little or no resources to fall back on when subject
to the shock of imprisonment. Their self-esteem had rested on a status and
respect that came with their positions, depended on their jobs, on being head of a
family, or similar external factors.[8]

The replacement of the complex value system evolved by the Eastern
Jews with values borrowed from the German petite bourgeoisie deprived
the Jews of the ability to function in moments of extreme self-doubt. The

value system they borrowed not only was never theirs in its entirety, but always contained elements inimical to them. The German always saw their adoption of it as merely a mask behind which glowered the unregenerate Jew. Sadly, for the German Jew the mask was the only reality. It is the acquisition of a new set of values which is portrayed at the close of the novel. That the Carnovsky family's new values are those of the Eastern European Jew, the values that Singer saw as those evolved by the Jews for themselves, should come as no surprise.

8

Sigmund Freud and
the Jewish Joke

I BEGIN WITH a parapraxis, a slip of the pen. In his autobiography, *From Berlin to Jerusalem*, Gershom Scholem, a man whose life was defined by books, makes surprisingly few references to those books that helped form his attitude toward literature as well as his Jewish identity. Scholem's life, played out in the scholarly world of texts, recreated the idealized world of the Jew as scholar in a Germany that had rediscovered these values of traditional Judaism only shortly before his birth in 1897. He describes discovering "some Hebrew books somewhere on the back shelves as well as other Hebrew books from the estate of my great-grandparents. . . . Otherwise I remember only two Jewish works of fiction that were very popular at the time, Israel Zangwill's *The King of Schnorrers* and the collection *Jüdische Witze* [Jewish Jokes] by Herrmann Noël. . . . I thought the latter book was magnificent, and to this day I feel it is noteworthy as one of the best formulated collections in the German language."[1] These two titles remained with Scholem for over sixty years as the first Jewish books he read. Zangwill's comic tales of London Jewry became classics among European Jews soon after they were published in 1894. They provided a comic romanticization of historic Western European Jewry similar to that which Shalom Aleichem provided for the contemporary Yiddish-reading public. But what of this "work of fiction," the Jewish jokebook by Herrmann Noël? No such author, no such book exists.

Scholem's memory has restructured the title and author of the collection. It was written or, perhaps better, compiled by a late nineteenth-century German-Jewish newspaperman named Manuel Schnitzer who published *The Book of Jewish Jokes* under the pseudonym M. Nuél in 1907.[2] Scholem christianizes Nuél's name to Noël and gives him the quintessential German first name of Herrmann. Scholem saw in this work, with its "German" author/compiler, a major force in shaping his Jewish identity. His parapraxis leads us to the somewhat unusual world of the German-Jewish joke book as a source for the definition of Jewish identity and the nature of the language in which that identity is clothed. Scholem's reference makes us, almost a century removed, aware of the power that the ethnic joke had (and has) in shaping communal as well as individual identity. For what we laugh at determines and is determined by our sense of self.[3]

Schnitzer's Jewish joke book evidently held a major place in the re-definition of the nature of Jewish humor, or at least the Jewish joke, after the turn of the century. In his introduction, Schnitzer comments that the "Jewish joke reveals the Jewish character, the weaknesses of which are the object of its mockery. But one must not forget, that it is always the Jews themselves who chastise their vanities."[4] Schnitzer sees in his collection, however, not a compilation of the weaknesses of the Jews to be read by the non-Jewish world, but a "folkloric" anthology of those stories "learned at grandmother's knee" which reveal the foibles of Jews in earlier, less enlightened times.[5] His audience is the ideal Jews of his time, who laugh not at their own "vanities" but at those of the past.

The program stated in the introduction to Schnitzer's collection of 1907 is expanded in the collection itself. The volume is divided into sociological categories that reflect an idealized, intact world of European Jewry, a world ascribed by 1907 to the Eastern Jew (*Ostjude*). For the Eastern Jew had come to fill the position of the "primitive" in the popular anthropology of Western Jewry. By observing the Ostjude, says the Western Jew, we can learn where we came from, just as Hegel uses the African black as the sign of the progress of European civilization. But also the Ostjude has preserved, better than we, an independent sense of self. Thus Schnitzer recounts tales about "important and unimportant rabbis," "students and pupils," "merchants and traders," "marriage brokers" and "beggars" (*schnorrern*). In all of these tales and jokes the language is clear, unambiguous German. Indeed, when he uses a Yiddishism in his tales, he provides footnotes explaining it to his Jewish audience:

The son of a famous German Jurist, who, although a baptized Jew, held the highest judicial posts and was ennobled, became engaged to the daughter of a banker, who likewise, even though in another area of endeavor, came from a famous Jewish family. He too, the Papa of the young bride-to-be, had been born Christian, for his father had been baptized. The mother of the bride-to-be was especially happy about this match, and said to her prospective son-in-law:

"You know, I had always wished for a son-in-law exactly like you . . ."

"And what should he have been like?" he asked smiling.

"You know . . . just a nice Christian young man from a *bekoweten** Jewish family."[6]

Schnitzer's note explains to his Jewish reader that *bekoweten* means "honorable." The presentation of this joke is typical of the volume, which presupposes absolutely nothing from its audience. Indeed, it reflects an apparent assumption that the audience would perceive the use of a Yiddishism (even terms such as *goy* (53) = non-Jew, or *gannef* (77) = thief, which had established themselves in German slang long before the turn of the century) as totally unintelligible. Schnitzer rejects any particularism in the discourse of the Jews. Evidently the ideal reader of his folkloric collection, which is supposed to be retrospective (and thus includes some Yiddishisms of the type "learned at grandmother's knee"), was removed from any language that could be classified as Jewish. Thus Schnitzer is at pains to point out that much of the comedy in the oral tales relied on the "tone-fall and gesture" of the speaker, both of which are lost in the written form and must, according to the compiler, be supplemented by a greater amount of narration.[7]

Schnitzer's ideal reader is an exclusively German-speaking Jew, one who, moreover, speaks German without a Yiddish accent (*mauscheln*) and without using Yiddishisms. Indeed, in the sequel to his collection, Schnitzer provides an extensive series of jokes about "the struggle for language and education" in which Eastern Jews are portrayed struggling with German, providing comic relief as they inevitably lose their struggles. The home of bad, comic German lies to the East, in Poland, in Galicia. Schnitzer begins the section with the following quotation from an apocryphal letter from a German teacher who is called to Posen to teach in a Jewish school there: "If they wish to say 'breit' (wide), they say 'braat'; if they wish to say 'Braten' (roast) then they say 'Broten'; if they wish to say 'Brot' (bread) then they say 'Braut'; and if they really have to say 'Braut' (bride), then they say 'Kalle.' "[8] *Kalle* is the Yiddish word for bride, but it is not Yiddish which is the butt of these tales, but rather mauscheln. By the turn of the century Yiddish had come to be seen by most Germans, as well as by such German-Jews as the language reformer Eduard Engels, as the primitive pidgin spoken by the Eastern Jew; and other German-Jews, such as Martin Buber, understood it as the true roots of a primitive, nonrational discourse. In either case it was exotic, distanced from the daily world of the German-speaking Jew. Mauscheln, the use of Yiddish intonation, accent, or vocabulary, was the mark of the Eastern Jew who wished to acquire the cultural status of a German-speaker but, by attempting to achieve this status, was revealed as the Jew as outsider. This Jew posed a threat to the integration of German-speaking Jews in the West by accentuating their "hidden" difference, the secret language ascribed to the Jews by Christian thought since the early Church fathers. The Eastern Jews were distanced by the German Jew into the world of the comic or the fictions of storytelling. They were thus placed in the past or at the fringes of Western "culture."[9]

Schnitzer's 1907 work parts company with other fin-de-siècle Jewish joke books in more than one respect. For not only is the language of his Jewish jokes cast in acceptable German, the language of his reference group, his stories are hygienically "clean." If we turn to the most widely read collections in the late 1890s we find quite a different image of the ideal reader. Written for a Jewish audience, these collections are, as the subtitle of one of them has it, "nothing for children." Containing many sexual double entendres, they are anthologies of "dirty" Jewish jokes. Four of the most widely circulated of these collections were compiled and published by Avrom Reitzer at the turn of the century.[10] Schnitzer's collections were evidently a reaction against such volumes as those published by Reitzer. All of Reitzer's jokes are told in mauscheln. The language of the jokes is the contemporary language of the Jews. There is absolutely no attempt to create a pseudoscientific matrix for the collection of the stories. Reitzer does not provide any "scholarly" apparatus qualifying his collections as "folkloric." Finally, these tales stress the sexual. As an example, here is the first tale in Reitzer's 1902 collection, entitled *Solem Alechem:*

Avrom Boschel and Schmule Josel leave the temple Friday evening. In the heavens a star [*Stern*] is shining. "Look at the lovely fixed star," says Avrom. "What do you mean," says Schmule, "dats not a fixed star, dats got a tail [*Schwaf*], dats a comet-star." "Na, na," says Avrom, "that I really like to know for sure. I'll tell you what. Come home with me, we'll ask my Elsa. She's educated, she'll tell us." "You're right, let's go." When they arrived home Avrom called his daughter Elsa. "Tell me my child, what is the name of the star [*Stern*] which has the long tail [*Schwaf*]." "Papa, that's Ephrain Stern from Leopoldstadt."[11]

The play upon the double meaning of *Schwaf* (tail and penis) in Yiddish is typical for this collection. What may not be clear from my translation is that the entire story, including the narrative intrusions, is written in mauscheln. Reitzer's tales presuppose an audience that can comprehend the double entendres presented in a German heavily laced with Yiddishisms. However, the knowledge of Yiddish actually required in these jokes is limited to those words and wordplays which exist in German, either because of parallel linguistic features in both languages or because of borrowings into colloquial German from the Yiddish. In other words, one certainly need not understand Yiddish (either written or spoken) to understand the jokes in Reitzer's collections. However, to the Jewish reader, the language appears to be transparent. For even those readers (read here Jews) who claim no Yiddish can understand the Jewish language of the joke. It is unimportant that non-Jewish readers of German, especially if they speak the slang of cosmopolitan areas such as Berlin, Vienna, or Frankfurt, could also understand these stories. For Jewish readers sensitive to their linguistic status as speakers of German, it would have seemed that there was some truth to the charge that, no matter what the surface polish, Jews spoke a secret language. Richard Wagner had formulated it in a manner widely quoted at the turn of the century: "The Jew speaks the language of the nation in whose midst he dwells from generation to generation, but always as an alien." This view is repeated endlessly during the late nineteenth century. In his overview of medical education in Germany and Austria, Freud's teacher Theodor Billroth summarized this view for Vienna: "Those whom one calls Jewish Germans are but those who happen to speak German, happen to have been educated in Germany, even if they write and think in better German than those Teutons of the purest water."[12] It is mauscheln which marks the Jew as the outsider (in German), especially to those Jews who perceived themselves as having achieved status in the German community which defined itself by the cultural implication of its language. In the Jewish joke book this was then linked to that other hidden language, the language of sexuality.

Before we further examine the function of the Jewish joke as a means of defining the special language of the Jews at the turn of the century, it is important to observe that the history of the Jewish joke book does not begin in the fin de siècle. The first joke books that collected jokes about Jews and were intended to be read by Jews appeared in Germany during the first generation after civil emancipation. The first seems to be L. M. Büschenthal's *Collection of Comic Thoughts about Jews, as a Contribution to the Characteristic of the Jewish Nation* (1812).[13] Six years later Sabattja Josef Wolff, the first biographer of Solomon Maimon, published a similar collection with an introduction by Büschenthal.[14] In both of his introductions, Büschenthal uses the eighteenth-century concept of *Witz* (humor) as the basis for his rationale in presenting this material. Humor calls upon the rational mind, and the Jews, Büschenthal comments, have been long noted for their rationality. It is this which the jokes reveal. But the Jews have been damned as well as praised for this characteristic. Their jokes reveal that hidden within the seeming rationalism may be yet another quality, a response to "centuries of persecution": "Necessity and weakness—this the female sex teaches us—give rise to deception and deception is the mother of humor. Therefore one finds this much more frequently among persecuted and poor rural Jews than among rich ones."[15] Büschenthal argues that what has previously passed for rationality, for the intense life of the mind among Jews, is simply a reaction to the persecutions they underwent. This false rationality, which bears more than a passing resemblance to the language of deception that Kant ascribed to women, can be revealed in the Jews' humor.[16] The joke thus reveals the truth about the language of the Jews, that it is a weapon used to defend them against the attacks of the Christian world.

Büschenthal's jokes are quite different from what his program would lead us to imagine. In the first joke in the collection which uses direct discourse, we can examine the spoken language attributed to the Jew and its implications:

A young Jewess sat in a loge in the theater in B———. A young rake entered and approached her in a familiar and aggressive manner. "Sir," said the young girl, "you evidently take me for someone else." "God forbid," he replied, "I can see very well that you are a young girl." He then became ever more impolite and finally brazen. The young girl, very upset, used her tongue, as only a young girl can. "Now, now," the rake cried, "don't eat me up!" "Sir, have no worries," she quickly replied, "I am a Jewess, and we are not allowed to eat pork."[17]

The story is told, as are all of the jokes in both early nineteenth-century collections, in the most cultured German. Indeed, the author-compiler is so sensitive to the linguistic implications of his text that when he uses the word for pork, *Schweinefleisch,* he prints it as "Schw——fleisch," since the term *Schwein,* pig, has a much more pejorative connotation in German than in English. He thus spares his readers from seeing a word that would be perceived as doubly offensive—indeed, that must have that implication in the context of the joke. This sensibility is not a Jewish linguistic sensibility but a German one. The joke has a sexual component that the author uses to illustrate his theme—that Jews, when oppressed, can attack only verbally. In that, they are like women, whose lack of strength is compensated for by their wit.

Büschenthal's collection, as well as Wolff's, also assumes a German-speaking reader. In these collections of stories written for a Jewish audience, no reference is made to dialect, for in this first generation after civil emancipation, mauscheln was still a widespread marker of the real difference between Jews and Germans. The entire non-Jewish literature that was aimed at satirizing the Jews during the first decades of the nineteenth century used mauscheln as a means of characterizing the language of the Jews. This was true not only of those writers who were clearly opposed to Jewish emancipation, such as Carl Borromaus Sessa, but of otherwise "liberal" writers such as Julius von Voss, who uses mauscheln in almost every representation of the Jew's language, but also prefaces his 1804 parody of Lessing's *Nathan the Wise* with a statement distancing himself from the conservative opponents of the Jews.[18] Büschenthal wishes to distinguish his "speaking" Jews from the image of the Jews' language which dominated both stage and fiction. Indeed, that image provided an explanation for the characteristic ascribed to the Jews, their rationalism, while distancing them from the language used to present this characteristic. Drawing on David Hume's concept of "national characters," he wishes to show that the specifically "Jewish" character is but a direct response to the way the Jew was treated in the past. His analogy is that of language. For he writes his anecdotes in the best possible German, showing that he has completely moved from the language associated with Jewish oppression (Yiddish) to the language of true emancipation (German). Likewise, he implies by the very act of collecting this material that such "national characteristics" as the Jews' wit will soon vanish and the Jew will become as dull and boring as the German.

The parallel between 1800 and 1900 should not be overlooked. For during each period a large group of Jews were identified by the nature of their language as different. In 1800, the Western Jew still spoke Western Yiddish within the walled ghetto; in 1900 a large number of Yiddish-speaking Eastern Jews fled the pogroms in Russia and settled in Germany and Austria. In both periods a Yiddish accent was the sign of a despised, incomplete symbiosis with the dominant common culture. The obtrusively different spoken language of the Jews kept alive the old charges of an inherently "Jewish" way of understanding the world as mirrored in the special language of the Jews. Both periods saw rampant and organized anti-Jewish movements in the German-speaking countries. After the defeat of Napoleon, riots caused the same type of insecurity in a Jewish community still very insecure about its status as did the rise of political anti-Semitism in the late nineteenth century. The joke book served in both periods as a means of defusing this anxiety. For it presents in softened and refined tones what the mobs in the streets were shouting about the Jews. And this discourse is given focus and distance by being placed within the covers of a book, a symbol of the higher culture. When, however, such books come too close to revealing the hidden, inner fears of their readers, when their mimetic quality reflects the wellsprings of their readers' anxiety, if only in distorted form, then even the book comes to be perceived as dangerous, as threatening. Such is the fin-de-siècle response to the Jewish joke book as a reflection of the hidden language of the Jew. This is especially true in the best-known study of the Jewish joke published by Freud in 1905.

Much of the recent discussion on Sigmund Freud's Jewish identity has been concerned with the role his father, Kallamon Jakob Freud, played in defining what it meant to be a Jew.[19] Freud's father was a Galician Jew who married into an established Austrian family and eventually moved to Vienna, the center of Austrian intellectual life. Even though Sigmund Freud moved to Vienna at the age of three, he never quite felt at home there.[20] This ambivalence, which manifested itself in many areas of Freud's personality, was evidently heightened by his work with Josef Breuer. Older than Freud, and more established in the Viennese intellectual and professional scene, Breuer contributed what came to be the paradigmatic case study, that of Anna O., to their joint *Studies in Hysteria* (1895). In this case study Breuer presents a reading of the "hidden" language of the Jew which may provide the matrix for Freud's own examination of this language in his later study of the Jewish joke. Breuer, also born in the provinces, is struck by Anna O.'s lack of religious feeling given her upbringing in a religious family.[21] Breuer deemed this observation important enough to record it in his casenotes. Thus one aspect of Anna O.'s illness, according to the observations of her physician, is a loss of identity as a Jew—a Viennese Jew, let it be noted.

While the symptoms of Anna O.'s illness included various types of physical impairment, such as the paralysis of her hand, Breuer's description of this case focuses again and again on the severe disruption of her language. During her illness, Bertha Pappenheim (Anna O.'s actual identity) lost her command of German. She began to communicate with her family and her physician, Breuer, exclusively in English, seemingly unaware that she had substituted English for German. Breuer's casenotes contain a letter written by her in English so stilted and academic that she clearly was neither fluent nor even comfortable with that adopted language. She had associated German with her father, with his long and intense illness, with his death cries. English, a purely academic tongue, had none of these associations for her. It was foreign to her, both literally and figuratively. Breuer reports that the central crisis in her illness occurred when she perceived herself threatened by a "snake." In her delusion she tried to pray, but all that came to her was an English children's rhyme. The prayer that Bertha Pappenheim could not remember would have been in Hebrew. Hebrew, the religious language of the Jews and her father, is repressed, forgotten, and is replaced by a rote rhyme in a tongue with no overt associations. Breuer stresses in his casenotes that Anna O. was "completely without belief." The loss of belief and the loss of language are one. Bertha Pappenheim repressed the two languages, German and Hebrew, which she associated with the world of her father. This is neither surprising nor unusual. What is interesting is that, following Bertha Pappenheim's failed analysis with Breuer, her career took her into the world of Eastern Jewry. She became highly involved combating the white slave trade, organizing a group that rescued young Eastern European Jewish women from the brothels. During this period, the 1920s and early '30s, she also published a series of German translations of some of the major popular Yiddish works, such as the *Maasebuch*, a collection of folk tales, and the *Tsena Uranah*, the Yiddish Bible written for Jewish women.[22] She became involved in the world that identified the Jew as a speaker of Yiddish, not German or Hebrew, and as female and a sexual object.

If Breuer's case study of Anna O. refers obliquely to her Jewish identity, it manages to avoid discussing her sexuality. Indeed, both the case study and Breuer's notes on the case comment that the patient seems without any overt sexuality. Breuer also, as is well known, avoids reporting his final confrontation with Anna O., during which she attributed her hysterical pregnancy to him. What is present in Breuer's case study is a detailed description of the collapse of Anna O.'s language.

Breuer, the provincial Jew as Viennese doctor, hears her German collapse into mauscheln. The syntax wavers, the conjugation of the verbs begins to disappear, until she finally uses only incorrect past tenses created from the past participle. This is, of course, a fantastic form of Yiddish, the language of the Jew which is neither German, the language of the assimilated Jew, nor Hebrew, the language of liturgy. Breuer labels this decay of German as "Jargon," the pejorative term used by German speakers when they referred to Yiddish.[23] Tacitly he associates the collapse of language, the loss of a Western Jewish identity, and the sexual Otherness of female discourse.

It was Sigmund Freud who made these associations overt. It was Freud, according to his own retrospective account, who saw the sexual etiology of the collapse of Anna O.'s language. It was Freud who first understood the sexual dimension of "hysteria" and the role of language in its cure. Freud's recounting of this central discovery, one of Frank Sulloway's "myths of psychoanalysis," links language and pathology.[24] But, as Breuer repressed the question of Anna O.'s sexuality, Freud represses the relationship between her illness and her rejection of her Jewish identity. In *The History of the Psychoanalytic Movement* Freud tells us two stories about the connection he drew between sexuality and the etiology of neurosis.[25] During his stay in Paris, Freud heard the great neurologist Jean Martin Charcot recount the case of a hysterical patient. Freud quotes Charcot concerning the source of the young woman's illness: " 'Mais, dans des cas pareils c'est toujours la chose genitale' " [But, in such cases, it's always the genitals]. He then recounts a case of hysteria about which he was consulted by the Viennese neurologist Rudolf Chrobak, and again he quotes Chrobak directly. The sole prescription for such a malady, Chrobak added, is familiar enough to us but we cannot order it. It runs:

> Rx. Penis normalis
> dosim
> repetatur!

Freud brings forward these two examples as proof that while the idea of a sexual basis for neurosis was evident, it had been treated as a joke, the punchline of which everyone knew. But Freud's recounting of these sexual jokes has an identical structure. Each story is told in German, and the punchline, a direct quote, is presented in a foreign language. This delivery may, on first reading, contribute to verisimilitude, or it may create the same slightly crabbed sensation one gets from reading Krafft-

Ebing's work on sexual pathology, in which all of the sexual references are presented in Latin. But there is a third dimension, one that provided the paradigm for Freud's sexual jokes, and that is the missing link of the Jewish joke and its role in defining Jewish identity in the 1890s.

As early as 1897, in his correspondence with Wilhelm Fliess, Freud reported that he had already compiled a "collection of profound Jewish stories."[26] Not merely jokes, but *Jewish* jokes, and this at the time when Freud was also collecting the reports of dreams which were to form the basis for his seminal study of the language of dreams. His collection can be reconstructed, at least in part, from the jokes published in *Jokes and Their Relation to the Unconscious* (1905). These stories reveal much of Freud's interest in presenting mauscheln in a scientific, that is, German, context. While the overall purpose of the books seems to be to analyze the nature of the joke (*Witz*), Freud actually limits most of the study to those jokes which he labels as "Jewish." Jokes "are capable of making us laugh and . . . deserve our theoretical interest. And both these two requirements are best fulfilled precisely by Jewish jokes."[27] Freud analyzes one of the "Jewish jokes," that of two Jews meeting near a bathhouse ("Have you taken a bath?" asked one of them. "What?" asked the other in return, "is one missing?"), in terms of its use of mauscheln. He is aware that the shift in stress from "taken" to "bath," which provides the ambiguity in the joke, is a quality of mauscheln. The origin of the displacement of meaning is thus in the language of the comic Jew, in the use of mauscheln. Freud analyzes a number of such jokes, all of which depend on the juxtaposition of "bad" German, mauscheln, with "good" German, the German in which Freud embeds the joke. The structure of the joke, as Freud describes it, is fulfilled in the very text Freud is writing.[28] The teller of the joke is Freud. He not only recounts the joke, but uses the form of the joke similar to that which is found later in Schnitzer's book of jokes. The joke is told in correct German. If there is any use of mauscheln it is limited to that part of the joke which is clearly delineated as the direct speech of the comic character. The joke's object vanishes in its telling. The object is the Eastern Jews who are trying to achieve status by speaking German but who reveal themselves through the nature of their language. Freud allies himself with a reader whom he expects to be conversant with the "modern" scientific discourse on the unconscious, the discourse, that is, of Freud himself. This projection reveals the identification that Freud, the provincial, has with those Eastern Jews who speak only in mauscheln. Freud's Galician father would have had at least a provincial accent which would have set him apart from Viennese Jews. Freud himself stated that his father served as his model of the persecuted Jew. Kallamon Jakob Freud would have also been his model for the Jews who revealed their nature through the difference of their speech. The special language of the Jew has another, major dimension for Freud. It is not merely that provincial Jews speak comically, but that this comic speech reveals their other hidden difference, their sexuality. The language of the Jewish joke is the language of sex. Marie Balmary centers her extraordinarily insightful reading of Freud's early life on the "hidden fault of the father," Kallamon Jakob Freud's unknown third marriage, and on Sigmund's birthdate, which was, in reality, two months earlier than his acknowledged date of birth.[29] The Ostjude, whether Jakob Freud or not, speaks a sexualized language, a language that reveals hidden truths in comic form. Kallamon Jakob's death in 1896 is seen by most critics (including Freud himself) as the catalyst for Freud's self-analysis, a self-analysis that led to the formulation of the new language of psychoanalysis. The actual language of his father, who was born in Tismenitz, Galicia, certainly played a role in the formulation of his image of the father, as did his association of this language with covert sexuality.

The association of the language of the Jews and sexuality is embedded in the collections of Jewish jokes available to Freud during the period from 1897 to 1905. In his work Freud mentions one specific contemporary source for his material (if we ignore his literary sources such as Heine's works), the Munich periodical *Flying Pages*. This periodical, a sort of German *Punch,* was consciously apolitical. It contains few dialect jokes, almost no Jewish jokes, and no sexual double entendres. (And yet this selfsame periodical republished in 1890 an 1877 collection of Jewish jokes written in mauscheln.[30] This collection is not much different from the anthologies of Avrom Reitzer.) Freud would have had access to most of the contemporary collections of jokes, both those (such as Reitzer's) written for a Jewish audience and the collection published by *Flying Pages*. He makes reference to none of these collections. Rather, he creates a new, scientific model (not unlike that later used by Schnitzer) in which he embeds these tales in an overtly scientific discourse. This scientific context heightens the difference between Freud's language, the language of the Jew as writer of scientific German, and the language, mauscheln, ascribed to the Jews in the jokes Freud presents.

In his study Freud dismisses the use of "Jargon," that is, Yiddish, as a source of humor. First in an analysis of jokes about marriage brokers (*Schadchen*), and then later in a discussion of a joke about Jews and alcohol, he observes that "Jargon" weakens the joke's effectiveness, since the tale relies on the effect of the language rather than on real content.[31] In dismissing the use of mauscheln, Freud undercuts the basis of the jokes he labels "Jewish." For the use of language in these jokes is as essential to their "Jewishness" as is their self-deprecating content. The Jews in Freud's jokes speak an easily identifiable language. This is true in the joke about the *Schadchen* (with its punchline "Do you call that living?") as well as in the first joke he cites from Heine's *Pictures of Travel,* in which Heine's Jewish upstart Hirsch-Hyacinth boasts of his relationship with the Rothschilds: "And as true as God shall grant me all good things, Doctor, I sat beside Solomon Rothschild and he treated me quite as his equal, quite *'famillionairely.'* "[32] The intonation of the first punchline and the punning misuse of German in the second are both qualities ascribed to the Jew speaking mauscheln, German with a Yiddish accent.

We are thus left with a complex set of paradoxes. Freud begins to collect "Jewish jokes" after his father's death, at a time in his career when he is trying to define his basic program. He records jokes in a very specific way: they are labeled by him as "Jewish," they are written in good German, and they contain direct or indirect discourse which uses mauscheln to characterize the speaker as a Jew. At the same time, according to Freud's own account, he discovers the basis for the neurosis of Breuer's star patient in two jokes, both of which share structural devices with the Jewish jokes he retells in his book on humor. They are told in good German, they contain direct or indirect discourse, and they use a foreign language to characterize the secretiveness of the speaker's *points.* All of this against a background of a German-speaking world in which the dominant image of the Jewish joke, at least in the 1890s when Freud is writing and collecting his material, is that of the off-color or "blue" story.

In his study of the nature of humor and its relationship to the unconscious, Freud separates two modes of storytelling, one that he illustrates with his "Jewish" jokes and the other, the sexually aggressive, that goes almost without illustration. The model for the joke about Jews that we discussed above, however, is not the model Freud perceives in his discussion of his "Jewish" jokes. Rather it is the model of the sexually aggressive joke told as part of the verbal seduction of the woman—the joke that causes the object of the story to vanish in the identification of the male storyteller with his male listener. The Jew in the "Jewish" joke in Freud's retelling thus becomes the woman, and vanishes in the presence of the idealized German self as both raconteur and listener, turning the teller's desire for identification with his reference group into hostility at the outsider, himself, who does not permit this. Freud rejects the very tales he tells as not "real" "Jewish" jokes because they are told in dialect, a dialect that triggers his own insecurity about his status as a provincial Jew in society. He is a provincial, one who speaks a different tongue, not only because of his "hidden" Jewish language, but because this language is sexual and reveals the true nature of the speaker to be the same as that of the caricatured Jew in the sexually suggestive Jewish joke.

The idea that the Jewish man in the nature of his humor (*Witz*) is identical with the woman is as old at least as Büschenthal's 1812 anthology of Jewish humor. Yet it is in a much more aggressive work of the fin de siècle that this parallel is repeated. Otto Weininger's *Sex and Character* (1903) is a work of intense self-hatred which, however, had an unprecedented influence on the scientific discourse about Jews and women at the turn of the century. Weininger's suicide shortly after the publication of this book helped publicize his views, but they were hardly new to the thinkers of the fin de siècle. His polemical restatement of Schopenhauer's views on women simply extended the category of the "female" to the Jew. What characterizes the woman is her language: "The impulse to lie is stronger in woman, because, unlike that of man, her memory is not continuous, whilst her life is discrete, unconnected, discontinuous, swayed by the sensations and perceptions of the moment instead of dominating them."[33] Women's language is lies; Jews' language is mauscheln: "Just as the acuteness of Jews has nothing to do with true power of differentiating, so his shyness about singing or even about speaking in clear positive tones has nothing to do with real reserve. It is a kind of inverted pride; having no true sense of his own worth, he fears being made ridiculous by his singing or his speech."[34] Women and Jews are thus parallel for Weininger, especially in the nature of their discourse. Both lack a "center" to their ego, according to Weininger, which accounts for the feminine characteristics of the Jewish male. Neither women nor Jews can possess true humor: "Jews and women are devoid of humor but addicted to mockery" (319). True humor is rooted in the ability to transcend the material, a gift possessed by Aryan males but not by Jews and women. Humor is thus a central marker of the difference between the self and the Other. It is a mode of truthful discourse which Jews and women cannot possess.

Since Weininger was a Jew, one must see in his very act of writing an attempt to disprove his thesis. He writes a laboriously pseudoscientific German, so convincing in its rhetoric in its own time that its polemical intent was initially overlooked and his work was viewed as a contribution to the science of racial anthropology. Freud read and used many of Weininger's views. One practice he seemed to accept as needful was drawing a distinction between his use of the language of science and the language attributed to the Jew. This hidden language, the language that Viennese society used to characterize the Jew, was the language of the outsider. It was part of the hostile labeling of the Jew as different. But Freud projects this universal labeling of the language of the Jews as different onto a subset of Jews. He characterizes the mauscheln of the Jew attempting to enter Austrian society from the East as the true sign of the different, hidden language of the Jew. In so doing he publicly identifies with the non-Jew rather than with the non-Jew's caricature of the Jew. Freud wishes to stand outside of the limited world-view attributed by this caricature to the Jew. He wishes to speak a different language. This is, of course, echoed much later in his creative career in his description of the basis for Moses' slowness of speech: "Moses spoke another language and could not communicate with his Semitic neo-Egyptians without an interpreter."[35] Freud, like his "Egyptian" Moses, speaks a language other than that of the image of the Jew which he rejects. It is the language of scientific discourse. Yet that discourse, as it manifests itself in Weininger, is itself contaminated. Freud's scientific German, at least when he sits down to write his book on humor, is a language tainted by Weininger's anti-Semitism. Thus even in this seemingly neutral medium of writing about Jews, Freud finds himself confronted with a new, hidden language of the Jew, the language of the Jew as anti-Semite, in which all of the charges brought against the Jew come home to haunt the author and lead him to the only possible escape, self-destruction.

In this medium Freud creates a language for himself which is neither that of women nor that of Jews. Freud replaces both of these languages with the new language, the language of the unconscious. It is a language present in all human beings, one unmarred by the sexual or anti-Semitic politics of his day, or at least so Freud hopes. The exercise of collecting and retelling the Jewish jokes, of removing them from the daily world in which Freud must live to the higher plane of the new scientific discourse, that of psychoanalysis, enables him to purge himself of the insecurity he feels by virtue of his status as a Jew in fin-de-siècle Vienna. He exorcises this anxiety by placing it in the closed world of the book and placing himself in the privileged position of the author employing the new language of psychoanalysis for an audience newly taught this discourse. It is no wonder that when Freud comes to remember his "discovery" of the sexual etiology of neurosis, the wellspring of this new language of psychoanalysis, his memory casts the source of his discovery in the structure of "Jewish" jokes. The very structure of the joke embodies the distancing of existing attitudes and their replacement by a new discourse, the universal discourse of psychoanalysis.

9

Sexology, Psychoanalysis, and Degeneration

Early Analogies of Sexuality and Degeneration

NO REALM OF human experience is as closely tied to the concept of degeneration as that of sexuality.[1] The two are inseparable in nineteenth-century thought. They evolved together and provided complementary paradigms for understanding human development.

A glance at the history of human sexuality as understood by the human sciences reveals that in the late eighteenth and early nineteenth centuries there was a fascination with the pathological rather than the normal.[2] Since much of the work on human sexuality was undertaken by medical practitioners who saw the pathological as the subject of their calling, it is not surprising that their central focus in examining human sexuality was the problem of deviancy; or that the subject claiming most of their attention was masturbation, since masturbation was deemed the major deviancy in late eighteenth- and early nineteenth-century medicine.

The initial interest in masturbation as a sexual pathology appeared in the early eighteenth century, and its impetus was clearly theological. The first widely circulated tractate on the subject, *Onania, or The Heinous Sin of Self-Pollution* (1726?), reads not as much like a series of medical case studies as like the testimony of sinners presented in the newest church on Grub Street, the Tabernacle of Public Opinion. Indeed the standard study of this subject assumes from the nature of the text that its author was probably a "clergyman turned quack."[3] Whether this conclusion is necessary can be left to individual judgment, but clearly the earliest popular or pseudomedical interest in sexuality was in sexuality as a manifestation of corruption in the child. The cases portrayed in *Onania* exclusively deal with children or young adults who began masturbating as children. Masturbation was an indicator of the potential for perversion inherent in humanity because of the fall from grace.

The first comprehensive nosology of human sexual pathology, Heinrich Kaan's *Sexual Pathology* (1844), departed from the focus on masturbation.[4] Kaan argued for a universal, comprehensive definition of sexual pathology based on observations of childhood sexual deviancy.[5] He drew an analogy between the sexuality of primitive humans and that of the child, a crude type of chronological primitivism similar to that argued by Hegel.[6] The child is the primitive form of human; the primitive manifests humanity's early sexuality. In this conflation of types of sexual Otherness the germ of the concept of sexual degeneration is present. Hidden within each individual, capable of being triggered by a fantasy in opposition to rational mind, is the tendency toward perversion. Perversion is the basic quality ascribed to the sexuality of the Other. Individual perversion is seen as a proof of the potential for the perversion of the group. Kaan, for example, even in postulating specific etiologies for masturbation in various hereditary, geographic, and environmental contexts, presents a mini-history of human sexuality in his discussion of sexual deviancy as a ubiquitous phenomenon.

The worm hidden within humanity and society is also the leitmotiv for B.-A. Morel's definition of "degeneration."[7] Morel argued that the degenerate bore the scars of a fall from grace.[8] He adduced the primitive as a straightforward proof that deviancy abided as a potential in all humankind, much as did his contemporary, Count Gobineau. The use of the anthropological model, Morel's greatest contribution to psychiatry, mirrored his understanding not only of individual human development but of societal development. The presence of the degenerate is as anagoge for the eternal potential for the fall from grace.[9] It is found in the child, whatever the child's manifestation, either as primitive or as pathology.

Kaan and Morel share more than a theologically based belief in chronological primitivism. Both draw on a model, that of the cretin, in which all the factors found in the models of deviant sexuality and degeneracy appear. B.-A. Morel initially formulated his concept of the degenerate based on his study of the cretin.[10] Kaan's major predecessor in Germany, an author whose work is little examined in studies of the history of human sexuality, was Johannes Häussler, whose work entitled *On the*

Relationship of the Sexual System to the Psyche in General and to Cretinism in Particular appeared in 1826.[11] The cretin was a common locus for various aspects of Otherness identified in the literature on masturbation as well as in the studies of the transmission of psychosexual pathologies. For the masturbator in a final state of collapse, mind gone, strength sapped, totally lethargic, is perceived as a type of mental defective. (The literature of masturbatory insanity never clearly assigns the roles of cause and effect to imbecility and masturbation.)[12] Morel presents parallel cases in his supplementary atlas. He introduced the case that follows as one of two selected from among a multitude he had amassed. The case and its mode of presentation are illustrative of that type of material which Morel believed to show the generalized typology of the cretin:

Marguerite Gros, twenty-three years old, from the village of Marcas, appears like a ten-year-old girl. She is not quite 977 mm tall and weighs about 20 kg. Noticeable is the lack of any sign of puberty and the retention of all her milk teeth. Her genitalia are no more developed than those of a seven or eight-year-old child. The pubis is totally hairless. The feeling of shame seems not yet to have been awakened.

The examination of Dr. Destrade, the family doctor, who accompanied me on my visit, actually seemed to cause her no embarrassment. Twenty-four teeth are present and Destrade had determined, as I did, that these were milk-teeth. This girl, whose organic development had come so completely to a stop, also had a very limited intelligence. She is unable to say how old she is nor does she know the value of various coins.[13]

The cretin is here both the child and the primitive. The cretin's physiognomy is that of the child, her sexual attitude that of the child and the primitive. The unrestrained sexuality, childlike appearance, and geographical and familial isolation of the cretin were an ideal basis for describing retrogressive sexuality. For Morel, as indeed for Kaan, the presence of shame is the proof of adult and therefore civilized sexual behavior. The cretin stands apart from civilization, as does the deviant, in a world inhabited by the sexual Other, the primitive and the child.

Sexual Politics and Degeneration

The "scientific" study of human sexuality is the equivalent of the "scientific" study of human history. Jakob Santlus in his *Psychology of*

Human Drives (1864) saw the origin of the "cultural history" of humanity in the combined "sexual and spiritual creativity" of humanity—a remark made in tracing the development of the history of human sexuality from the muck of pre-Christian myth to the "ethical perfection" of Christianity.[14] Christianity's introduction of the feeling of shame or modesty was viewed in the mid-nineteenth century as the major indicator of the move from the primitive to the civilized. And just as three decades later Ernst Haeckel was to see the development of human society in the light of his embryological model of ontogeny recapitulating phylogeny, so too did those mid-nineteenth-century thinkers concerned with the development of human sexuality begin to see human history writ fine in the development of sexuality from the child into the adult.

A similar analogy was drawn by Rudolf Virchow in his *Cellular Pathology* (1858).[15] Virchow likened the interaction of the cells in the body to the interaction of citizens in the body politic. Disease arose from only two sources: an active external source ("irritation") and a passive internal source. The latter Virchow labeled "degeneration." So within the human body as well as within the body politic forces are constantly at work which expose hidden weaknesses of the body and can cause its eventual collapse.

The concept of sexual degeneracy as a political force in the flow of human history was expressed at mid-century in J. J. Bachofen's *Mother Law* (1870). While *Mother Law* does not overtly discuss the medical aspects of human sexuality but rather the development of history in the light of human sexuality, it does analyze the question of sexual degeneracy. Rather than concerning himself with models of masturbatory or cretinous degeneracy, Bachofen based his analysis of sexual degeneracy on lore about the Amazon—a point of departure that stirred early twentieth-century feminist criticism of his model of history. Bachofen perceived the movement from the hetaeristic age to the age of exploitative promiscuity to matriarchy and, finally, to patriarchy as proof of the maturation of human society. Within this seemingly linear movement of history are ambiguous eddies, such as the violence of the Amazon, and this was labeled by Bachofen as "savage degeneration."[16] The cruel and unnatural domination of the male by the woman warrior in Amazon society was a vestige of an aberrant but necessary stage in human development. Bachofen's belief that such a condition once characterized all cultures echoes Kaan's discussion of the ubiquitousness of human sexual pathology.[17] Bachofen saw this form of deviancy as the result of psychic aberration, stemming not from the dominance of the irrational (as in

Kaan's model) but rather from the natural dialectic of political repression.[18] Hegel's master-slave dyad had been used by John Stuart Mill in 1869 to describe the status of the woman in a male-dominated society.[19] Bachofen's use of the same idea to explain the Amazon's nature, however, is a remarkable recycling of Hegel's idea. For Hegel had cited the Amazon as the nadir of sexual degradation. A legend of the fabulous state dominated by women that Hegel related in his *Lectures on the Philosophy of Religion* told of a world even more destructive than Kleist's *Penthesilea:*

Tradition alleges that in former times a state composed of women made itself famous by its conquests: it was a state at whose head was a woman. She is said to have pounded her own son in a mortar, to have besmeared herself with the blood, and to have had the blood of pounded children constantly at hand. She is said to have driven away or put to death all the males, and commanded the death of all male children. These furies destroyed everything in the neighbourhood, and were driven to constant plunderings, because they did not cultivate the land. Captives in war were taken as husbands; pregnant women had to betake themselves outside the encampment; and if they had borne a son, put him out of the way. This infamous state, the report goes on to say, subsequently disappeared.[20]

Hegel used this image of the Amazons not primarily to illustrate the history of the degenerate sexuality of the female but as an instance of the horrors that can take place among the blacks, whom Hegel describes not only as "pre-historic," that is, outside of the concept of history, but also as an "infantile nation."[21] Bachofen's discussion places the Amazon back in history, but at a moment of degeneration. But degeneration is not merely retrogression to a more primitive mode of sexual expression—on the contrary, Bachofen sees in this moment a progressive force. Society can be improved through a dialectic in which the antithesis is "savage degeneracy."[22] This sense of the creativity inherent in the primitive underlies yet another perception of the nineteenth century concerning the close analogy between sexual deviancy and the nature of the state. The state can be undermined or revolutionized by retrogressive models of sexuality, and the state bears within its own history this potential just as the body does. The state must have the means to control or harness this force. Bachofen's assimilation of this idea can be seen in his view of the necessary progression from the Amazonian reaction against the bondage of woman in the hetaeristic state to the matriarchy: from lawlessness through lawlessness to mother law.

The arena of mid-nineteenth-century thought in which the analogy of the political and sexual models of degeneracy was most clearly played out was that of public health. Eduard Reich can stand as representative of writers on this subject in the German-speaking lands. Reich, a medical doctor turned polyhistor, authored a remarkable series of books during the latter half of the nineteenth century, books that were widely read and translated and were quite influential in public health reform. What they had in common was the view that the study of human history illustrates the repression of sexuality and an advocacy of the movement of sexuality from the private into the public sphere. Reich saw as the basic problem confronting society in the late nineteenth century the need for public control of human degeneracy, specifically through the control of sexual activity. Beginning with his study *History, Natural Laws, Laws of Hygiene in Matrimony* (1864), Reich saw the movement from the promiscuity of primitive people to modern institutions of matrimony as a means of eliminating potential causes of illness and perversion.[23] In *On Immorality* (1866) his historical understanding of marriage was applied to the root causes of the potential of degeneracy, which he however still saw within the limits of the masturbatory mode.[24] Such deviant behavior, according to Reich, demanded the intervention of the state before the entire society succumbed to immorality. In 1868 Reich authored one of the first major German works on degeneracy, *Degeneracy of Man: Its Source and Prevention*.[25] Among the causes of individual degeneration as well as the eventual collapse of the state, according to Reich, is the moral climate of society. Like Bachofen, Reich believes that an immoral state causes the corruption of its members. Not surprisingly, one of Reich's examples for the immorality of the state is the institution of slavery. The form of slavery he is concerned with is not that represented by Hegel's master-slave dyad but, more specifically, black slavery, an issue that had defined this problem during the first half of the nineteenth century. Slavery can lead to degenerate sexuality as it can lead to other forms of degeneracy.

What can the state do to prevent this degeneracy from appearing and thus undermining the state itself? It can, of course, eliminate those features that further degeneracy, such as slavery, but it can and must also police itself to prevent the excesses that lead to sexual degeneration. Public control and supervision of prostitution, which reduced the spread of venereal disease, was one important arena of the intervention of the state, but Reich also saw the control of the form of government as a vital area of intervention.[26] Indeed he ended his work on degeneration with a discussion of the potential degenerative effect of democracy and monarchy. In democracy degeneration can occur when the wealth is unequally distributed and the state strives to expand itself too greatly through war. This leads to a "worsening of morals." Under a monarchy, the prime threat is the rigidity of the class structure and the "all too great striving for money."[27]

Reich's view that social and moral illness are inextricably linked was already echoed in the French discussion of racial and social degeneracy during the 1860s. Both Morel and Gobineau saw the analogy between class and race as a valid one. Class mobility was perceived as almost as dangerous as "hybridization" or, to use the mid-nineteenth-century term of American racial pseudoscience, "miscegenation." Indeed the attraction of the Other as a sexual being in nineteenth-century fiction was enhanced by the Other being of either another race or another class.[28]

The most influential statement of the analogy between history and sexuality was the opening chapter of Richard von Krafft-Ebing's *Psychopathia sexualis* (1888). This chapter, entitled "Fragments of a System of the Psychology of Sexual Life," is a skeletal history of humanity according to sexual principles. Like Bachofen, Krafft-Ebing perceived the history of humanity in stages of social development extrapolated from the stages of its sexual development. He began with the most "shameless" level of human development, seeing in contemporary "primitive" societies proof of the biblical view of the earliest stages of human society.[29] In his sketch of human sexuality Krafft-Ebing relied heavily on Edward Westermarck's *History of Human Marriage*.[30] Westermarck, however, saw a continuity of human institutions, such as monogamous marriage, as a means of overcoming aberrant promiscuity. For Krafft-Ebing the second state is the movement from the swamp, to use Bachofen's term, of universal promiscuity to a male-dominated world of human law.[31] It is only with Christianity that abstract principles begin to regulate human sexual activity:

Christianity raised the union of the sexes to a sublime position by making woman socially the equal of man and by elevating the bond of love to a moral and religious institution. Thence emanates the fact that the love of man, if considered from the standpoint of advanced civilization, can only be of a monogamic nature and must rest upon a stable basis. Even though nature should claim merely the law of propagation, a community (family or state) cannot subsist without the guarantee that the offspring thrive physically, morally and intellectually. From the moment when woman was recognized the peer of man, when monogamy became a law and was consolidated by legal, religious and moral conditions, the Christian nations obtained a mental and material superiority over the polygamic races, and especially over Islam.[32]

This movement from chaos to human law to divine law is the basic view of history found in Hegel. It reappears in various guises in Bachofen, Reich, and later writers about human sexuality such as August Forel. It is this paradigm that Lewis H. Morgan (1877) and Friedrich Engels (1884) adopt in their extension of the argument that the human control of human sexuality is but another means of state control.[33] Krafft-Ebing, unlike Westermarck, adds yet another feature to the discussion of the history of human sexuality: the potential of degeneration. He, like Bach-ofen and Reich, sees the potential for degeneration as omnipresent and under the influence of the state. He sees advanced rather than primitive cultures as the generators of degenerate sexuality.[34] The fluctuation that Bachofen perceives within the dialectic of history, that Reich sees within the potential faults of the state, is also articulated by Krafft-Ebing. In a reversal of Virchow's likening of humanity to society, society is likened to humanity.[35] It contains the potential for decay within its systems, and its decay is manifested in the deviancy of the basic human drives. But decay is not embodied in the Amazon or in the prostitute, but in the Other as homosexual.[36] In Reich's views, as in the early literature on masturbation, the potential for other deviancies, including homosexuality, was present within the effect of childhood masturbation on adult sexuality. Krafft-Ebing, who sees childhood masturbation as an extremely minor and rare manifestation, discounts it. He replaces it with homosexuality as the exemplary sexual degeneracy. The homosexual is the prime violator of "natural drives."

The idea of the basic drives as the structures of natural law is from the eighteenth century. Indeed both Reich and Krafft-Ebing refer to Friedrich Schiller's poem "The Worldly Wise," in which Schiller sees the "drive for Hunger and Love" as that "which holds the structure of world-philosophy" together.[37] The basic drives can be perverted through the state, and their perverted expression in turn undermines the state. Bachofen's positive model is thus made manifest. Degeneracy, especially degenerate sexuality, is a positive force as it moves humanity to the necessary changes in forms of human interaction. Society thus benefits from its own repression as it dialectically causes changes within itself. Even Engels, who adapts this basic model, sees in the development of female gender identity within capitalism the negative result of the exploitation of the woman within the family structure and thus as the seeds for revolutionary change. Although he views the history of humanity as paralleling the development of the economic systems on which its societal structures are based, rather than seeing it by analogy with the history of its sexual development, Engels still retains the basic dialectic paradigm concerning sexual repression and its potential. Bachofen, Reich, and Krafft-Ebing incorporated the predominant view of the sexual basis for human society into their understanding of the dilatory effects of that society, a view that is given medical validity through the creation of a disease entity that manifested the sexual pathology of nineteenth-century society.

The American Disease

Richard Krafft-Ebing's argument that civilization regularly brings forth degenerate forms of sexuality because of the "more stringent demands which circumstances make upon the nervous system" and which manifest themselves in the "psychopathological or neuropathological conditions of the nation involved" summarizes the etiology of one of the phantom diseases of the late nineteenth century, neurasthenia. A disease with no rigid symptomatology, it was defined negatively as not being hysteria, madness, melancholia, epilepsy, or any of the numerous other endogenous or degenerate illnesses catalogued in the late nineteenth century.[38] In fact, the definition of neurasthenia stated by its formulator, George M. Beard, can be seen as embracing almost all "psychopathological or neuropathological conditions." "Nervousness," he wrote, "is nervelessness—a lack of nerve-force."[39] He saw neurasthenia as a physiological deficit of nerve-function, for he took quite literally the late nineteenth-century analogy between electrical systems and the nervous system. Neurasthenia was the decreased capacity to carry nervous stimuli or a decrease in the wattage of the nervous system.

What is striking about neurasthenia is that it quickly becomes—even more than its companion in medical arms, hysteria—the classic illness of the late nineteenth century. Its very amorphousness permitted it to be all things to all practitioners. What it was understood to be in practical terms can be seen in Beard's partial catalogue of symptoms, which he claimed could be extended infinitely. This catalogue is equivalent to that attributed by Voltaire (and many other eighteenth-century commentators) to the effects of masturbation. Beard presents the following list in his second volume on neurasthenia, *American Nervousness* (1881):

Insomnia, flushing, drowsiness, bad dreams, cerebral irritation, dilated pupils, pain, pressure and heaviness in the head, changes in the expression of the eye, neurasthenic asthenopia, noises in the ears, atonic voice, mental irritability, tenderness of the teeth and gums, nervous dyspepsia, desire for stimulants and narcotics, abnormal dryness of the skin, joints and mucous membranes, sweating hands and feet with redness, fear of lightning, or fear of responsibility, of open places or of closed places, fear of society, fear of being alone, fear of fears, fear of contamination, fear of everything, deficient mental control, lack of decision in trifling matters, hopelessness, deficient thirst and capacity for assimilating fluids, abnormalities of the secretions, salivation, tenderness of the spine, and of the whole body, sensitiveness to cold or hot water, sensitiveness to changes in the weather, coccyodynia, pains in the back, heaviness of the loins and limbs, shooting pains simulating those of ataxia, cold hands and feet, pain in the feet, localized peripheral numbness and hyperaestesia, tremulous and variable pulse and palpitation of the heart, special idiosyncrasies in regard to food, medicines, and external irritants, local spasms of muscles, difficulty of swallowing, convulsive movements, especially on going to sleep, cramps, a feeling of profound exhaustion unaccompanied by positive pain, coming and going, ticklishness, vague pains and flying neuralgias, . . . [ad infinitum].[40]

Voltaire's catalogue of the signs of masturbatory illness, taken from the *Philosophical Dictionary,* sets up much the same relationship between somatic and psychological symptoms and includes "loss of strength, impotence, degeneration of the stomach and bowel, shaking, dizziness, idiocy and an early death."[41] Masturbatory insanity, insanity *ex onania,* has evolved into neurasthenia. Masturbation was also viewed as sapping the essence of the body. The key quality of both sets of symptoms is abulia or passivity; its cause is social as well as sexual.

Neurasthenia is to a great degree insanity *ex onania* in a new guise. Its paradigm is highlighted by much of the same sexual etiology and symptomatology. Indeed, Beard authored a separate monograph, *Sexual Neurasthenia: Its Hygiene, Causes, Symptoms and Treatment* (1884), in which he stated quite baldly:

Seminal emissions are frequently the cause of nervous and other diseases.

In science, as in other departments, serious mistakes are made by confounding effects with causes.

Seminal emissions are the effects as well as the causes of disease, and should be so considered.

Anything that weakens the nervous system may bring on seminal emissions. Exhausting fevers, dyspepsia, diseases of the brain and spinal cord, constipation, etc., etc., may give rise to over-frequent seminal emissions. Persons recovering from exhausting diseases oftentimes experience this trouble for several weeks. It usually lasts for a short time only, and disappears as the patient resumes his usual strength. The great fact to be remembered is that seminal emissions, when in excess, are symptoms of general debility, as well as causes of debility.

There is no question that in turn they do have a debilitating influence on the system, but only when they are in considerable excess, and by no means to the extent that is commonly supposed.

The great majority of cases of seminal emissions can by proper treatment and hygiene be substantially cured.[42]

Beard follows a discussion of "sexual hygiene" with a set of forty-three "illustrative cases" that recapitulate the catalogue of symptoms presented in *American Nervousness*.

It is indeed the sexual aspects of neurasthenia which captured the interest of German specialists. As Beard noted, the publication of his first volume on neurasthenia created great interest in Germany: "Within less than nine months after the publication of my work on Nervous Exhaustion, two independent requests for authority to translate it into German were made of me and my publishers by German physicians; this could not probably have happened if the disease were not increasing in Germany."[43] The German medical community immediately adopted the new illness as another means of understanding deviant sexual patterns. The fact that neurasthenia's antecedent was the familiar model of masturbation made it easy for them to recognize this illness as the catchall needed to deal with degenerate sexuality.

Perhaps the first major writer to address the question of nervousness and sexuality in German was Eduard Reich. His *Neurasthenia in Women: Its Causes and Prevention* (1872) illustrated the wide abyss between women in "primitive" and modern society. Reich still saw masturbation in modern society as one of the primary causes of degeneration,[44] but he also discussed the role that the interplay of fantasy and emotionality has in causing the decay of entire nations through neurasthenia. He observed that while the Indians and Arabs are believed to have the strongest fantasy, the absence of "strong emotions" among them prevents neurasthenia from occurring. For neurasthenia is "the night-side of civilization."[45] This leitmotiv has its roots in Beard. It is modern society, the society of America and Europe in the late nineteenth century, which provided the sole context for degeneracy and neurasthenia. Beard states this directly in the preface to *American Nervousness:*[46]

The chief and primary cause of this development and very rapid increase of nervousness is modern civilization, which is distinguished from ancient by these five characteristics: steam-power, the periodical press, the telegraph, the sciences, and the mental activity of women.

   Civilization is the one constant factor without which there can be little or no nervousness, and under which in its modern form nervousness in its many varieties must arise inevitably. Among the secondary and tertiary causes of nervousness are, climate, institutions—civil, political, and religious, social and business—personal habits, indulgence of appetites and passions.

Nervousness, neurasthenia, is a cultural manifestation that triggers an inherent weakness in the individual and thus can ultimately lead to the destruction of the society that produced it. In Germany this was perceived as the moment of degeneration. Otto Dornblüth in his *Nervous Tendencies and Neurasthenia* (1896) stressed the role that physical degeneration of the individual plays in providing the target for neurasthenia.[47] Wilhelm Erb, in his *The Growing Nervousness of Our Time* (1894), again saw masturbation as a source of the sexual degeneration of the late nineteenth century.[48] In Franz Carl Müller's *Handbook of Neurasthenia,* Rudolph von Hösslin's discussion of the "essence of neurasthenia" presented masturbation as one of the major etiologies of neurasthenia but also as one of its major symptoms.[49] Paul Julius Möbius, in his pamphlet *Neurasthenia* (1882), presented "modern civilization" as the cause of neurasthenia. Specifically, he blamed the increased speed of modern life for the decay of modern humanity: "It has been correctly observed that the use of steam is the signature of our time. Indeed the introduction of the steam engine has made the steam increase the tempo of modern life, we live with steam."[50] Christian Ufer in his *Neurasthenia and the Education of Girls in the Home and School* (1890) pinpointed the cause of neurasthenia even more specifically, attributing it to faulty modern education.[51] Education is for him the reflex of the general ills of modern society.[52] Among the most vehement philippics on the subject was Max Nordau's *Degeneration* (1892). Society, according to Nordau, produces certain signs and symptoms, the degenerate stigmata not only of the individual, but of the culture.[53] Degenerate individuals can be recognized as degenerate by their very appearance: protruding jaw, low forehead, large ears, fleshy lips—that is, the Western European stereotype of the Other, whether the Other is the lower class or the exotic. Degenerates can also be known by their sexuality. They are masturbators par excellence, and masturbation is the path to all other sexual deviation. The society produces similar stigmata in the abulia and irrationality of its cultural productions. Nietzsche, Zola, Wagner are signs of cultural neurasthenia. But it is also society which triggers the weakness of the individual. Its turbulence, its excitement, what August Forel in his *The Sexual Question* (1905) calls its "Americanism," leads to degenerate neurasthenia:

Americanism.—By this term I designate an unhealthy feature of sexual life, common among the educated classes of the United States, and apparently originating in the greed for dollars, which is more prevalent in North America than anywhere else. I refer to the unnatural life which Americans lead, and more especially to its sexual aspect.

The true American citizen despises agricultural work and manual labor in general, especially for women. His aim is to centralize labor by means of machinery and commerce, so as to concern himself only with business, intellectual occupations and sport. American women consider muscular work and labor in the country as degrading to the sex. This is a relic of the days of slavery, when all manual labor was left to negroes, and is so to a great extent at the present day.

Desirous of remaining young and fresh as long as possible, fearing the dangers and troubles of childbirth and the bringing up of children, the American woman has an increasing aversion to pregnancy, childbirth, suckling and the rearing of large families.

Since the emancipation of negroes has caused domestic servants in the United States to become expensive luxuries, family life has been to a great extent replaced by life in hotels and boarding-houses, and this has furnished another reason for avoiding conception and large families.

It is evident that this form of emancipation of women is absolutely deleterious and that it leads to degeneration, if not to extinction of the race. The mixed Aryan (European) race of North America will diminish and become gradually extinguished, even without emigration, and will soon be replaced by Chinese or negroes. It is necessary for woman to labor as well as man, and she ought not to

avoid the fulfillment of her natural position. Every race which does not understand this necessity ends in extinction. A woman's ideal ought not to consist in
reading novels and lolling in rocking chairs, nor in working only in offices and
shops, so as to preserve her delicate skin and graceful figure. She ought to
develop herself strongly and healthily by working along with man in body and
mind, and by procreating numerous children, when she is strong, robust and
intelligent. But this does not nullify the advantage that may accrue from limiting
the number of conceptions, when the bodily and mental qualities are wanting in
the procreators.[54]

Forel's critique of "Americanism," taken primarily from Beard's criticism of modern society and sounding much like such late nineteenth-
century critics of modern society as Henry George, distilled the speed
and direction of history that discomforted many thinkers into a pattern
of disease. This disease, neurasthenia, was perceived as the product of
modern society and had its prime effect through the decay of the body, in
the sexual realm. Neurasthenia displaced masturbation as the means of
presenting the interrelationship of degeneracy, sexuality, and society.
While neurasthenia was catalogued as a "psychoneurosis" rather than as
a "psychic degeneration," the line between the two categories was
blurred. Both were seen as communicable from generation to generation, psychoneurosis slightly less so than psychic degeneracies. Both
were caused by external stimuli and both were protean in their symp-
tomatologies. It was therefore not surprising that neurasthenia was perceived as an illness that paradigmatically revealed the degenerative effects
of society. For societal degeneration contained the seeds for the decay of
the individual, just as the degeneration of the individual embodied degeneration of the society.

Freud and Degeneracy

Sigmund Freud, like many of his contemporaries, even those
not trained in science, saw the world in terms of the biological model.[55]
After Darwin the description of the biological world became what the
chemical model had been to the eighteenth century and the psychoanalytic model would be for the twentieth century—the source of a
universal explanation of causality through analogy. Such biologists as
Ernst Haeckel were so convinced by the power of their explanatory
model that they wrote philosophies of history as if the biological analo-

gies were literally true.[56] Historians, especially conservative ones like Houston Stewart Chamberlain, littered their works with the crudest parallels between history and biological development.[57] For the models with which they operated were models of progress and decay. There arose simultaneously a historical model for biology and a biological model for history. Degeneracy became as key for explaining the negative moments of human history as it was for explaining evolutionary retrogression in biology.

The concept of degeneracy appears in Freud's earliest work on neurological diseases in childhood. Freud, whose work on cerebral diplegia and multiple sclerosis put him in the forefront of thinkers on the neurological diseases of childhood, went to Paris in 1885–86 specifically to study the "secondary atrophies and degenerations that follow on affections of the brain in children."[58] Although the term *degeneration* was used strictly within the neurological sense given by Virchow, it is this early linkage between the concept of degeneration and childhood illness which colored Freud's thinking during this period. While he was in Paris under the tutelage of Jean Martin Charcot at the Salpêtrière, his interest moved from this original problem to the problem of hysteria. In his essay on neurosis (1894) Freud distinguished between degenerative neurosis, which had a primarily psychological etiology, and hysteria:

In fact, hysterical illnesses even of troublesome severity are no rarity in children of between six and ten years. In boys and girls of intense hysterical disposition, the period before and after puberty brings about a first outbreak of the neurosis. In infantile hysteria the same symptoms are found as in adult neuroses. Stigmata, however, are as a rule rarer, and psychical changes, spasms, attacks and contractures are in the foreground. Hysterical children are very frequently precocious and highly gifted; in a number of cases, to be sure, the hysteria is merely a symptom of a deep-going degeneracy of the nervous system which is manifested in permanent moral perversion. As is well known, an early age, from fifteen onwards, is the period at which the hysterical neurosis most usually shows itself actively in females.[59]

Most earlier work on childhood hysteria, as well as on the other endogenous illnesses catalogued by nineteenth-century medicine, had seen all childhood psychopathologies as proof of an inherent failing in the child.[60] In the model of insanity *ex onania*, the weakness was seen within the child and was usually triggered by outside causes. Hermann Smidt, in his dissertation (1880) on childhood hysteria, argued for such a purely somatic understanding of hysteria in children.[61] Freud questioned the somatic etiology of childhood psychopathologies in his earliest work. Nevertheless the concept of "degeneracy" remained linked to childhood, to illness, and to childhood sexuality.

The French tradition ran parallel to this view. Jean Martin Charcot saw all neurosis, including hysteria, as "neuropathic"; and in Pierre Janet's view, which was only a slight refinement on Charcot's, the neurotic was marked by an inability to synthesize (what Janet called a "psychical stigma") and by evidence of degeneracy characteristic of "hysterical individuals."[62] Freud maintained that the neurotic individual has some type of "pathological disposition," although such a disposition is quite distinct from individual or hereditary "degeneracy."[63] He saw the roots of neurosis as existing prenatally. But he also equated the French formulation of this view, a view that had almost universal acceptance, with the concept of degeneration itself. Indeed in all of the later retrospective discussions of the history of psychoanalysis, Freud felt it necessary to draw the distinction between this earlier, more rigid manner of understanding the etiology of neurosis and his own views.[64] Quite often he will use the term *dégénération* rather than the equivalent German term (*Entartung*) to stress the French origin of this concept.

During this period, the problem of sexual degeneracy as the model for psychopathology arose often in Freud's correspondence with Wilhelm Fliess. In his draft outline "On the Etiology and Theory of the Major Neuroses," Freud attempted to distinguish between psychopathologies that are the product of degeneracy and those that are the product of disposition (1:187). Psychopathologies of both kinds originate within the patient; those of the latter category demand an external stimulus before the illness manifests itself. Even with this modification, degeneracy remains the primary etiology. But Freud had postulated that trauma played a part in the initial stages of some psychopathologies. As late as 21 May 1894, in a letter to Fliess, Freud still reduced the roots of all neurosis to four primary sexual etiologies, and degeneration remained central to all four categories (1:188). Degeneracy remained the basis for the sexual etiology of neurosis. But because they excluded the possibility of psychological influence, degeneracy and disposition were too rigid for Freud. Eventually he simply equated degeneracy with inherent genetic error, and by August 1894 began to move away from the concept of degeneracy as the root of sexual "enfeeblement" and toward the need for some type of psychological motivation for neurosis (1:196; see also 3:48). Yet in his paper on anxiety neurosis (1895), his first major attempt to undermine the concept of neurasthenia with its strong linkage to the role of degeneracy, Freud still gave credence to Paul Julius Möbius's category of "hereditarily degenerate individuals" as one of the explanations for neurasthenia (3:90; 1:106). In his paper on this question, "Heredity and the Neurosis" (1896), he still retained "syndromes constituting mental degeneracy" as a valid category, but excluded obsessions from it (3:146). This was a qualification of his rejection of degeneracy in the beginning of his paper "Obsessions and Phobias" (1894), which stressed the special place these neuroses had outside the category of degeneracy (3:74). But there Freud still retained a place in his nosological system for degeneration. He still attributed certain psychopathologies (but not neurosis) to it.

Freud worked on the concept of degeneracy, trying to recast it for his own needs, and in a letter to Fliess of January 1897 completely restructured it.[65] He moved from the idea of somatic "disposition," the relationship between inherent somatic factors and some type of psychological stimulus, to a more purely psychological explanation of degeneracy.[66] Degeneracy, whose visible manifestation is a set of maladaptive behaviors, can be passed nongenetically from one generation to the next. Freud's positing of such earlier psychological structures played a major role in his moving the moment of degeneracy from prenatal influence to early childhood experience:

An idea about resistance has enabled me to put straight all those cases of mine which had run into fairly severe difficulties, and to start them off again satisfactorily. Resistance, which finally brings work to a halt, is nothing other than the child's past character, his degenerate character, which (as a result of those experiences which one finds present consciously in what are called degenerate cases) has developed or might have developed, but which is overlaid here by the emergence of repression. I dig it out by my work, it struggles; and what was to begin with such an excellent, honest fellow, becomes low, untruthful or defiant, and a malingerer—till I tell him so and thus make it possible to overcome this character. In this way resistance has become something actual and tangible to me, and I wish, too, that, instead of the concept of repression, I already had what lies concealed behind it. (1:266–67)

Character and not biology structures Freud's understanding of degeneracy. Character is linked with the fantasy world of masturbation, following Kaan, and the concept of degeneracy has a specifically sexual context, as it does in late nineteenth-century discussions of neurasthenia.

It is in the *Studies on Hysteria* (1895), written together with Joseph Breuer, that Freud comes to terms with the pejorative implications of the term *degeneration*. His patients, even though hysterics, are in no way congenitally predisposed to hysteria (2:104, 161). In the case of "Fräulein Elisabeth von R.," Freud rejected the label of degenerate for the hysteric. Indeed this case prefigured much of his later discussion of the role that the concept of degeneracy should play in the diagnosis of psychosexual pathologies. In "Little Hans" (1909) Freud's argument evoked a rhetorician who condemns the child as hopelessly mired in the swamp of his own ancestry:

> But before going into the details of this agreement I must deal with two objections which will be raised against my making use of the present analysis for this purpose. The first objection is to the effect that Hans was not a normal child, but (as events—the illness itself, in fact—showed) had a predisposition to neurosis, and was a young "degenerate"; it would be illegitimate, therefore, to apply to other, normal children conclusions which might perhaps be true of him. I shall postpone consideration of this objection, since it only limits the value of the observation, and does not completely nullify it. . . .
>
> I think, therefore, that Hans's illness may perhaps have been no more serious than that of many other children who are not branded as "degenerates"; but since he was brought up without being intimidated, and with as much consideration and as little coercion as possible, his anxiety dared to show itself more boldly. With him there was no place for such motives as a bad conscience or a fear of punishment, which with other children must no doubt contribute to making the anxiety less. (10:100, 141)

By 1917 this voice, condemning all through the use of the term *degeneracy,* is the voice of "psychiatry" as opposed to the voice of the psychoanalyst:

> Psychiatry, it is true, denies that such things mean the intrusion into the mind of evil spirits from without; beyond this, however, it can only say with a shrug: "Degeneracy, hereditary disposition, constitutional inferiority!" Psychoanalysis sets out to explain these uncanny disorders; it engages in careful and laborious investigations, devises hypotheses and scientific constructions, until at length it can speak thus to the ego: —
>
> "Nothing has entered into you from without; a part of the activity of your own mind has been withdrawn from your knowledge and from the command of your will. (17:142)

Degenerate is the label for the Other, specifically the Other as the essence of pathology (3:280). It carries a sense of hopelessness and helplessness. Thus Freud rejected clinical psychiatry's label of the sexually deviant as the degenerate, again through the rhetoric of the prototypical "psychiatrist." In his paper on female homosexuality (1920), one of Freud's last uses of the term *degenerate* appears in this context (18:149). The authority of medicine is the condemning voice Freud mockingly quotes to illustrate its own limits:

Perhaps you would like to know in advance, having in mind our earlier talks, what attitude contemporary psychiatry adopts towards the problems of obsessional neurosis. But it is a meagre chapter. Psychiatry gives names to the different obsessions but says nothing further about them. On the other hand it insists that those who suffer from these symptoms are "degenerates." This gives small satisfaction; in fact it is a judgement of value—a condemnation instead of an explanation. We are supposed to think that every possible sort of eccentricity may arise in degenerates. Well, it is true that we must regard those who develop such symptoms as somewhat different in their nature from other people. But we may ask: are they more "degenerate" than other neurotics—than hysterical patients, for instance, or those who fall ill of psychoses? Once again, the characterization is evidently too general. Indeed, we may doubt whether there is any justification for it at all, when we learn that such symptoms occur too in distinguished people of particularly high capacities, capacities important for the world at large. It is true that, thanks to their own discretion and to the untruthfulness of their biographers, we learn little that is intimate about the great men who are our models; but it may nevertheless happen that one of them, like Émile Zola, may be a fanatic for the truth, and we then learn from him of the many strange obsessional habits to which he was a life-long victim.

Psychiatry has found a way out by speaking of "dégénérés supérieurs." Very nice. But we have found from psycho-analysis that it is possible to get permanently rid of these strange obsessional symptoms, just as of other complaints and just as in people who are not degenerate. I myself have succeeded repeatedly in this. (16:260; see also 3:201, 7:160)

The locus of this voice of authority is problematic. Is it merely the French medical tradition, at that time generally accepted in Germany, against which Freud is arguing, or is he striving to overcome an element of his own system of belief? If it is the latter, the internalized voice of the biologist in a struggle with the psychoanalyst, then it should be possible to find other residual elements of this conflict in Freud's work.

Hidden by Freud's rejection of the hereditary origin of psychopathology in general is a fascination that links heredity to sexual pathology. The pejorative sense of "degeneration" which Freud saw in the use of this label distanced the essence of the Other. In an essay on Jensen's *Gradiva* (1906), Freud noted medical science's need to differentiate between the normal and the degenerate as a means of drawing the line between the perfect self and the perverse Other (9:45). This observation crystallized the problem that runs parallel to his own rejection of the medical/biological concept of the degenerate.

In *The Interpretation of Dreams* (1900) Freud continued to evolve a model of infantile sexuality as the basic developmental model of humanity. This view of chronological primitivism traced the movement of the infant from "egoist" to "moralist," a view compatible with earlier views of the acquisition of shame as the wellspring of morality: "For we may expect that, before the end of the period which we count as childhood, altruistic impulses and morality will awaken in the little egoist and (to use Meynert's terms) . . . a secondary ego will overlay and inhibit the primary one. It is true, no doubt, that morality does not set in simultaneously all along the line and that the length of non-moral childhood varies in different individuals. If this morality fails to develop, we like to talk of 'degeneracy,' though what in fact faces us is an inhibition in development" (4:250). *Degeneracy* comes to be for Freud a faulty designation for the sexually pathological, inherent, immutable (7:50). With his *Three Essays on the Theory of Sexuality* (1905) the seemingly separate strands of childhood sexuality, the etiology of neurosis, perversity, and degeneracy merge, and the major shift prefigured in the above passage becomes evident, the shift from the model of sexuality to its historical analogy (7:138–39). While Freud attributed his shift in interest to Iwan Bloch's semipopular studies of sexuality in history, clearly he was to no little degree influenced by the contemporary debates concerning the nature of homosexuality and the role of hereditary predisposition in the development of the homosexual.[67] Yet his discussion of degeneracy in this passage treats it as a disease of civilization, parallel to the discussions of neurasthenia during the late nineteenth century. For Freud perversity is not necessarily degenerate (except in the ultimate sense that polymorphous perversity is inherent in all infants), but degeneracy is an illness of civilization.[68] There are yet further contemporary overtones in this passage on degeneration and civilization.

Freud adopts a view of trauma in his theory of sexual psychopathology which would seem much more at home in Ibsen's *Doll's House,* in the figure of Dr. Rank, or in the central figure in *Ghosts,* Oswald Alving. It

is the trauma of civilization, the illness that characterized it and condemns it, syphilis. For Freud civilization in its most degenerate sexuality
passed the fear of syphilis, syphilophobia, from generation to generation
(7:236). The hidden decay of syphilis, its mythic relationship to sexuality
(assumed but not yet scientifically proven), its ability to destroy across
generations, made it one of the late nineteenth-century paradigms for
degenerative sexuality. Freud had already made this fear the subject of
one of his illustrative anecdotes in the *Interpretation of Dreams* (1900)
(4:300–301). He transferred sexual pathology from the private, masturbatory sphere to the public, venereal one. Eduard Reich, as well as many
other writers on public health during this period, displaced at least some
of their anxiety concerning sexuality and sexual pathology from masturbation to syphilis, moving from a degenerate endogenous model to a
degenerate exogenous one. In masturbation the evil lies in the degeneracy of the individual; in syphilis, in the degeneracy of the Other, the
prostitute. Sexuality can become contaminated through an external
source, rather than by virtue of any inherent failure of the individual.
Late nineteenth-century discussions of the prostitute centered around the
question of whether she was inherently degenerate (the view of Lombroso) or merely had a disposition for prostitution which was triggered by
her economic circumstances (the view of Parent-Duchatelet).[69] Freud
favored the former view. Libido theory, which posits the inherent polymorphous perversity of the infant, is not far removed from the view that
perversity is the disposition of all human beings, including the prostitute.[70] This is an extrapolation from the view that a special subclass of
degenerates carries the stigmata of perverse sexuality rather than a rejection of that view.

But sexuality is not "degenerate." Reversing the paradigm of degeneracy makes sexuality the antithesis of degeneracy. Freud undermined the
view that sexuality in most of its forms leads to decay. He noted that a
ciliate infusorian had been observed to reproduce to the 3059th generation with "no signs of . . . degeneration."[71] Later, in *Beyond the Pleasure
Principle* (1920), he drew on a similar example in arguing against the idea
that sexuality *per se* was degenerative:

Let us, however, return to the self-preservative sexual instincts. The experiments
upon protista have already shown us that conjugation—that is, the coalescence of
two individuals which separate soon afterwards without any subsequent cell-
division occurring—has a strengthening and rejuvenating effect upon both of
them. In later generations they show no signs of degenerating and seem able to

put up a longer resistance to the injurious effects of their own metabolism. This single observation may, I think, be taken as typical of the effect produced by sexual union as well.[72]

Thus in both his earliest and his last reference to degeneracy Freud played on an idea of cellular decay akin to that originated by Rudolf Virchow. Freud, however, denied the pathological nature of sexuality and its importance within the degenerative model.

Freud needed to draw on historical data to more clearly delineate the ideas concerning perversion that he had developed partly from the study of generation theory. The cyclical occurrence of perversion only within highly developed cultures still implied degeneration. In 1917, in the *Introductory Lectures,* he reformulated his reading of Bloch from 1905, seeing perversion as a universal presence, limited neither in its historical manifestation nor in its geographical locus.[73] The degenerate cannot exist within human nature. Freud had already stressed this in his dismissal of the false rhetoric of psychiatry, which used the concept of the degenerate to defame the Other. In the striking opening paragraph to his "Thoughts for the Times on War and Death" (1915) Freud had attributed to the "anthropologists" this labeling of the Other as degenerate:

In the confusion of wartime in which we are caught up, relying as we must on one-sided information, standing too close to the great changes that have already taken place or are beginning to, and without a glimmering of the future that is being shaped, we ourselves are at a loss as to the significance of the impressions which press in upon us and as to the value of the judgements which we form. We cannot but feel that no event has ever destroyed so much that is precious in the common possessions of humanity, confused so many of the clearest intelligences, or so thoroughly debased what is highest. Science herself has lost her passionless impartiality; her deeply embittered servants seek for weapons from her with which to contribute towards the struggle with the enemy. Anthropologists feel driven to declare him inferior and degenerate, psychiatrists issue a diagnosis of his disease of mind or spirit. Probably, however, our sense of these immediate evils is disproportionately strong, and we are not entitled to compare them with the evils of other times which we have not experienced.[74]

It is indeed to the scientistic French anthropological tradition of modern psychiatry that the term *degeneracy* is most indebted. In dismissing this label as false rhetoric, Freud is able to move the category of degenerate from its sexual context and place it where it belongs, in the realm of political rhetoric. Freud sees the degenerate not as a real biological category but as a concept revealing of a specific understanding of the historical process.

Summary

History, sexuality, and degeneracy are inextricably linked in late nineteenth-century thought. Through Hegel's model of history, in which each age succeeds and replaces, on a higher level, the one that preceded it, human sexuality was perceived teleologically. Welded to this movement from the concrete to the abstract is another paradigm. The theological model of the Fall as the wellspring of history and of Christ's sacrifice as mankind's redemption served as an explanation for human degeneration and regeneration. These historical analogies were perceived within the model of human development as understood in the nineteenth century. If the most advanced stage of human sexuality following the redemption of Christ is that of the adult, male European, rather than the child or the Other (woman, black) as child, this is proof that the most primitive sexuality must correspond to the most primitive stage of human history. The Other's sexuality, labeled as perverse because it was seen as retrogressive, was soon identified with all modes of sexuality other than those prescribed for adult Europeans. The child's masturbation is perverse. The Other's sexuality is perverse because it is childlike. Here the linkage among all modes of deviant sexuality can be found. Masturbation, homosexuality, promiscuity (in primitive societies), prostitution (in advanced societies) are all degenerate forms of adult sexual experience, since they are ascribed to the Other.

The projection of deviant sexuality onto the Other during the nineteenth century was understood in theological as well as teleological terms. The aberrant sexuality of the child was proof of humanity's fall from grace. It seldom manifested itself, as humanity had been saved through Christ's sacrifice, but its rare appearance was proof of the potential within each adult of regression to the state before redemption. Here the idea of the degeneracy of the Jew fitted quite nicely. Hegel could not understand the Jews' tenacity at existing following their contribution to a specific stage of Western culture. Nineteenth-century science tried to explain it in terms of medicalization. This categorized the Jews at a stage of sexual development which was understood as primitive and perverse and therefore degenerate.

It was, however, not merely the child, the woman, the homosexual, the Jew, who were seen in terms of degenerate sexuality. Embedded within all nineteenth-century concepts of the Other is the concept of class and a consciousness of potential class conflict. Hegel took the rhetoric for his model of the "master-slave" dyad from the nineteenth-century focus on black slavery. Inherent in the slaveowners' perception of the institution was the "paranoid" fear of slave uprisings.[75] Fear of seizure of power by the Other is inherent in all images of Otherness. The idea that revolutionary change is accompanied by the most horrible of sexual excesses finds its liberal echo in such thinkers as Bachofen and its conservative denial in such thinkers as Westermarck; it is reflected in the nineteenth century's understanding of such institutions as prostitution and marriage.

The city becomes the icon of "modern life" and the locus of degenerate sexuality. The Rousseauan idea that "idyllic" life is contaminated by social institutions lasts through the nineteenth century and directs the fear of revolt to one specific locus of "modern life," the city.[76] The city, as opposed to the image of the garden, is yet another image of the fall from grace. The city—an icon of the rejection of redemption, of Abraham's failure in Sodom and Gomorrah, of the Jerusalem of Herod—permeates the image of civilization and is represented as the breeding ground of perverse and unnatural sexuality.

Even as medicine during the course of the nineteenth century saw itself more and more as an adjunct to the science of biology, medicine's prime interest in human sexuality remained focused on its pathological aspects. Discussion of normal reproduction and human sexual potential was generally repressed in favor of the protean image of the diseased. The presentation of reproduction, of sexual anatomy, of sexual activity within the medical textbooks of the period was in terms of what could and evidently often did go wrong, rather than in terms of what was labeled as "healthy" or "normal." The normal was understood simply as that which was not degenerate, and the sexually normal was defined by the most powerful of contrastive models, that of deviant human sexuality.

Society's power to define the Other was articulated through an explanatory model of human pathology. But all of this distancing reflected only the deep-seated anxiety stemming from the consciousness that power (including the power to stigmatize) can be lost, leaving its erstwhile possessor in danger of becoming the Other. This anxiety affected biologists and physicians as well as other members of society. The magic of any overarching explanatory model such as degeneracy disguises, but does not eliminate, the potential loss of power. The only buffer "science" could provide against the anxiety that remained because of this inherent flaw, the fear of oneself eventually being labeled as degenerate, was to create categories that were absolutely self-contained. Thus disease-entities were invented which defined a clearly limited subset of human beings as the group solely at risk. For such diseases were labeled as inherited to one degree or another. The inherited diseases, whether masturbation, hysteria, neurasthenia, congenital syphilis, or even incest, all had one thing in common. In all cases the etiology and the symptomatology are identical. All begin with some type of sexual deviancy and result in sexual perversion. Here we again have the repetition of the Fall. The Fall stems from the sexuality introduced into Eden and is proven by the pains that attend every labor. But also proving the Fall by a necessary, eternal repetition of it is the regular descent into degeneracy of women (and by analogy, Jews). Thus the group at risk was different, inherently, ineluctably separate from the group providing the label (at least in the fantasy of the latter).

Sigmund Freud was in a very special position to question this model of degeneracy. The late nineteenth century saw the organization of large numbers of individuals who had been stigmatized through the projections of the majority. Jews, women, homosexuals reified the majority's fear of losing their dominance in defining the normal by demanding the label of "normal" for themselves. The role of the child as the paradigm of Otherness had to be reexamined, and Freud was able to draw the very paradigm of the Fall, of degeneration, into question. He was helped to no little degree by his perceived peripherality to Western cultural and scientific traditions.[77] As an "Eastern" Jew in "Western" Vienna, he saw himself as the Other, at least in his perception of the world. This "myth" of persecution was more than the question of the specific treatment of the single individual; it was inherent in the rhetoric of Western society, a rhetoric that was also present within the scientific model of degeneracy. What is most interesting about Freud's struggle with the concept of degeneracy is that he was never able to abandon it completely even when he saw its implications. Indeed, his latter works on history, *Totem and Taboo* (1912–13) and *Civilization and Its Discontents* (1930), were largely rooted in variations on the theme of degeneracy, either its reversal or the use of aspects of the model (such as incest) as the foundation of a model of historical development. The dark center of human history, like the mirage of degeneracy, is explicable in terms of the projection of fears onto the world. Freud's necessary grappling with the model of degeneracy gave him a deeper understanding of the implications of the rhetoric of science and sent him to the power of language as a means of understanding not only the individual but society. Both Freud and his great contemporary adversary Karl Kraus repudiated the model of degeneracy because they saw within themselves the qualities ascribed to the Other. Inasmuch as the wellspring of these projections is universal, Freud's and Kraus's discovery is not surprising. But they also sensed the potentially destructive power of such projections linked to the political power of an explanatory model such as biological degeneracy. Central to the model and to the understanding of the Other is the definition of the Other in sexual terms, for no factor in nineteenth-century self-definition was more powerful than the sense of sexual pathology. The stigma of the Fall, of the rejection of Christ's redemption, is the stigma of sexuality, hidden within oneself and projected onto the Other. *Degenerate* was for the nineteenth century the central term of sexual opprobrium categorizing the inner nature of the Other. It remains so even today.

The Mad as Artists

The Psychopath as Artist

ARE CRAZY PEOPLE more creative than others? R. D. Laing, the British psychiatric guru of the 1960s, affirmed this more forcefully than most.[1] He saw (and sees) madness as a creative response to an untenable world: the family (or perhaps even society) is destructively mad; those whom society labels as insane are only responding to the craziness that surrounds them by creatively reworking it. The diseased world (or family) labels this response an "illness," and this view determines how the individual is perceived and, more important, treated. Society denies this creative response of the mentally ill even though it presents the roots for any true understanding of the nature of insanity. To use Michel Foucault's formulation, the mad are denied their own voice.[2] They are forced to speak through either those institutions that caused their madness, such as the family, or those that deny them insight, such as medicine.

In the 1960s Laing undertook an experiment to show that the insane could be treated and restored if they were, in a sense, reprogrammed. Laing's creation was Kingsley Hall, a community of patients and therapists which attempted to return "ill" individuals to that stage in life at which they were exposed to the pernicious influence of the sick world about them. They were encouraged to return to infancy and relive their early life in a new, caring, protective, "healthy" world, the world of Kingsley Hall.

Kingsley Hall had a favorite patient, Mary Barnes. Together with her therapist, the American psychiatrist Joe Berke, she wrote an account "of a journey through madness."[3] Now most psychiatrists or mental healers who see themselves as establishing a new order have "pet" patients who serve them as the ideal example of the efficacy of their method. From Philippe Pinel, the father of modern psychiatry, to Jean Martin Charcot, Freud's teacher, from Anton Mesmer, who first used hypnotism in creating psychological disorders, to Laing, the exemplary patient seems a standard feature of all psychiatric systems that style themselves as innovative. These patients illustrate the "creative" response that the new system enables them to make to their own madness. This is clearly the case with Mary Barnes. Barnes validates Laing's treatment by literally becoming a creative artist, a painter. She shows that she has recovered by painting her vision of the world rather than internalizing it in her psychotic fantasies.

Joe Berke conceived of art as the key to unlocking Mary Barnes's madness. He saw in her regression to childhood a "creative" pattern: "Mary smeared shit with the skill of a Zen calligrapher. She liberated more energies in one of her many natural, spontaneous and unself-conscious strokes than most artists express in a lifetime of work. I marvelled at the elegance and eloquence of her imagery, while others saw only her smells" (1949). Mary Barnes is a real artist since she is unfettered by the limitations of the very world that drove her into madness; she is the romantic artist par excellence, following her own inner sense of the creative, and Joe Berke is the true critic, able to perceive the truth in art, while all others in the philistine mob see only shit. But this is only part of the model for the artist which Berke has internalized and which Barnes accepts and carries out in her desire to please her therapist. Berke continues this description of the role which art can play in communicating with patients (and having patients communicate with the world) by telling an anecdote about another psychotherapist, John Thompson, and an unnamed patient who had withdrawn totally into his world of madness. Thompson presented him with pen and paper and "the man grasped hold of the pen tightly and, in a few minutes, fashioned a technically proficient, Giacometti-like drawing of a thin, tortured individual" (250). This mode of communication continued, Berke informs us, since "the man had found his mode of expression. Later he became a well known painter" (250). Thus the artist for Berke not only is the true prophet of inner feeling but also is rewarded for this ability to articulate this insight with success and status. Mary Barnes was given crayons and paper in November 1965. Her first products were given to her therapist as a gift and he encouraged her through his praise to continue to produce (134). By February 1969 Barnes had moved from crayons to other media, had sold some of her paintings, and was preparing a "one-woman exhibition" (325). Its success was overwhelming. Articles appeared in such British intellectual journals as *New Society* which were clearly in sympathy with Laing's views, and the show was covered by newspapers and television. All of this Barnes records in her autobiographic recollections with great pleasure. At the preopening party "Joe came, glorious in a huge robe of gold dragons. The big bear who had caused all the Painting. 'It's really wonderful, what you have done for Mary,' Mrs. Nix, an old friend, was saying. Joe replied, 'Oh, Mary teaches me'" (331). Whatever Mary can teach us about madness, it is not the lesson that Joe Berke drew. For Joe was pleased with Mary's success as an artist within the approved institutional framework in which art (even art produced by the romantic artist) is judged. Mary has simply accepted Berke's presuppositions and lived them out. Her success as an artist must be measured against her status as the "pet" patient of Kingsley Hall and the climate in which this answer to the treatment of mental illness was seen as the most socially acceptable one.

The Mad Artist through the Nineteenth Century

The case of Mary Barnes raises one of the central questions about the myth linking madness and artistic production (or creativity). Are madness and creativity necessarily linked? Aristotle believed they were. In his *Problemata* he asked, "Why are men of genius melancholics?"[4] Melancholia, the dominance of one of the humors, black bile, was seen as the root of most mental illnesses from the time of the ancient Greeks through the Renaissance. Aristotle saw mythological figures such as Heracles as possessing a melancholic constitution but also saw "most of the poets" as being "clearly melancholics." Creative minds are diseased or, at least according to the ancients, are housed in a body dominated by black bile, the source of madness. Creative individuals set themselves apart from the normal not only by their actions but also by the source of these actions. Their uniqueness is perceived as the result of some greater, overwhelming force, such as madness. This view was accepted in the West for over two thousand years, and it attained the status of a truism in the nineteenth century. With the reform of the asylums in the early nineteenth century and the parallel literary glorification of the mad as the only ones possessing true insight (in the writings of Romantics such as E. T. A. Hoffmann), attention is thrown for the first time on the artistic production of the insane. For if the creative are mad, must it not also be true that the mad are creative?

Philippe Pinel, credited with "freeing the mad from their chains" (and replacing them with more "humane" treatment such as the newly developed "English straight waistcoat," the strait jacket), in his textbook of psychiatry (1801) mentions in passing the artistic production of some hospitalized patients.[5] Benjamin Rush, one of the signers of the American Declaration of Independence, who had the most original mind in the history of American psychiatry, reported in 1812 that his patients at the Philadelphia Hospital showed uncommon capacity for poetry, music, and art.[6] Indeed, as a result of Rush's interest, there are preserved the poetry and watercolors of one of his patients, Richard Nisbett, which reflect this deranged individual's interest in drawing detailed maps. But Nisbett's use of maps as a way of presenting his vision of the world was no more unusual than his physician's use of the model of government in presenting his model of the mind in his 1791 lectures on the institutes of medicine: "The passions are the deputies of the supreme executive, and carry into effect all the good and evil which are fabricated by the legislative powers."[7] Both maps and governments were powerful images in post-Revolutionary America and permeated the way in which all, mad and sane, saw the world. Rush must have seen Nisbett's art as providing some type of opening into the nature of madness, or else he would not have preserved it. But what Rush saw we do not know, for he never commented on this case.

In 1845 Pliny Earle, one of the founders of the organization that became the American Psychiatric Association, published an essay on the artistic production of the insane in which he presented for the first time the theoretical presuppositions medicine had developed to deal with the aesthetic products of the mad. He censured society's quarantine of the insane as brutal and brought as proof of their innate humanity the fact that they too produce works which can be seen as "elevated." He sees in these works by the mentally ill the truths of some prelapsarian state of humanity:

It has been asserted, by one who was laboring under mental derangement, that the only difference between the sane and the insane, is, that the former conceal their thoughts, while the latter give them utterance. This distinction is far less erroneous than might be supposed, and is not destitute of analogy to the remark of Talleyrand, that "language was invented for the purpose of concealing thought." The contrast between lunatics and persons retaining the use of reason, is not so broad and striking as would appear to such as are but little acquainted with the former. It seems to me that one of the most prominent points of difference, having the general character in view, is that with the insane, "the shadow has receded upon the dial-plate of time," and they are, truly, "but children of a larger growth." In their attachments and antipathies, their sources of pleasure and of pain, their feelings, motives, all their secret springs of action, they appear to have returned again into childhood. But childhood and early life are emphatically the poetical age of man, when hope is unclouded and care is but a name, when affection is disinterested, the heart unsullied, and imagination untrammeled by the serious duties of a working world.[8] (195–96)

Earle sees mad-poets as child-poets unable to repress the inner truths they have seen. But this poet as child also sees more intensely than do the sane: "It is well known that insanity not infrequently develops, or gives greater activity to powers and faculties of the mind, which, prior to its invasion, had remained either dormant or but slightly manifested. No other power is more frequently thus rendered prominent than that of poetical composition" (197). The mad poet sees more deeply and is able to articulate this perception. Earle's examples, however, are quite contradictory. For while he can (and does) quote from poets who became insane (such as the "melancholic" William Cowper), the poetry he cites from his patients he labels as either confused or banal.

Shortly after the publication of Pliny Earle's essay, the British "alienist" (the terms "psychiatrist" as well as "psychiatry" were coined in the 1830s and took a while to catch on) Forbes Winslow continued the argument in a paper "on the insanity of men of genius" in which he noted resemblances among paintings by the mentally ill which he collected from various British asylums over a period of twenty years.[9] Likewise, Cesare Lombroso, in his first major work on the subject, Genius and Madness (1864), drew analogies between geniuses, whom he saw in an Aristotelian manner as mad, and the work by the insane which he had seen in his work in the Turin clinic.[10] Lombroso's book, and his subsequent fame as the best-known medical champion of the concept of "degeneracy" as the central explanation of deviancy (from sociopathic and psychopathic to creative acts), moved this question into the center of the concerns of contemporary psychiatry. It is only following Lombroso that the two questions are clearly separated: one line leads to the examination of the "great" in order to find the psychopathological origin of their greatness (as in Paul Möbius's "psychographs" or Freud's "psychobiographies"); the other to examination of the aesthetic products of the mentally ill to establish the creativity of the mad (and discover their greatness in their illness).

Lombroso's *Genius and Madness* examines 107 mentally ill patients, of whom about half spontaneously painted. The author sees in these paintings proof of his basic tenet, which is that sociopathic and psychopathic acts reflect a throwback to a more primitive stage of human development. In the art of his patients he sees an atavistic form of representation which he parallels with the "art" of the "primitive": both exhibit a fixation on the obscene and a stress on the absurd. He also sees, however, that his patients' art fulfills no function either in the world of the asylum or in the greater world. It seems to be merely the reflection of the madness of the patient and has therefore only overt meaning, without any deeper significance. What Lombroso is interested in, however, is the seemingly spontaneous act of painting, which he sees as parallel to the seemingly spontaneous act of painting among "savages." The act of creation rather than the product of creation is central to Lombroso's concern.

There is another shift when the late nineteenth-century medical establishment turns to the aesthetic productions of the insane. While most discussions of the creativity of the mad in the early part of the nineteenth century revolved around the poetry of the insane (Pliny Earle's title), the late nineteenth century, beginning with Forbes Winslow, became fascinated by the visual art produced by the insane. In 1872 Ambroise Tardieu published his "medico-legal study of madness," in which he commented that "although our attention to the present has been concentrated on the writings of the mad, I do not shy away from saying that I am interested in examining the drawings and paintings produced by the insane. What one can associate in ideas, what one perceives in one's fantasy, the most impossible things, the most bizarre images, which one would not have even in one's own delirium, are drawn by the mad. These creations contain nightmares and cause one's head to swim."[11] Tardieu's conclusion is that the art of the insane, which he also describes as somehow or other different from the art of the sane, gives greater insight into the nature of the insane's perception of the world.

Why does the emphasis shift from poetry to art? The shift, as we can see in Tardieu's observation, is one of which the "scientific" investigators are quite aware. It can on one level be understood as a direct reflex of the role experimentation plays in impinging various modes of aesthetic communication on the popular consciousness. Romantic poetry was the face of Romanticism as far as the popular understanding of that revolution in perception was concerned.[12] For the 1860s and early 1870s, especially in Paris, it was art in which the most visible and controversial experimentation was taking place. Art became the appropriate vehicle for experimentation, just as poetry had been some four decades prior. It is not that experimentation in art had not taken place during the early nineteenth century (as for example in the work of Théodore Géricault or Caspar David Friedrich) or that experimentation in poetry was lacking in the late nineteenth century (think of Baudelaire and Mallarmé), but that the popular view of where experimentation was present had shifted. Thus the central questions asked concerning the creativity of the insane both preselected that medium in which experimentation was then taking place and imposed upon the products of the insane the ideology of the avant-garde. By the end of the nineteenth century, the art of the insane represented not only the lost world of childhood but also the utopia (or distopia) of aesthetic experimentation.

Only four years after Tardieu published his first halting speculations on the art of the insane, Max Simon used the art of the mentally ill as the basis for a set of diagnostic categories.[13] Simon discovered specific, formal qualities in the art of the insane corresponding to six of the categories of late-nineteenth-century psychiatric diagnosis (melancholia, chronic mania, megalomania, general paralysis of the insane, dementia, and imbecility). Thus paintings by the "demented" are childish or foolish while those by "chronically manic" patients are incoherent and disregardful of reality in their use of color. Simon was also struck, as was Lombroso, by some of the "bizarre" content of these works, specifically their sexual imagery. His intent was to use paintings and drawings by the mentally ill as diagnostic tools. His attempt was bound to fail since his categories of illness were as much a reflex of his time as was his formalist methodology. Simon was working with the critical tools of his age. He approached the work of art in the asylum much as his eye had been trained to see the work of art in the museum. Robbed of all context except one that is self-consciously neutral, the work of art in the museum demanded to be seen as a closed structure referring only to itself. Embeddedness was either excluded or consciously repressed. Simon's view was rigidly formalist. He commented on composition and to a much lesser degree (because they point toward the context of the work) on the themes of the works of art. However, as the medical director of the asylum at Bron, Simon had set the limits for the examination of art by the insane in his application of contemporary aesthetic standards taken from the fine arts to objects that he labeled as aesthetic objects. Thus the artistic production by the insane was given the status of "ART."

In 1882 Emmanuel Regis published a detailed reflection on the art of the insane in which he carried Simon's argument yet further.[14] He focused on the orthographic component present in much of the "art" of the insane. As early as Lombroso's work, it was evident that the clear line between the "writing" and the "art" of the insane was an artifact of the beholder. Pliny Earle himself discussed the first published clinical study of an "influencing machine," described by John Haslam in 1810, and is fascinated as much by Haslam's reproduction of his patient's sketch of the machine as he is by the vocabulary the patient used to describe it. Regis, reflecting to no little degree the late nineteenth-century fascination with graphology, concentrated on the formal aspects of embellishment and structure rather than on the broader context of the relationship between words and image. Indeed, he tended to see the shape of the words as more important than their meaning. As a reaction to this attempt (no matter how superficial) at a new synthesis of word and image, Marcel Réja published the first comprehensive overview of the "art of the mad: drawing, prose, poetry" (1901), in which he argued that there can be no direct, overwhelming relationship between mental illness and the total aesthetic production of the insane.[15] It is only in the world of words, in literature, that this influence can be judged. Réja's work is clearly an attempt to "save" art as a haven from the synthesizing attempts of writers such as Regis and the American psychiatrist Aleš Hrdlička, whose little-known essay "Art and Literature in the Mentally Abnormal" had appeared in 1899.[16]

A New Madness

In psychiatric circles during the closing decades of the nineteenth century, there was a great deal of interest in the artistic production of the insane. Part of this interest was rooted in an overall shift in the definition of mental illness. By the definition of mental illness, I do not merely mean what is considered to be crazy, but what aspects of being crazy are seen as standing in the center of a "scientific" consideration of madness.

What diagnostic criteria are emblematic for madness? It is clear that for the greater part of the late nineteenth century, the "disease" that defined madness was "general paralysis of the insane." Madness was perceived as an alteration of mind rather than of emotions and thus fitted very nicely into the model of mental illness which dominated late-nineteenth-century psychiatry. Seen as some type of a reflex of a disease of the brain (indeed it was shown, shortly after the beginning of this century, to be the final stage of syphilitic infection), it fulfilled the aperçu of Wilhelm Griesinger, dean of nineteenth-century biological psychiatrists, that "mind illness is brain illness." But by the closing decades of the nineteenth century the basic definition of mental illness began to change. Psychiatrists such as Jean Martin Charcot in Paris and Sigmund Freud in Vienna turned to the study of the emotions. The new illness which begins to take center stage in the 1890s is dementia praecox, a term coined by the French psychiatrist Bénédict-Augustin Morel in 1856. In Emil Kraepelin's revitalization of this diagnostic category in 1896, modern psychiatry found that "disease" which best defined its center of mental illness.[17] In 1911 the Swiss psychiatrist Eugen Bleuler restructured what for Kraepelin had been a static concept (dementia praecox), a disease having an inevitably negative outcome, into a more dynamic category (schizophrenia), a category that has been the focus of twentieth-century psychopathology. Twentieth-century psychiatry has been greatly interested in the implications of the artistic and poetic products of the schizophrenic. Bleuler's major contribution was to separate what he considered the basic structure of schizophrenia—disassociation of thought, loss of appropriate affect, ambivalence, autism—from the accessory symptoms such as hallucinations, alterations of personality, and changes in language and handwriting as well as the seemingly unique artistic productions of the schizophrenic. Bleuler also countered Kraepelin's view that schizophrenia necessarily ended in total idiocy; he saw the potential for a return of the schizophrenic patient to society.

Interest in the artistic production of the insane was not lacking in the decades preceding Kraepelin's and Bleuler's works, but was greatly heightened with the popularization of the concept "schizophrenia." Joseph Rogues de Fursac's 1905 monograph, *Writing and Drawing in Mental and Nervous Illness,* presented the idea that the work of art produced by the mentally ill served as a "translation" of the illness into concrete form.[18] Such views served as a bridge to Bleuler's theory of the accessibility of the underlying structures of schizophrenia through its peripheral products. This is a far cry from Emil Kraepelin's statement that these products, which he called "word or picture salad," were meaningful only as a gross sign of the dementia, much as a rash signifies the presence of measles. For such thinkers as Rogues de Fursac and Friedrich Mohr (in essays published between 1906 and 1909), the illness could be *interpreted* through the work of art itself.[19]

The shift in perspective had implications not only for the understanding of schizophrenia, but for treatment. Following in Freud's footsteps, Bleuler listened to, observed, and attempted to analyze his schizophrenic patients while seeing them as suffering not from some type of physical alteration of brain structure (a disease of the mind) but from a severe disorder of the psyche. As such, the artistic products of the schizophrenic assumed a greater and greater role in both diagnosis and treatment. Schizophrenics were perceived as suffering from some type of alteration in their relation to their sense of self. According to the new theories, this relationship could be extrapolated from the nature of their art.

The idea of a dynamic psychopathology as evolved by Bleuler influenced a new generation of psychiatrists, who began to concentrate on the products of the schizophrenic as a means of examining and eventually treating the illness. The center of interest moved from Bleuler's hospital, the Burghölzli outside of Zurich, to the university clinics at Heidelberg. These had been run by Emil Kraepelin until the end of World War I. Following the war they were headed by Karl Wilmanns, later the editor of the comprehensive handbook on schizophrenia produced by the Heidelberg group in 1932. During the 1920s Heidelberg became the center for the study of the products of schizophrenia as means of access to the central problems of mental illness. In 1922 Hans Prinzhorn published his study of the "art of the insane" based on the Heidelberg collection, which he helped found; in 1924 Wilhelm Mayer-Gross, who would become the founder of British dynamic psychopathology, published his study of the "autobiographies of the mentally ill."[20] These endeavors stood under the influence of Wilmanns as well as the most original mind of the Heidelberg school, Karl Jaspers, whose systematic handbook, *General Psychopathology* (1913), both summarized the existing literature and indicated the paths that should be taken by future students of psychopathology.[21] Jaspers's existential phenomenology as well as that of the philosopher Ludwig Klages, Prinzhorn's main influence, saw the peripheral products of the mentally ill as a tool to explore the alienation of humans from their essential self. In a sense, Jaspers and Klages were reacting against what they perceived as the biological basis of Freud's thought. They wished to replace Freud's biological model with a purely psychological explanation for psychopathology. Prinzhorn and Mayer-Gross picked up the challenge to examine the artistic and literary products of the mentally ill in the light of this new manner of understanding the insane.

Hans Prinzhorn had initially approached the art of the insane in an essay published in 1919.[22] This essay was superficially little more than a summary of the literature, but like Jaspers's great work of six years earlier, it used a survey of the literature as a device for defining the direction the investigation must take. Prinzhorn perceived four stages in the "scientific" treatment of the art of the insane: first, the awareness that the insane do produce works of art (Tardieu); second, that these works of art could have value in diagnosis (Simon); third, that the approach appropriate to the study of this material was an intrinsic one (Mohr); fourth, that the question of the relationship of this art to "real" art should be part of the investigation (Réja). The program outlined in 1919 was carried out in his 1922 volume, *Artistry of the Mentally Ill*.[23] In undertaking a formalistic analysis of the some 5000 works by 450 individuals, Prinzhorn stressed the inner structure of the works of art as the key to their meaning. Following Bleuler, he assumed that these works had a hidden meaning, inasmuch as they related to the inner world of the schizophrenic. He outlined six major formal criteria of the art of the schizophrenic which point directly to the nature of the psychological disruption in the illness: the compulsive need to express inner feelings, playfulness in expressing them, the need to ornament (the horror felt at leaving any corner of the paper undecorated), the need for order, the drive to copy or imitate, and finally, the self-conscious development of complex systems of visual (and literary) symbols or icons. In spite of his development of these categories (which he understood as the reflection of the basis of schizophrenia as a disorder of the character), he warned at the conclusion of his work against using them simply as a means of labeling a given work of art as the product of the mentally ill. Prinzhorn's seeming contradiction is in reaction to a series of monographs beginning with Paul Schilder's study of madness and knowledge (1918), which drew parallels between the art of his patient "G.H." and the avant-garde, specifically the works of Kandinsky.[24] Prinzhorn was quite aware that he could all too easily fall into the type of fallacy that characterized some earlier studies. They took a group of patients labeled as insane, examined their products (as medieval doctors had examined the urine of fever patients), and determined that the patients were insane. Prinzhorn believed that the art of the schizophrenic shows certain qualities, but that without the patient (or a diagnosis) before one, one cannot determine whether the work reflects a disease process or not. This break with the rigid equation between artistic production and diagnosis does not evolve from Prinzhorn's formalistic analysis of his patients' paintings. It must be understood in the context of a specific concept of the mythopoesis of mental illness which dominated the German intellectual scene in the opening decades of the twentieth century.

The Artist as Psychopath

During the opening decades of the twentieth century, German expressionism reveled in the exotic. The "discoveries" of African art by Carl Einstein very much paralleled the "discovery" of the insane by such diverse writers and poets as Ernst Stadler, Georg Trakl, Alfred Döblin, and the dadaist Richard Huelsenbeck.[25] This discovery was precipitated by the need to define the avant-garde as the antithesis of the established order. Artifacts imported from the Wilhelminian Empire's colonial empire in Africa during the 1880s had been embedded in the "anthropological museum," where they gave the German middle class proof of its inherent superiority over the primitive. Einstein simply reversed things, seeing the isolated works of African art as proof of the superiority of the primitive vision over that of technological society. The Wilhelminian Empire created a massive system of state asylums, centering about the huge hospital at Bielefeld (founded in 1867) which housed upward of 5000 patients. If the state found it necessary to isolate the insane, the avant-garde would integrate them, or at least integrate the myth of insanity into their image of an ideal world. Hugo Ball, the dadaist and expressionist, in a sonnet entitled "Schizophrenia" placed himself in the position of a patient, a patient given a new identity as "the schizophrenic":

> A victim of dismemberment, completely possessed
> I am—what do you call it—schizophrenic.
> You want me to vanish from the scene,
> In order that you may forget your own appearance.
> I will press your words
> Into the sonnett's dark measure
> My acid arsenic

Has measured the blood in you to the heart.
From the days' light and custom's permanence
Protect yourselves with a secure wall
From my madness and jarring craziness.

But suddenly sadness will overcome you.
A subterranean shudder will seize you
And you will be destroyed in the swinging of my flag.[26]

Ball, who is not mad even though the bourgeoisie labels the avant-garde as "crazy" and "ill," uses the identity of the mad poet to comment on the true nature of society. The schizophrenic becomes a device, used in much the same way as other exotics have been traditionally used to present a critique of society. Wieland Herzfelde, a publisher and the brother of the inventor of the modern photomontage, John Heartfield, states this position quite boldly in an essay published during 1914 in the leading expressionist periodical *Action*:

We call people mentally ill who do not understand us or whom we do not understand. I shall speak about the latter. Normally one does not make this distinction. The patients in an asylum are crazy. That's enough. . . . One is sorry about these poor unfortunates, one laughs at them and is horrified by their fate. . . .

The mentally ill are artistically gifted. Their works show a more or less unexplained, but honest sense for the beautiful and the appropriate. But since their sensibility differs from ours, the forms, colors and relationships of their works appear to us as strange, bizarre and grotesque: crazy. Nevertheless the fact remains that the possessed can work creatively and with devotion. Thus they remain protected from boredom, the most apparent reason to be unhappy, even though there is little tradition or influence on them. They only integrate into themselves that which is in harmony with their psychological changes, nothing else. They keep their own language: it is the statement of their psyche, and yet orthography, punctuation, even words and turns of phrase, which do not reflect their feelings, they avoid. Not out of forgetfulness but out of unwillingness. The mad are not forgetful. What has impressed itself on their psyche, remains forever in their memory. For everything which impresses them, they have a better memory than do we, but they have no memory for unimportant things. A similar gift has caused the artist to be considered as a dreamer who avoids reality and lives without any structure.[27]

Herzfelde sees the mad as model artists. The German expressionists saw in the image of the insane the reification of their own definition of the artist in conscious opposition to the structures of society. In 1921 Walter Morgenthaler had presented the work of the schizophrenic artist Adolf Wölfli within the format of the "art historical monograph."[28] Wölfli was presented not as a clinical case, masked behind a pseudonym (Breuer's "Anna O." or Freud's "Dora") or initials (Schilder's "G.R."), but as an artist whose work merited serious attention as art. It is against this tendency that Prinzhorn reacted by arguing that the mad may produce art but are not artists per se. He was concerned about the extension of the self-conscious confusion between artist and patient which is embodied in the metaphoric language of the expressionists. He saw the patients as not creating "works of art" as part of free creation but as a direct result of the process of illness. But this aspect of the creativity of the mentally ill could not be measured by a formalistic analysis of their products. Indeed through the confluence of similar sources (naive and votive art among them) and the growth of interest in the productions of the insane (and their increased accessibility through works on this topic for the lay public), the line between the works of the mentally ill and the artistic avant-garde was blurred. But this was true only if the context of the work was ignored. Thus Prinzhorn found himself in a dilemma. He saw the limitations of his approach, but did not see a resolution of the problem.

Prinzhorn's search for the essence of the art of the schizophrenic was doomed. But his presentation articulated many problems concerning the nature of artistic production and the role of the artist-patient as the outsider. Unlike the patient, of course, artists must create for themselves the persona of the outsider, which they don like a helmet to do battle with society. Prinzhorn was quite aware of this attitude and of how it compromised the understanding of the disease process.

Prinzhorn's Patients

The material in the Heidelberg collection was preselected in a very specific manner. In the letter that Karl Wilmanns, and his then assistant Hans Prinzhorn, circulated to all of the major asylums in Germany, Austria, and Switzerland in 1920, the intent of the project was made very clear. They wished to collect "drawings, paintings and sculptures by the mentally ill, which are not merely copies or memories of better days, but rather an expression of their own experience of illness." They were specifically interested in "1. exceptional accomplishments, 2. representations which clearly arose from the influence of psycho-pathology, so-called 'catatonic drawings,' 3. every type of sketch, even the most primitive, which may have no value in itself, but which can have comparative value." Thus Wilmanns and Prinzhorn solicited only interesting and "crazy" material from their sources. They excluded the repetitive, the boring, the ordinary. The fascinating nature of their mate-rial is the result not only of the psychopathology of the patients but also of the preselection by the institutions that supplied it. The Heidelberg project was interested in the insane as artist, with all of the ideological implications which that term had for the educated bourgeoisie.

Prinzhorn's patients were ill. They were not shamans speaking an unknown tongue, nor were they Romantic artists expressing through their art conscious disapproval of modern society. These patients were ill, and their artistic productions reflected the pain and anguish caused by that illness. This fact was often overlooked by earlier commentators on the art of the mentally ill as well as by those writers who used the persona of the mad as their alter ego. We can see this anguish in the case notes to the work of that artist whom Prinzhorn calls "August Klotz." The al-teration of his name from "August Klett" to "Klotz" is of interest, since "Klotz" is a pejorative term for an idiot. During Klotz's hospitalization, as reflected in the original case notes rather than in Prinzhorn's selective interpretation of them, the patient's constant pain is stressed. Since Klotz was not Prinzhorn's patient, but was at the asylum in Göppingen, Prinz-horn's views were based on the case material rather than on a firsthand knowledge of the patient. We can reread the material, preserved in the Heidelberg archives, and see what caught Prinzhorn's eye when he wrote his analysis.

The case notes begin on 4 June 1903, when Klotz was thirty-nine years old, and describe the patient's excitement, his hallucinations and fear of imminent death. He had tremors in his hands, headaches, nightmares. He was fearful, informing his doctors of his supposed "syphilitic" infec-tion. (Syphilophobia was among the most vivid terrors of the nineteenth century.) He showed no physical sign of infection, however. He at-tempted suicide on 12 June by slashing his abdomen. It was only at the end of August that anything that could be perceived as "artistic" was recorded in the case notes: in his manic exaltation the patient "scratches the walls." In July 1904 Klotz began to hallucinate about the pattern of his wallpaper. (Here the "real" and the "literary" world approach one another, for this motif is central to Charlotte Perkins Gilman's tale of madness, "The Yellow Wallpaper" [1892].) In September he began to smear figures and secret signs in grease on the walls of the asylum. From that point, Klotz produced "artistic" works, detailed letters, highly complex symbolic systems, ornate drawings and sketches. But all of these were achieved in the context of the turmoil of his illness. The pain Klotz experienced in the asylum, the pain that defined his illness, made any formalistic analysis of his work meaningless. Klotz's case notes (one of the two sets of case notes preserved in the Prinzhorn collection in Heidelberg) describe his "illness." Only in the absence of such information could the work be interpreted on strictly formalistic grounds; Prinzhorn, who had much of this material, saw the constraints built into his critical model. For missing from it is the personal, individuated illness of each patient, the patient's response to the illness, and the unbridgeable anguish. These dimensions are equally missing from the image of the insane entertained by the German avant-garde.

Race, Madness, and Politics

The avant-garde's use of the outsider as a mask was a commonplace by the 1920s. In Germany, however, there was a parallel development in the creation of a mask for the quintessential outsider in that society, the Jew. As has been discussed, the theories of degeneration advanced by the French psychiatrist Bénédict-Augustin Morel, honed on Darwin's view of the development of the species, led to the labeling of many somatic pathologies and psychopathologies as "degenerate." They were explained by the "decline" of the group afflicted because of its inability to compete successfully in society. This was, of course, a means of labeling perceived differences in outsider groups as both pathological and immutable. Thus the idea of inherent differences among races is slowly replaced in the nineteenth century by the idea that it is somatic characteristics that differentiate these groups. In other words: "We are healthy; they are sick." As we have seen, many different diseases were ascribed to the Jews, but the label that most effectively summarized the perception of the Jews in Germany was "crazy." Belief that the Jew was generally predisposed to mental illness became a commonplace throughout the early twentieth century. This myth, unlike the self-constructed myth of the artist as mad, had a very specific set of consequences in the real world. First, the Jews themselves became convinced of the slur's validity because it was embedded in a scientific (and therefore reliable) dogma. Second, there was now a plausible rationale for isolating Jews from society. The ghetto was no more, but the asylum could serve as a surrogate ghetto in which to put these "crazy" Jews. Here the myth had a pragmatic consequence in associating two outsiders, the insane and the Jew.

Such views are not on the fringe of late nineteenth- and early twentieth-century medicine. They stand at the center of "liberal" German science. Krafft-Ebing, after all, represented the left-liberal political tradition within German and Austrian medicine. But the association of Jews and madness became so powerful that it defined the perception of the Jew within yet another context: the role that the Jew was seen to play in the world of the arts. For many complicated reasons, German Jews were perceived as dominating the artistic and literary avant-garde in Germany from the close of the nineteenth century.[29] Part of the reason for this was indeed the presence of highly visible German-Jewish artists (or artists labeled by the anti-Semitic press as Jewish) such as the impressionist Max Liebermann. There were, however, equally well-known non-Jewish impressionists such as Wilhelm von Uhde, and it is clear that the perception of the avant-garde as predominantly "Jewish" was partially owing to the cultural outsider status shared by the Jew and the avant-garde. The irony of course is that many Jews, for example the conductor Hermann Levi, played a major role in the conservative aesthetic tradition of Wilhelminian Germany, yet conservatism was never perceived as "Jewish." When the expressionists began to adopt their role as "mad," the association of the Jew, the artist, and the mad was complete. What was initially a pose or theory became part of the political program of German anti-Semitism.

In 1924, in the Landsberg prison in Bavaria, the leader of a failed coup d'etat against the young Weimar Republic dictated his political philosophy. Adolf Hitler added Bolshevism to the equation of Jews, artists, and the mad since the revolution in Russia was seen by the German right wing as the most recent success of the international Jewish conspiracy:

Even before the turn of the century an element began to intrude into our art which up to that time could be regarded as entirely foreign and unknown. To be sure, even in earlier times there were occasional aberrations of taste, but such cases were rather artistic derailments, to which posterity could attribute at least a certain historical value, than products no longer of an artistic degeneration, but of a spiritual degeneration that had reached the point of destroying the spirit. In them the political collapse, which later became more visible, was culturally indicated.

Art Bolshevism is the only possible cultural form and spiritual expression of Bolshevism as a whole.

Anyone to whom this seems strange need only subject the art of the happily Bolshevized states to an examination, and, to his horror, he will be confronted by the morbid excrescences of insane and degenerate men, with which, since the turn of the century, we have become familiar under the collective concepts of cubism and dadaism, as the official and recognized art of those states. Even in the short period of the Bavarian Republic of Councils, this phenomenon appeared. Even here it could be seen that all the official posters, propagandist drawings in the newspapers, etc., bore the imprint, not only of political but of cultural decay.

No more than a political collapse of the present magnitude would have been conceivable sixty years ago was a cultural collapse such as began to manifest itself in futurist and cubist works since 1900 thinkable. Sixty years ago an exhibition of so-called dadaistic "experiences" would have seemed simply impossible and its organizers would have ended up in the madhouse, while today they even preside over art associations. This plague could not appear at that time, because neither would public opinion have tolerated it nor the state calmly look on. For it is the business of the state, in other words, of its leaders, to prevent a people from being driven into the arms of spiritual madness. And this is where such a development would some day inevitably end. For on the day when this type of art really corresponded to the general view of things, one of the gravest transformations of humanity would have occurred: the regressive development of the human mind would have begun and the end would be scarcely conceivable.

Once we pass the development of our cultural life in the last twenty-five years in review from this standpoint, we shall be horrified to see how far we are already engaged in this regression. Everywhere we encounter seeds which represent the beginnings of parasitic growths which must sooner or later be the ruin of our culture. In them, too, we can recognize the symptoms of decay of a slowly rotting world. Woe to the peoples who can no longer master this disease![30]

Hitler thus enters and shapes the dialogue concerning the artist as outsider. It is impossible to avoid the conclusion that Hitler, the failed Austrian watercolorist, saw the glorification of patients such as Wölfli or indeed the entire interest in the art of the insane as proof of the "crazy" direction the avant-garde had taken. While there is no direct evidence that Hitler read Prinzhorn's work, he would have been exposed to its central thesis through reviews and polemics published in a wide range of sources, including the newspapers of the far right. Hans Prinzhorn's work, published two years before Hitler completed his own, could well have served as a catalyst for these views. The irony is that Prinzhorn's book reflects the political conservatism associated with his mentors, Ludwig Klages, the philosopher, and the conservative Munich art historian Conrad Fielder. Both stressed the "intuitive" nature of creativity and perception; both tied their theories to the politics of the day. For example, Prinzhorn stresses the "tribal" identity of each of his patients. August Klotz, for example, is described as having the typical persona of the Swabian. Like many conservatives, Prinzhorn flirted with the Nazis. Indeed, because of his death in June of 1933, it is quite impossible to judge what his long-range response to them would have been. Prinzhorn's support of the Nazi state, like that of many of the intellectual conservatives who, at first, rejoiced at its "stability," might well not have been welcomed by the Nazis in the long run.

Had *Mein Kampf* remained merely the political platform of a group of cranks, the interest that Hitler showed in the state of German art would have become an unimportant footnote to any reading of the historical context of Prinzhorn's work. But on 30 January 1933 Hitler was asked to form a new government, and by the end of that spring he had turned Germany into a Nazi state. In the mid-1930s there was a purge of Jews from all state and academic functions, including the few Jewish museum directors and teachers at the various universities and art academies. Gallery directors began to arrange shows that contrasted the "degenerate" art of the "Jewish" avant-garde with the "healthy" art of German conservatism. In Nuremberg the director of the city art museum arranged a show he called "the horror chamber of art."[31] In Chemnitz, where the director of the museum was fired by the Nazis, Dr. Wilhelm Rüdiger arranged a similar show under the title: "Art Which Does Not Speak to Our Soul." But these regional shows were but previews for the massive exhibition "Degenerate 'Art'" staged by Joseph Goebbels's Ministry for Popular Enlightenment and Propaganda on 30 June 1937. Adolf Ziegler put together a show of 750 objects in rooms in the anthropological museum in Munich (officially designated "the city of the movement"). Among the artists "exhibited" were Ernst Ludwig Kirchner (25 paintings), Emil Nolde (26 paintings), Otto Müller (13 paintings), Franz Marc, and Lionel Feininger, as well as Mondrian, Kandinsky, Lissitzky, and Marc Chagall. What is striking about this exhibition is that it employed a basically ethnological approach. It did not consider the paintings "works of art" but rather representative of the atavistic nature of the Jewish avant-garde. (Even though many of the artists represented—such as Nolde—were not Jewish, their role in the avant-garde enabled the Nazis to label them as such.) The catalogue accompanying the exhibit used the comparative approach to illustrate the degeneracy represented by the works of art. African masks were used to show the "racial" identity of the avant-garde as identical to blacks. But most important, the art of the avant-garde is related to the art of the mentally ill. And the prime witnesses called for the prosecution were Adolf Hitler and Wieland Herzfelde. Hitler's programmatic statement at the opening of the "Hall of German Art" in Munich on 19 July 1937 is juxtaposed with Herzfelde's expressionistic call for the art of the mentally ill to be recognized as valid.[32] The Nazis took the equation of artist = mad = Jew as a program of action. The museums were stripped of this "degenerate" art, some of which was sold at auction during 1939 in Lucerne and some of which was simply destroyed.

The Nazis did not create the categories of "degenerate" and "healthy" art. It was the seventeenth-century critic Giovanni Pietro Bellori, in an attack on Vasari and Michelangelo, who first used Machiavelli's label "corruzione" to describe art. Friedrich Schlegel, the German Romantic critic, in his lectures on Greek poetry (1795/1796), labeled the works he did not favor as "degenerate." But it was only in the nineteenth century, following the work of the medical anthropologist Bénédict-Augustin Morel (1857) and Max Nordau's popular book *Degeneration,* that the medical category of the "pathological" was linked with the artistic category of the "degenerate." By the time the Nazis used the term in their 1937 exhibition it had become a fixture in any discussion of the avant-garde. They simply appropriated the contrast of "healthy" and "degenerate" and placed into each category those works of art that the audience, no matter what its aesthetic predilections, would have expected. The "healthy" was the traditional; the "degenerate" was the avant-garde. Each group wore its label with a certain smug satisfaction. Each group thus defined itself negatively.

Hans Prinzhorn had officially left the Heidelberg clinic in 1921 even before the publication of his work on the artistic production of the mentally ill. He was following up the interest of the Heidelberg psychiatrists in psychotropic drugs such as mescaline, when he contracted an illness in the field which led to his premature death in June 1933. His collection, however, remained in the Heidelberg clinic (or at least in its basement). Wilmanns was stripped of his directorship of the clinic in 1933 because of his outspoken anti-Nazi views, and Jewish psychiatrists such as Mayer-Gross were dismissed. Wilmanns's successor was Carl Schneider, a member of the Nazi party from 1932 and, after the Nazi seizure of power, the political officer of the newly purged Heidelberg professoriat. Schneider was invited by Goebbels to speak at the opening of the exhibit of "Degenerate Art." His speech, though it was not delivered at the time, was published under the title "Degenerate Art and the Art of the Insane."[33] Schneider's crudely political statement reified the association of the art of the avant-garde and the art of the insane by simply dismissing Prinzhorn's ambiguous but careful use of this material and returning to a pre-Bleulerian view of "picture salad." Schneider's position was a clear reflection of his understanding of the implications of the Heidelberg approach to the mentally ill. Jaspers had been stripped of his position in 1937, by which time all of the followers of the "Jewish science" of psychoanalysis were exiled from the German scholarly world. Schneider was distancing himself from an area that had come to be labeled as "Jewish." He saw the entire attempt to understand the art of the insane, beginning with the "Jew Lombroso" (139), as part of the Jewish corruption of Western art and science, a process that culminated in Freud and Adler's attempt to explain art as pathological rather than as the healthy expression of a healthy society. Again it is the metaphor of the mad as artists as articulated by Wieland Herzfelde before World War I which Schneider cites as his proof of the corruption of the avant-garde, a corruption exploited by those who wish to destroy the body politic, the Jews and the Communists. Schneider argued against the definition of art as form, a definition that Prinzhorn borrowed from Klages, and stressed the question of whether the art of the mentally ill could ever be perceived as having "successful" form or whether it is a parody of "healthy" art. Schneider denies the insane, like the Jew and the black, any true aesthetic sensibility. The new perception of the insane as unable to communicate on any level permitted the Nazis to begin their first experiment in mass murder, the "euthanasia" of the inmates of the German asylums.[34] Schneider served as one of the most important experts in the sterilization and murder of the mentally ill until the intercession of the Catholic Church in the person of Cardinal von Galen shortly after the program had begun in 1939. The movement from killing the insane to killing Jews was but a short step, because the interchangeability of the mad and the Jews had long been established in the popular mind in Germany.

The historical context for Hans Prinzhorn's study of the art of the mentally ill spans a series of radical changes in the political, social, and intellectual history of Germany. That study must be read in the light of its context as well as its reception within this web. The flaws that Prinzhorn himself saw in his approach and the veiled political use to which the popularization of the art of the insane was put both colored the structuring of his work. In addition, the shift in the medical and popular understanding of madness, its acceptance as an appropriate alter ego for the artist in Wilhelminian and Weimar Germany, figured in the frightening use to which this material was eventually put. Prinzhorn did not live to see the horrors of Nazi Germany and the use that was made of his project, but he certainly sensed the possibility inherent in examining art labeled as the products of the mentally ill. This is one of the reasons he calls his study an examination of the *Bildnerei,* artistic production, rather than the *Kunst,* art, of the mentally ill. The Nazis, however, reduced all of the avant-garde to *Bildnerei,* demoting it from art. Their answer to the question of the creativity of the insane was to deny it, reducing the insane to a subhuman level, denying them the status of members of a "cultural entity," and eventually murdering them. Jews too are seen in this light, as degenerates whose pathology is evident in the madness of their *Bildnerei.* The supposed inability to create works of art thus assumes a major function in defining the outsider, a position it had held since Hegel's mid-nineteenth-century discussion of the nature of African art. The difference is, of course, that by the 1940s direct measures were taken to excise the "disease" from the "body politic."

Conclusion

IN HIS "Theses on the Philosophy of History," Walter Benjamin observed that "every image of the past that is not recognized by the present as one of its own threatens to disappear irretrievably."[1] But the power of these ever-receding images should not be underestimated. They remain impressed on a culture as on a palimpsest, shaping and coloring all of the images that evolve at later dates. The representations of the world, those structured ideological statements about the way the world should be, have a history. And it is this history that has been sketched in the present volume.

Benjamin is aware, indeed more than most, that as ideologies shift, the representations that are associated with and formed by those ideologies fade. But the recapturing of older systems of representations is not merely an exercise in historical "fact-finding." Rather it provides us with some insight into the forces that shaped the past and continue to shape the present. Louis Althusser spoke of that which "is represented in ideology [as] . . . not the system of the real relationship which governs the existence of individuals, but the imaginary relation of those individuals to the real relations in which they live."[2] The internalized representations of reality mirror the fantasies of the individual, but are always shaped by the individual's place in the stream of history.

We can learn from the study of stereotypes not only why we need stereotypes but how they function, how we use them to manipulate our world. Neither we nor any of our cultural artifacts are free of this taint, as Benjamin goes on to observe: "There is no document of civilization which is not at the same time a document of barbarism. And just as such a document is not free of barbarism, barbarism taints the manner in which it was transmitted from one owner to another" (256). Benjamin sees himself, as a historical materialist, in a special position to "brush history against the grain" in order to make such "barbarism" visible. Indeed, any contrasting ideological system will make the presuppositions inherent in our representations of the world overt—if only because such a contrasting system needs its own seemingly unique vocabulary of images.

In studying the web of stereotypes that exists in texts, I have chosen a new perspective with which to examine the "barbarisms" of the past. But it would be a mistake to assume, with a crude type of historicism, that we are free of ideology, that our observations are pure and true. We examine those images that have meaning for us (as women, as Jews, as blacks) or those images that speak to our heightened awareness of these groups not because of our suddenly activated liberal's consciousness, but because, as historians of representation, we need to understand the unstated assumptions our own world view entails. We cannot eradicate images of difference, but we can make ourselves aware of the patterns inherent in these images.

The goal of studying stereotypes is not to stop the production of images of the Other, images that demean and, by demeaning, control. This would be the task of Sisyphus. We need these stereotypes to structure the world. We need crude representations of difference to localize our anxiety, to prove to ourselves that what we fear does not lie within. The images we generate are also associated for us in a meaningful manner and thus present a closed system. Although this system is built upon our special, private needs, the fact that those around us have the same needs and are therefore likely to have the same perceptions lends it an appearance of legitimacy and self-evident truth. Our internal, mental representations of the world become the world. We act as if this world were real, external to ourselves; as Albert Einstein observed, "To the discoverer . . . the constructions of his imagination appear so necessary and so natural that he is apt to treat them not as the creations of his thought but as given realities."[3] The flux of reality is made static, and the stasis that we produce further hardens our sense that our world view is "real." The stereotypical categories that we use are rarely without some point of tangency with reality (biological, social, medical), but their interpretation is colored by the ideology that motivates us.

In studying stereotypes we can examine how ideologies (including those in which we ourselves are implicated) structure our universe. The examples of shared systems of ideological representation presented in this volume are "antiquarian" in that their remoteness from our own world view is readily apparent to us. But although most of these systems of representation, whether of Athens or Heidelberg, seem remote—who assumes anymore that the mad can be cured by specific musical tones or that there is a special quality to the artistic work of the mentally ill?—the association of creativity and pathology (to take one example), of the artist and the outsider, exists as strongly today as it did in ancient Greece or Weimar Germany. We may use the distancing effect of this stereotype of the "mad" as artists (and artists as mad) to different ends. We may place the anxiety generated by the avant-garde in its disruption of our accepted patterns of representation (and thus of our definition of our culture and our fixed place in that culture) in a different ideological mode. But we still need to distance this anxiety. We may color our views with a different rhetoric applied to the pathological nature of the artist, indeed we may redefine the artist in terms quite different from those used by Aristotle or Hans Prinzhorn, but we still use this internal representation of the avant-garde as different to externalize our fear of innovation.

The ideal of historical inquiry espoused by Leopold von Ranke was to know "how it really was." Our goal in tracing the history of a stereotype, similarly, is to understand how it really was perceived.[4] Following the history of perception, with all of its class- and culture-bound limitations, is the means of tracing our own icons of representation, seeing their evolution, decay, revitalization, and, last but not least, their effect. For in tracing the history of images we are not merely undertaking an exercise in the history of ideas, a history divorced from action. Rather, in understanding the stereotype within the model of interpersonal relationships, we understand that such images both result from and result in action. Our fantasies about difference, our anxieties about our status, can result in medical theories about the Other which relegate human beings to the status of laboratory animals (in Auschwitz or in the American South); in racial theories that reduce the Other to the status of exotic, either dangerous (as in present-day South Africa) or benign (as in the treatment of the indigenous population of New Zealand); in social codes that ostracize specific groups as inherently, unpleasantly different (as in the anti-Semitic codes in housing and university admissions in twentieth-century America). For the structure of our universe is the basis for our actions in this universe. We view our own images, our own mirages, our own stereotypes as embodying qualities that exist in the world. And we act upon them.

Stereotypes can be blueprints for action or, at least, for the fantasy of action. Here the comparative study of stereotypes, such as has been attempted in this volume, has its value. For parallel cultures or parallel discourses in a given culture may well refunction a specific mental representation in very different ways. Why is British eugenics so very different in its program of action from German eugenics? Such questions lead us to the specific mentality of a given moment in history as found in a specific system of icons. A comparative study of images, an understanding of the subtle shadings present in their codification (or, indeed, in their homogeneity), can bring to light differences, parallels, and patterns of action. Texts provide us with a rich bounty of materials upon which to base these observations. But the texts must not be perceived as separate from the world that generated them. They also give us the key to decoding courses of action based upon the presuppositions inherent in our mental representation of the world.

Pascal said that "the more intelligence one has the more people one finds original. Commonplace people see no difference between men."[5] Intelligence can here be understood in the sense of "information," and "commonplace people" in the sense of "people who stereotype." One can only hope that the study of the history of stereotypes can indeed contribute to our "intelligence," even if it cannot quite keep us from being "commonplace."

Notes

Introduction: What Are Stereotypes and Why Use Texts to Study Them?

1. For an overview of the literature see Arthur G. Miller, ed., *In the Eye of the Beholder: Contemporary Issues in Stereotyping* (New York: Praeger, 1982), esp. pp. 1–40.

2. An excellent overview of this question is given in Manfred S. Fischer, *Nationale Images als Gegenstand vergleichender Literaturgeschichte: Untersuchungen zur Entstehung der komparatistischen Imagologie,* Aachener Beiträge zur Komparatistik, 6 (Bonn: Bouvier, 1981). For a summary of the literature see the extensive bibliography in Wolfgang Manz, *Das Stereotyp—Zur Operationalisierung eines sozialwissenschaftlichen Begriffs* (Meisenheim: Hain, 1968), pp. 399–412.

3. See, for example, Jack Levin, *The Functions of Prejudice* (New York: Harper & Row, 1975).

4. I am indebted to Otto Kernberg's work for this discussion. See especially his *Internal World and External Reality: Object Relations Theory Applied* (New York: Jason Aronson, 1980) and *Severe Personality Disorders: Psychotherapeutic Strategies* (New Haven, Conn.: Yale University Press, 1984). I thank Dr. Kernberg for making the manuscript of this volume available to me prior to publication. Kernberg builds upon the work of Margaret Mahler, *On Human Symbiosis and the Vicissitudes of Individuation,* vol. 1, *Infantile Psychosis* (New York: International Universities Press, 1968), and Edith Jacobson, *The Self and Object World* (New York: International Universities Press, 1964). Jay R. Greenberg and Stephen A. Mitchell, in *Object Relations in Psychoanalytic Theory* (Cambridge, Mass.: Harvard University Press, 1983), p. 328, quite correctly see Kernberg's views as "moving drive theory toward a more 'social' view of man."

5. Hans Kohut, *The Analysis of the Self* (New York: International Universities Press, 1971).

6. I am drawing here on the relationship Freud postulates between "anxiety" and "neurosis" as reformulated in Karen Horney, *The Neurotic Personality of Our Time* (New York: W. W. Norton, 1937). On its application to the generation of texts see Harold Bloom, *The Anxiety of Influence: A Theory of Poetry* (New York: Oxford University Press, 1973).

7. One of the best examples of this tradition of seeing the Other is the study of the history of ethnology. I have used the work of James A. Boon, *The Anthropological Romance of Bali, 1597–1972: Dynamic Perspectives in Marriage and Caste, Politics and Religion* (Cambridge: Cambridge University Press, 1977) and *Other Tribes, Other Scribes: Symbolic Anthropology in the Comparative Study of Cultures, Histories, Religions and Texts* (Cambridge: Cambridge University Press, 1982). Boon is extraordinary in his ability to read the texts of a "science" as representational systems. His work can serve as a model for the historical examination of stereotypical systems.

8. Gordon W. Allport, *The Nature of Prejudice* (New York: Doubleday Anchor, 1958), p. 364.

9. I am here following the direction set by George Lakoff and Mark Johnson, *Metaphors We Live By* (Chicago: University of Chicago Press, 1980).

10. Oscar Wilde, "The Decay of Lying," in *The Soul of Man under Socialism and Other Essays,* ed. Philip Reiff (New York: Harper & Row, 1970), p. 72.

11. Stephen Pepper, *World Hypothesis* (Berkeley: University of California Press, 1966), p. 91.

12. These are categories suggested by George L. Mosse in his rich work on texts that contain culturally embedded stereotyped images. See his recent essay, "Nationalism and Respectability: Normal and Abnormal Sexuality in the Nineteenth Century," *Journal of Contemporary History* 17 (1982): 221–46.

13. Bartolome de las Casas, *Historia de las Indias,* 5 vols. (Madrid: M. Ginesta, 1875–76); Susan Sontag, *Illness as Metaphor* (New York: Farrar, Straus & Giroux, 1977). Again, Sontag is interested in the language of texts that represent disease.

14. While I disagree with his overall thesis, Michel Foucault's strong presentation of the Western response to insanity is a major resource in understanding the power of the image of the insane. See his *Histoire de la folie à l'âge classique* (Paris: Gallimard, 1972).

15. I draw here on H. T. Engelhardt, Jr., "The Concepts of Health and Disease," in H. T. Engelhardt, Jr., and S. F. Spicker, eds., *Evaluation and Explanation in the Biomedical Sciences* (Dordrecht: D. Reidel, 1975), pp. 125–41.

16. See the theoretical introduction in Michel Foucault, *Histoire de la sexualité,* vol. 1, *La volonté de savoir* (Paris: Gallimard, 1976).

17. Here I draw on the work of Elias Canetti, *Masse und Macht* (Düsseldorf: Classen, 1981), which discusses the typology of mass responses and the loss of autonomy. Like Boon, Canetti knows how to read the texts upon which he bases his argument.

18. Compare the discussion in Hans Mayer, *Aussenseiter* (Frankfurt: Suhr-

kamp, 1975), in which, again, textual evidence is used to study the nature of stereotyping.

19. The best discussion of the relationship between object and representation is D. Boesky, "Representation in Self and Object Theory," *The Psychoanalytic Quarterly* 52 (1983): 564–83. On the function of representations in literary theory and history see the work of Barbara Herrnstein Smith, *On the Margins of Discourse: The Relation of Literature to Language* (Chicago: University of Chicago Press, 1978); Jonathan Culler, *On Deconstruction: Theory and Criticism after Structuralism* (Ithaca: Cornell University Press, 1982); Dominick LaCapra, *Rethinking Intellectual History: Texts, Contexts, Language* (Ithaca: Cornell University Press, 1983); Martin Meisel, *Realizations: Narrative, Pictorial, and Theatrical Arts in Nineteenth-Century England* (Princeton: Princeton University Press, 1983).

20. Leo Steinberg, *The Sexuality of Christ in Renaissance Art and in Modern Oblivion* (New York: Pantheon, 1984).

21. For example, see Henry L. Gates, Jr., "The 'Blackness of Blackness': A Critique of the Sign and Signifying Monkey," *Critical Inquiry* 9 (1983): 685–723.

22. Stephen Heath, "Difference," *Screen* 19 (Autumn 1978): 53. I am grateful to Mary Jacobus for this reference.

23. On the power of systems of metaphor in science see Roger S. Jones, *Physics as Metaphor* (Minneapolis: University of Minnesota Press, 1982), and Carl Friedrich von Weizsäcker, "Wissenschaft, Sprache und Methode," in his *Die Einheit der Natur* (Munich: C. H. Beck, 1971), pp. 17–148.

24. Hilary Putnam, *Reason, Truth and History* (Cambridge: Cambridge University Press, 1981), p. 185.

25. The debate between E. H. Gombrich, *The Image and the Eye* (Ithaca: Cornell University Press, 1982), and Nelson Goodman, *Ways of Worldmaking* (Hassocks: Harvester, 1978) has mainly concerned the means by which conventions of representation create the work of art. Not explicitly addressed in their debate is the broader question of the function of systems of conventions as icons within the work of art itself. Ulrich Weisstein's extensive "Bibliography of Literature and the Visual Arts, 1945–1980," *Comparative Criticism* 4 (1982) contains some discussion of the special position of the work of art as separate from other aspects of society (pp. 324–34). This is a holdover from the era of *Geistesgeschichte*, in which special attention was paid to the interaction between aesthetic objects. The special role of the aesthetic can be seen in the alternative case of works of aesthetic provenance which are, however, part of the medical discourse. One thinks immediately of the anatomical works of Leonardo and Stubbs, and paintings containing medical references such as Rembrandt's *Dr. Tulp* and Géricault's paintings of the insane. It is striking how most analysis of these works remains embedded either in the discourse of aesthetic objects (viewing anatomical drawing, for example, as a "subjective" study of human form) or within medical discourse (viewing anatomical illustration as a "scientific" tradition). That both of these modes of discourse exist simultaneously in the context of social history is lost on most critics. An exception is the recent book by William Schupbach, *The Paradox of Rembrandt's "Anatomy of Dr. Tulp,"*

Supplement 2 to *Medical History* (London: Wellcome Institute for the History of Medicine, 1982). On the background of this general question see Catherine Gallagher, "The Politics of Culture and the Debate over Representation," *Representations* 5 (1984): 115–47.

26. See Leon Eisenberg, "The Subjective in Medicine," *Perspectives in Biology and Medicine* 27 (1983): 48–61.

27. Frantz Fanon, *Black Skins, White Masks* (New York: Grove, 1967), p. 188.

28. Prosper Mérimée, *Carmen,* trans. Walter F. C. Ade (Woodbury, N.Y.: Barron's, 1977), p. 42.

29. Houston Stewart Chamberlain, *Foundations of the Nineteenth Century,* trans. John Lees (London: John Lane, 1910), 1:388–89. The intellectual context of Chamberlain's work has been outlined by Geoffrey G. Field, *Evangelist of Race: The Germanic Vision of Houston Stewart Chamberlain* (New York: Columbia University Press, 1981).

30. Cited by Fritz Stern, *Gold and Iron: Bismarck, Bleichröder, and the Building of the German Empire* (London: George Allen & Unwin, 1977), p. 498.

31. Paul Weber, *Geistliches Schauspiel und kirchliche Kunst in ihrem Verhältniss erläutert an einer Ikonographie der Kirche und Synagogue* (Stuttgart: Neff, 1894), and Paul Hildenfinger, "La figure de la synagogue dans l'art du moyen âge," *Revue des Etudes Juives* 47 (1903): 187–96.

32. Adam G. de Gurowski, *America and Europe* (New York: D. Appleton, 1857), p. 177.

33. Erik H. Erikson, *Childhood and Society* (New York: W. W. Norton, 1950), pp. 301, 311–15. For the context of Erikson's work and life see Robert Coles, *Erik Erikson: The Growth of His Works* (Boston: Little, Brown, 1970).

34. The relevant passages are to be found in Ralph Manheim's translation of *Mein Kampf* (Cambridge: Houghton Mifflin, 1943), pp. 325, 624, 629. Erikson's reading of *Mein Kampf* is very clearly a post–World War II reading, presented in the light of the victory against Nazi racism. For a parallel reading by an anti-Nazi Social Democrat *during* the late 1930s see the recently published manuscript by Hans Staudinger, *The Inner Nazi: A Critical Analysis of 'Mein Kampf,'* ed. Peter M. Rutkoff and William B. Scott (Baton Rouge: Louisiana State University Press, 1981).

35. E. D. Morel, "The Employment of Black Troops in Europe," *Nation* (London), 27 March 1920, p. 893.

36. Reiner Pommerin, *Sterilisierung der Rheinlandbastarde: Das Schicksal einer farbigen deutschen Minderheit, 1918–1937* (Düsseldorf: Droste, 1979). On the Nazis' image of the black and its relationship to their image of the Jew see F. Zumpt, *Kolonialfrage und nationalsozialistischer Rassenstandpunkt* (Hamburg: Hartung, 1938), and Walter Kucher, *Die Eingebornenpolitik des Zweiten und Dritten Reiches* (Königsberg: Graefe & Unzer, 1941).

37. On the background and implication of this image see Neil Hertz, "Medusa's Head: Male Hysteria under Political Pressure," *Representations* 4 (1983): 27–54. Compare the study of invective and taboo in Edmund Leach, "Anthropological Aspects of Language: Animal Categories and Verbal Abuse,"

in Eric H. Lenneberg, ed., *New Directions in the Study of Language* (Cambridge, Mass.: MIT Press, 1964), pp. 23–63.

1. Male Stereotypes of Female Sexuality in Fin-de-Siècle Vienna

1. Steven Marcus, "Introduction" to Sigmund Freud, *Three Essays on the Theory of Sexuality*, trans. James Strachey (New York: Basic Books, 1962), p. xxxix. All cited works of Freud are from *The Standard Edition of the Complete Psychological Works of Sigmund Freud*, trans. James Strachey (London: Hogarth, 1953–74); here, Marcus quotes from 7.191. Except where otherwise noted, other translations are mine.

2. Contrast Renato Tagiuri and Luigi Petrullo, eds., *Person Perception and Interpersonal Behavior* (Stanford: Stanford University Press, 1958), and Peter W. Sheehan, ed., *The Function and Nature of Imagery* (New York: Academic Press, 1972).

3. The relationship between Freud's idea of infantile sexuality and earlier medical and theological views of masturbation has been well documented in Henri F. Ellenberger, *The Discovery of the Unconscious: The History and Evolution of Dynamic Psychiatry* (New York: Basic Books, 1970), pp. 295–303. The general background is outlined in E. H. Hare, "Masturbatory Insanity: The History of an Idea," *Journal of Mental Science* 108 (1962): 1–25. For the more general background see Jos van Ussel, *Sexualunterdrückung: Geschichte der Sexualfeindschaft* (Reinbek: Rowohlt, 1970), and Michel Foucault, *Histoire de la sexualité, I: La volonté de savoir* (Paris: Gallimard, 1976).

4. Voltaire, "Onan, Onanisme," *Oeuvres complètes*, vol. 20, *Dictionnaire philosophique* (Paris: Garnier, 1879), 4:133–35.

5. D. M. Rozier, *Lettres médicales et morales* (Paris: Bechet, 1822).

6. Richard Krafft-Ebing, *Psychopathia Sexualis with a Special Reference to Antipathic Sexual Instinct*, trans. C. G. Chaddock (London: Rebman, 1899), pp. 48–49. For the general background to this question see Annemarie Wettley, *Von der "Psychopathia sexualis" zur Sexualwissenschaft*, Beiträge zur Sexualforschung 17 (Stuttgart: Enke, 1959).

7. Hermann Rohleder, *Vorlesungen über Sexualtrieb und Sexualleben des Menschen* (Berlin: Fischer, 1901), pp. 15–16.

8. Albert Fuchs, "Zwei Fälle von sexueller Paradoxie," *Jahrbuch für Psychiatrie und Neurologie* 23 (1903): 207–13.

9. The Romantic image of childhood in German letters is best summarized in Rainer Stöcklie, "Die Rückkehr des romantischen Romanhelden in seine Kindheit" (diss., Fribourg, 1970). More specific but skeletal is the chapter "Jugend in Wien" in Hermann Glaser, *Literatur des 20. Jahrhunderts in Motiven* (Munich: Beck, 1978), pp. 21–25. The general literature on this topic is collected in Manuel Lopez, "A Guide to the Interdisciplinary Literature of the History of Childhood," *History of the Child Quarterly* 1 (1974): 463–94.

10. Jakob Christoph Santlus, *Zur Psychologie der menschlichen Triebe* (Neuwied:

Heuser, 1864), pp. 87 ff. The idea that female sexuality begins at the moment of menarche continues throughout the nineteenth century. In one of the standard textbooks of German clinical psychiatry during the 1890s, Theodor Kirchhof observed a close relationship between "faulty education" and insanity in "very young girls"; the etiology of insanity could not be "unsatisfied sexual desire, inasmuch as so many of the patients have hardly entered upon the period of puberty." In contrast, Kirchhof sees sexuality as a dominant causal factor in the insanity of equally young males. Theodore (sic) Kirchhof, *Handbook of Insanity for Practitioners and Students* (New York: William Word, 1893), p. 24.

11. Frances Finnegan, *Poverty and Prostitution: A Study of Victorian Prostitutes in York* (Cambridge: Cambridge University Press, 1979), p. 81n.

12. Josef Schrank, *Die Prostitution in Wien in historischer, administrativer und hygienischer Beziehung* (Vienna: Selbstverlag, 1886), 2:202–7.

13. William Tait, *Magdalenism: An Inquiry into the Extent, Causes, and Consequences of Prostitution in Edinburgh* (Edinburgh: P. Rickard, 1852), p. 32.

14. Abraham Flexner, *Prostitution in Europe* (New York: Century, 1914), p. 430.

15. Friedrich Hügel, *Zur Geschichte, Statistik und Regelung der Prostitution. Social-medicinische Studien in ihrer praktischen Behandlung und Anwendung auf Wien und andere Grosstädte* (Vienna: Zamarski & Dittmarsch, 1855), pp. 155–56.

16. Ibid., pp. 205–17.

17. William Acton, *Prostitution, Considered in Its Moral, Social, and Sanitary Aspects* (London: J. Churchill, 1857), pp. 165–66. Acton's comments on the immorality in Vienna are indicative of that city's reputation in the 1850s (147–48). The majority of useful studies on late nineteenth-century cultural attitudes toward sexuality have dealt with British views, but the British experience is not unique. The major studies and rebuttals in this area which have been of use to me are: Steven Marcus, *The Other Victorians: A Study of Sexuality and Pornography in Mid-Nineteenth Century England* (New York: Meridian, 1974); Morse Peckham, "Victorian Counterculture," *Victorian Studies* 18 (1975): 257–76; Flavia Alaya, "Victorian Science and the 'Genius' of Woman," *Journal of the History of Ideas* 38 (1977): 261–80; Peter Gay, *The Bourgeois Experience: Victoria to Freud,* vol. 1, *Education of the Senses* (New York: Oxford University Press, 1984). (Peter Gay argues quite convincingly that there is a disparity between the actual sexual practice during this period and the stereotypes of sexuality. I would maintain that, disparate though they are, the two are intimately linked, and it is this tension that makes sexuality one of the prime sources of metaphors in late nineteenth-century Western culture.) The major study of fin-de-siècle Austrian thought which deals with parallel issues is Carl Schorske, *Fin de Siècle Vienna: Politics and Culture* (New York: Knopf, 1980).

18. Acton, *Prostitution,* p. 73. See Nina Auerbach, *Woman and the Demon: The Life of a Victorian Myth* (Cambridge: Harvard University Press, 1982), pp. 150–84.

19. The roots of this concept are exposed by Ursula Friess, *Buhlerin und*

Zauberin: Eine Untersuchung zur deutschen Literatur des 18. Jahrhunderts (Munich: Fink, 1970). The problem in the late nineteenth century is sketched in the structure of one literary type by Ariane Thomalla, *Die 'femme fragile': Ein literarischer Frauentypus um die Jahrhundertwende.* Literatur in der Gesellschaft 15 (Düsseldorf: Bertelsmann, 1972). More recently the polemical implications of this problem have been stressed by Silvia Bovenschen, *Imaginierte Weiblichkeit und weibliche Imagination: Die Frau in literarischer Diskurs* (Frankfurt: Suhrkamp, 1978), and Rajiva Wijesinha, *The Androgynous Trollope: Attitudes to Women amongst Early Victorian Novelists* (Washington, D.C.: University Press of America, 1982).

20. Schrank, *Die Prostitution in Wien,* 2:324–25.

21. The relationship between the real age of menarche in the late nineteenth century and the legal fiction of the age of consent has never been properly discussed. While the age of menarche dropped, the general fertility rates in the large cities, especially among the lower classes, also dropped. See John E. Knodel, *The Decline of Fertility in Germany, 1871–1939* (Princeton: Princeton University Press, 1974), pp. 88–90. See also J. Richard Udry, "Age at Menarche, at First Intercourse, and at First Pregnancy," *Journal of Biosocial Science* 11 (1979): 433–42. For the cultural background to this question see Janice Delaney et al., *The Curse: A Cultural History of Menstruation* (New York: Dutton, 1976), and Penelope Shuttle and Peter Redgrove, *The Wise Wound: Eve's Curse and Everywoman* (New York: Marek, 1978).

22. The author of *Josefine Mutzenbacher* is unknown. While Felix Salten is mentioned as the reputed author by many reference books as well as by the editor of the reprint cited below (n. 28), he clearly denied this to a contemporary. See Paul Englisch, *Geschichte der erotischen Literatur* (1927; reprint Magstadt: Verlag für Kultur und Wissenschaft, 1963), p. 291.

23. The standard history remains Englisch, *Erotische Literatur,* pp. 290–93. See also Gustav Gugitz, "Die Wiener Stubenmädchenliteratur von 1784," *Zeitschrift für Bücherfreunde* 6 (1902): 137–50.

24. See Oswald Wiener's introduction to the reprint of *Meine 365 Liebhaber* (Reinbek: Rowohlt, 1979), pp. 5–7.

25. Knodel, *Decline of Fertility,* p. 70.

26. Gottlieb Schnapper-Arndt, *Sozialstatistik* (Leipzig: Werner Klinkhardt, 1908), p. 235.

27. "Aus dem Proletariate recrutiren sich die Verbrecher und die Prostituirten." Schrank, *Die Prostitution in Wien,* 1:308.

28. All references are to the reprint *Josefine Mutzenbacher: Geschichte einer wienerischen Dirne* (Munich: Non-Stop, 1971), here, p. 10. I have compared this reprint with the first edition (1906) and with other reprints.

29. Some sense of the social reality can be seen in Ronald Pearsall, *The Worm in the Bud: The World of Victorian Sexuality* (New York: Macmillan, 1969) as well as in Hans Ostwald's turn-of-the-century series *Grossstadt-Dokumente:* Alfred Deutsch-German, *Wiener Mädel,* Grossstadt-Dokumente 17 (Berlin: Hermann Seemann, n.d.); Alfred Lasson, *Gefährdete und verwahrloste Jugend,* Grossstadt-

Dokumente 49 (Berlin: Hermann Seemann, n.d.); Wilhelm Hammer, *Zehn Lebensläufe Berliner Kontrollmädchen, Grossstadt-Dokumente* 23 (Berlin: Hermann Seemann, n.d.).

30. See here the various tales that appeared in the pornographic journal *The Pearl* during 1879–80. The modern reprint (New York: Grove, 1968) does not reprint the "Christmas number" for 1879, which has an extensive fantasy concerning the sexual nature of children. Here and in other pornographic sources it is evident that adults' sexual fantasies concerning children revolve about the incest taboo. The literature on the historical perception of incest and its statistical occurrence has been summarized by Herbert Maisch, *Inzest* (Reinbek: Rowohlt, 1968).

31. See Alexander Thomas and Samuel Sillen, *Racism and Psychiatry* (New York: Brunner/Mazel, 1972), pp. 101–2.

32. All references are to the first edition, Peter Altenberg, *Wie ich es sehe* (Berlin: S. Fischer, 1896), here, p. 3.

33. See Inta Miske Ezergailis, *Male and Female: An Approach to Thomas Mann's Dialectic* (The Hague: Martinus Nijhoff, 1975), esp. pp. 47–71, and Claus Sommerhage, *Eros und Poesis: Über das Erotische im Werk Thomas Manns* (Bonn: Bouvier, 1982), pp. 90–97.

34. Ria Claassen, *Das Frauenphantom des Mannes,* Züricher Diskussionen (Zurich: n.p., 1898), 4:4.

35. See K. Reidmüller, "Felix Salten als Mensch, Dichter und Kritiker" (diss., Vienna, 1950).

36. Felix Salten, *Wurstelprater* (Vienna: Rosenbaum, 1911), pp. 111–15.

37. *Illustrirtes Extrablatt,* 23 June 1880, cited by Schrank, *Die Prostitution in Wien,* 1:308.

38. A first-rate study of Schnitzler's stereotypical perception of the female is available in Barbara Gutt, *Emanzipation bei Arthur Schnitzler* (Berlin: Volker Spiess, 1978).

39. All references are to Arthur Schnitzler, *Gesammelte Werke: Erzählende Schriften, Ergänzungsband IV* (Berlin: S. Fischer, 1922), here, p. 246.

40. Gordon W. Allport, *The Nature of Prejudice* (New York: Doubleday Anchor, 1958), p. 351.

41. Hugo von Hofmannsthal, *Gesammelte Werke: Die Erzählungen* (Stockholm: Bermann-Fischer, 1946), pp. 117 ff.

42. Cesare Lombroso and Guglielmo Ferrero, *La donna deliquente: La prostituta e la donna normale* (Turin: Roux, 1893). In this context see Annemarie Wettley, "Bemerkungen zum Entartungsbegriff im Hinblick auf den Alkoholismus und die sexuellen Perversionen," *Archivo ibero-americano de historia de la medicina* 9 (1957): 539–42.

43. Christian Ströhmberg, *Die Prostitution . . . Eine social-medicinische Studie* (Stuttgart: Enke, 1899), p. 65.

44. See Gisela Brude-Firnau, "Wissenschaft von der Frau? Zum Einfluss von Otto Weiningers 'Geschlecht und Charakter' auf den deutschen Roman," in

Wolfgang Paulsen, ed., *Die Frau als Heldin und Autorin* (Bern: Francke, 1979), pp. 136–49.

45. All references are to Otto Weininger, *Sex and Character* (London: William Heinemann, 1906), here, p. 235.

46. Sigmund Freud, *The Complete Letters of Sigmund Freud to Wilhelm Fliess, 1887–1904*, trans. and ed. Jeffrey Moussaieff Masson (Cambridge, Massachusetts: The Belknap Press of Harvard University Press, 1985), p. 249.

47. I am here echoing the more detailed discussion of this question in Juliet Mitchell's *Psychoanalysis and Feminism: Freud, Reich, Laing and Woman* (New York: Vintage, 1975), esp. pp. 5–16, 401–35. For a more in-depth study of one specific aspect of Freud's views discussed by Mitchell see also Stephen Kern, "The Discovery of Child Sexuality: Freud and the Emergence of Child Psychology" (diss., Columbia University, 1972); for a discussion of Freud's image of the woman see Zenia Odes Fliegel, "Half a Century Later: Current Status of Freud's Controversial Views on Women," *The Psychoanalytic Review* 69 (1982): 7–28.

48. See the work done by Josef Sajner, "Sigmund Freuds Beziehung zu seinem Geburtsort Freiburg (Pribor) und zu Mähren," *Clio Medica* 3 (1968): 167–80, and his "Drei dokumentarische Beiträge zur Sigmund Freud-Biographik aus Böhmen und Mähren," *Jahrbuch der Psychoanalysis* 13 (1981): 143–52. On the interpretation of this seduction see Marie Balmary, *Psychoanalyzing Psychoanalysis: Freud and the Hidden Fault of the Father*, trans. Ned Lukscher (Baltimore: Johns Hopkins University Press, 1982).

49. Jeffrey Moussaieff Masson, *The Assault on Truth: Freud's Suppression of the Seduction Theory* (New York: Farrar, Straus & Giroux, 1984).

50. Freud, *Letters to Fliess*, p. 241.

2. The Nietzsche Murder Case; or, What Makes Dangerous Philosophies Dangerous

1. All references to Wedekind's Lulu plays are to the translation by Stephen Spender, *The Lulu Plays and Other Sex Tragedies* (London: John Calder, 1972), here, p. 23. Except where otherwise noted, other translations are mine.

2. See Richard Frank Krummel, *Nietzsche und der deutsche Geist* (Berlin: de Gruyter, 1974).

3. See the recent attempt by Donald M. Lowe to write a *History of Bourgeois Perception* (Chicago: University of Chicago Press, 1982).

4. Eugen Weber, "The Reality of Folktales," *Journal of the History of Ideas* 42 (1981): 93–114. Weber is not interested in using the text to document social reality; he is interested in using social reality in reading the text.

5. See the systematic introduction and anthology of criticism edited by Jörg Salaquarda, *Nietzsche*, Wege der Forschung 521 (Darmstadt: Wissenschaftliche Buchgesellschaft, 1980).

6. See the relevant passages by his contemporaries in my *Begegnungen mit Nietzsche* (Bonn: Bouvier, 1981).

7. See Ruth Friedlander, "Bénédict-Augustin Morel and the Development of the Theory of *dégénérescence* (The Introduction of Anthropology into Psychiatry)" (diss., University of California, San Francisco, 1973).

8. The testimony is quoted in *Deutsche Warte,* 4 December 1901.

9. The testimony is quoted in *Der Tag,* 4 December 1901.

10. Ibid.

11. For a detailed account of the nature and course of Nietzsche's final illness, one which corrects much of the conjecture of recent biographies, see my essay "Friedrich Nietzsche's 'Niederschriften aus der spätesten Zeit' (1890–1897) and the Conversation Notebooks (1889–1895)," in Bernd Urban and Winfried Kudzus, eds., *Psychoanalytische und psychopathologische Literaturinterpretation,* Ars Interpretandi (Darmstadt: Wissenschaftliche Buchgesellschaft, 1981), 10:321–46. While Binswanger was the director of the clinic and therefore in titular charge of Nietzsche's case, Nietzsche's actual supervising psychiatrist was Theodor Ziehen, later a noted philosopher.

12. Public interest in the Fischer case was so great that Binswanger published his "Criminal-psychologische Ausführungen zu dem 'Fall Fischer' " in the popular journal *Deutsche Rundschau* 110 (1902), here, 302.

13. Ibid., p. 307. Binswanger's testimony was seen by the contemporary press as the key to the case. See the report of the case in the *Leipziger Tageblatt und Anzeiger,* 4 February 1902.

14. *Berliner Börsen Courier,* 6 December 1901.

15. *Die Post,* 5 December 1901.

16. *Deutsche Warte,* 6 December 1901.

17. The best contemporary summary of German, Austrian, and Swiss legal definitions of insanity is to be found in Eugen Bleuler's *Lehrbuch der Psychiatrie* (Berlin: Julius Springer, 1918), pp. 476 ff. For further discussion of this question see Jerome Neu, "Minds on Trial," and Michael Moore, "Legal Conceptions of Mental Illness," both in Baruch A. Brody, ed., *Mental Illness: Law and Public Policy* (Dordrecht: D. Reidel, 1980), pp. 73–105, 25–69.

18. See the discussions of Wedekind and Nietzsche throughout Artur Kutscher's monumental monograph on Wedekind (*Frank Wedekind: Sein Leben und sein Werk,* 3 vols. [Munich: G. Müller, 1922–31]) as well as R. A. Firda, "Wedekind, Nietzsche and the Dionysian Experience," *Modern Language Notes* 87 (1972): 720–31, and J. L. Hibbard, "The Spirit of the Flesh: Wedekind's 'Lulu,' " *Modern Language Notes* 79 (1984): 336–55.

19. Compare R. Hinton Thomas, "Nietzsche, Women and the Whip," *German Life and Letters: Special Number for L. W. Forster* 34 (1980): 117–25.

20. See for example the discussion of prostitution in Christian Ströhmberg, *Die Prostitution . . . Eine social-medicinische Studie* (Stuttgart: Enke, 1899), pp. 35–66.

21. Cesare Lombroso and Guglielmo Ferrero, *La donna deliquente: La prostituta e la donna normale* (Turin: Roux, 1893).

22. See Edward Westermarck's classic answer to Darwin and Engels, *The History of Marriage* (London: Macmillan, 1903).

23. See Robin Odell, *Jack the Ripper in Fact and Fiction* (London: G. G. Harrap, 1965).

24. See J. E. Chamberlin, "An Anatomy of Cultural Melancholy," *Journal of the History of Ideas* 42 (1981): 691–705.

25. Michel Foucault, *Discipline and Punish: The Birth of the Prison,* trans. Alan Sheridan (New York: Pantheon, 1977). For a parallel use of historical material to offer a key to the mode of perception see Foucault's presentation of *I, Pierre Rivière, Having Slaughtered My Mother, My Sister, and My Brother . . . : A Case of Parricide in the 19th Century,* trans. Frank Jellinek (New York: Pantheon, 1975), in which ample discussion of the "medico-legal" opinions and their role in understanding the perception of the crime is presented. (See pp. 122–36, 175–98, 212–18.) For the German context see also Henner Hess et al., eds., *Sexualität und soziale Kontrolle: Beiträge zur Sexualkriminologie* (Heidelberg: Kriminalistik Verlag, 1978).

26. Alvin V. Sellers, *The Loeb-Leopold Case with Excerpts from the Evidence of the Alienists . . .* (Brunswick, Ga.: Classic Publishing, 1926), pp. 180 ff.

27. See Henri F. Ellenberger, *The Discovery of the Unconscious: The History and Evolution of Dynamic Psychiatry* (New York: Basic Books, 1970), pp. 439 ff.; Frank J. Sulloway, *Freud: Biologist of the Mind* (New York: Basic Books, 1979), pp. 44–45.

28. See my testimony before the National Commission on the Insanity Defense, *Myths and Realities: Hearing Transcript of the National Commission on the Insanity Defense* (Arlington, Va.: National Mental Health Association, 1983), pp. 116–33.

29. André Mayer and Michael Wheeler, *The Crocodile Man: A Case of Brain Chemistry and Criminal Violence* (Boston: Houghton Mifflin, 1982). An even more grotesque example of arguments for a necessary link between pathology and violence is that made by V. H. Mark and F. R. Ervin, *Violence and the Brain* (New York: Harper & Row, 1970). See the general critique of this view in R. C. Lewontin, Steven Rose, and Leon J. Kamin, *Not in Our Genes: Biology, Ideology, and Human Nature* (New York: Pantheon, 1984). Such ideas are also quite alive in France and West Germany: see Patrick Moreau, "Die neue Religion der Rasse: Der Biologismus und die kollektive Ethik der Neuen Rechten in Frankreich und Deutschland," in Iring Fetscher, ed., *Neokonservative und 'Neue Rechte'* (Munich: C. H. Beck, 1983), pp. 117–62.

3. The Hottentot and the Prostitute: Toward an Iconography of Female Sexuality

1. George Hamilton, *Manet and His Critics* (New Haven: Yale University Press, 1954), pp. 67–68. I am ignoring here the peculiar position of George Mauner, *Manet: Peintre-Philosophe: A Study of the Painter's Themes* (University

Park: Pennsylvania University Press, 1975) that "we may conclude that Manet makes no comment at all with this painting, if by comment we understand judgment or criticism" (99).

2. For my discussion of *Olympia* I draw on Theodore Reff, *Manet: Olympia* (London: Allen Lane, 1976), and for my discussion of *Nana,* on Werner Hofmann, *Nana: Mythos und Wirklichkeit* (Cologne: Dumont Schauberg, 1973). Neither of these studies examines the medical analogies. See also E. Lipton, "Manet: A Radicalized Female Imagery," *Artforum* 13 (1975): 48–53.

3. George Needham, "Manet, Olympia and Pornographic Photography," in Thomas Hess and Linda Nochlin, eds., *Woman as Sex Object* (New York: Newsweek, 1972), pp. 81–89.

4. P. Rebeyrol, "Baudelaire et Manet," *Les temps modernes* 5 (1949): 707–25.

5. Georges Bataille, *Manet,* trans. A. Wainhouse and James Emmons (New York: Skira, 1956), p. 113.

6. Edmund Bazire's 1884 view of Nana is cited by Anne Coffin Hanson, *Manet and the Modern Tradition* (New Haven: Yale University Press, 1977), p. 130.

7. See my *On Blackness without Blacks: Essays on the Image of the Black in Germany* (Boston: G. K. Hall, 1982). On the image of the black see Ladislas Bugner, ed., *L'image du noir dans l'art occidental* (Paris: Bibliothèque des Arts, 1976 ff.). The fourth volume, not yet published, will cover the post-Renaissance period. In the course of the nineteenth century the female Hottentot becomes the black female *in nuce,* and the prostitute becomes representative of the sexualized woman. Each case represents the creation of a class with very specific qualities. While the number of terms for the various categories of the prostitute expanded substantially during the nineteenth century, all were used to label the sexualized woman. Likewise, while many groups of African blacks were known in the nineteenth century, the Hottentot continued to be treated as the essence of the black, especially the black female. Both concepts fulfilled an iconographic function in the perception and representation of the world. How these two concepts were associated provides a case study for the investigation of patterns of conventions within multiple systems of representation.

8. See the various works on Hogarth by Ronald Paulson as well as R. E. Taggert, "A Tavern Scene: An Evening at the Rose," *Art Quarterly* 19 (1956): 320–23.

9. M. N. Adler, trans., *The Itinerary of Benjamin of Tudela* (London: H. Frowde, 1907), p. 68.

10. See John Herbert Eddy, Jr., "Buffon, Organic Change, and the Races of Man" (diss., University of Oklahoma, 1977), p. 109, as well as Paul Alfred Erickson, "The Origins of Physical Anthropology" (diss., University of Connecticut, 1974), and Werner Krauss, *Zur Anthropologie des 18. Jahrhunderts: Die Frühgeschichte der Menschheit im Blickpunkt der Aufklärung,* ed. Hans Kortum and Christa Gohrisch (Munich: Hanser, 1979). See also George W. Stocking, Jr., *Race, Culture and Evolution: Essays in the History of Anthropology* (Chicago: University of Chicago Press, 1982).

11. Johann Friedrich Blumenbach, *Beyträge zur Naturgeschichte* (Göttingen: Heinrich Dietrich, 1806). Even though a professed "liberal" who strongly ar-

gued for a single source for all the races, Blumenbach was puzzled about the seemingly radical difference in the anatomy of the African (read: black woman).

12. Guillaume Thomas Raynal, *Histoire philosophique et politique des éstablisse-ments et du commerce des Européens dans les deux Indes* (Geneva: Chez les libraires associés, 1775), 2:406–7.

13. William F. Bynum, "The Great Chain of Being after Forty Years: An Appraisal," *History of Science* 13 (1975): 1–28, and his dissertation, "Time's Noblest Offspring: The Problem of Man in British Natural Historical Sciences" (Cambridge University, 1974).

14. *Dictionnaire des sciences médicales* (Paris: C. L. F. Panckoucke, 1819), 35:398–403.

15. J. J. Virey, *Histoire naturelle du genre humain* (Paris: Crochard, 1824), 2:151. My translation.

16. George M. Gould and Walter L. Pyle, *Anomalies and Curiosities of Medicine* (Philadelphia: W. B. Saunders, 1901), p. 307, and Eugen Holländer, *Äskulap und Venus: Eine Kultur- und Sittengeschichte im Spiegel des Arztes* (Berlin: Propyläen, 1928). Much material on the indebtedness of the early pathologists to the reports of travelers to Africa can be found in the accounts of the autopsies presented below. One indication of the power the image of the Hottentot still possessed in the late nineteenth century is to be found in George Eliot's *Daniel Deronda* (1876). On its surface the novel is a hymn to racial harmony and an attack on British middle-class bigotry. Eliot's liberal agenda is nowhere better articulated than in the ironic debate concerning the nature of the black in which the eponymous hero of the novel defends black sexuality (376). This position is attributed to the hero not a half-dozen pages after the authorial voice of the narrator introduced the description of this very figure with the comparison: "And one man differs from another, as we all differ from the Bosjesman" (370). Eliot's comment is quite in keeping with the underlying understanding of race in the novel. For just as Deronda is fated to marry a Jewess and thus avoid the taint of race mixing, so too is the Bushman, a Hottentot equivalent in the nineteenth century, isolated from the rest of humanity. That a polygenetic view of race and liberal ideology can be held simultaneously is evident as far back as Voltaire. But the Jew is here contrasted to the Hottentot, and, as has been seen, it is the Hottentot who serves as the icon of pathologically corrupted sexuality. Can Eliot be drawing a line between outsiders such as the Jew and the sexualized female in Western society and the Hottentot? The Hottentot comes to serve as the sexualized Other onto whom Eliot projects the opprobrium with which she herself was labeled. For Eliot the Hottentot remains beyond the pale, showing that even in the most Whiggish text the Hottentot remains the essential Other. (George Eliot, *Daniel Deronda,* ed. Barbara Hardy [Harmondsworth: Penguin, 1967].)

17. De Blainville, "Sur une femme de la race hottentote," *Bulletin des Sciences par la société philomatique de Paris* (1816), pp. 183–90. This early version of the autopsy seems to be unknown to William B. Cohen, *The French Encounter with Africans: White Response to Blacks, 1530–1880* (Bloomington: Indiana University Press, 1980) (see esp. pp. 239–45, for his discussion of Cuvier). See also Stephen Jay Gould, "The Hottentot Venus," *Natural History* 91 (1982): 20–27.

18. Quoted from the public record by Paul Edwards and James Walvin, eds., *Black Personalities in the Era of the Slave Trade* (London: Macmillan, 1983), pp. 171–83. A print of the 1829 ball in Paris with the nude "Hottentot Venus" is reproduced in Richard Toellner, ed., *Illustrierte Geschichte der Medizin* (Salzburg: Andreas & Andreas, 1981), 4:1319. (This is a German reworking of Jacques Vie et al., *Histoire de la médecine* (Paris: Albinmichel-Laffont-Tchon, 1979.) On the showing of the "Hottentot Venus" see Percival R. Kirby, "The Hottentot Venus," *Africana Notes and News* 6 (1949): 55–62, and his "More about the Hottentot Venus," *Africana Notes and News* 10 (1953): 124–34; Richard D. Altick, *The Shows of London* (Cambridge, Mass.: Belknap Press of Harvard University, 1978), p. 269; and Bernth Lindfors, " 'The Hottentot Venus' and Other African Attractions in Nineteenth-Century England," *Australasian Drama Studies* 1 (1983): 83–104.

19. Georges Cuvier, "Extraits d'observations faites sur le cadavre d'une femme connue à Paris et à Londres sous le nom de Vénus Hottentote," *Memoires du Musée d'histoire naturelle* 3 (1817): 259–74. Reprinted with plates by Geoffrey Saint-Hilaire and Frédéric Cuvier, *Histoire naturelle des mammifères avec des figures originales* (Paris: A. Belin, 1824), 1:1 ff. The substance of the autopsy is reprinted again by Flourens in the *Journal complémentaire du dictionnaire des sciences médicales* 4 (1819): 145–49, and by Jules Cloquet, *Manuel d'anatomie de l'homme descriptive du corps humain* (Paris: Béchet jeune, 1825), plate 278. Cuvier's presentation of the "Hottentot Venus" forms the major signifier for the image of the Hottentot as sexual primitive in the nineteenth century. This view seems never really to disappear from the discussion of difference. See the discussion of the "bushmen" among French anthropologists of the 1970s, especially Claude Rousseau, as presented by Patrick Moreau, "Die neue Religion der Rasse," in Iring Fetscher, ed., *Neokonservative und 'Neue Rechte'* (Munich: C. H. Beck, 1983), pp. 139–41.

20. See for example Walker D. Greer, "John Hunter: Order out of Variety," *Annals of the Royal College of Surgeons of England* 28 (1961): 238–51. See also Barbara J. Babiger, "The *Kunst- und Wunderkammern*: A *catalogue raisonné* of Collecting in Germany, France and England, 1565–1750" (diss., University of Pittsburgh, 1970).

21. Adolf Wilhelm Otto, *Seltene Beobachtungen zur Anatomie, Physiologie und Pathologie gehörig* (Breslau: Wilibald Holäafer, 1816), p. 135; Johannes Müller, "Über die äusseren Geschlechtstheile der Buschmänninnen," *Archiv für Anatomie, Physiologie und wissenschaftliche Medizin* (1834), pp. 319–45; W. H. Flower and James Murie, "Account of the Dissection of a Bushwoman," *Journal of Anatomy and Physiology* 1 (1867): 189–208; Hubert von Luschka, A. Koch, and E. Görtz, "Die äusseren geschlechtstheile eines Buschweibes," *Monatsschrift für Geburtskunde* 32 (1868): 343–50. The popularity of these accounts is attested by their republication (in extract) in *The Anthropological Review* (London), which was aimed at a lay audience (5 [1867]: 316–24, and 8 [1870]: 89–318). These extracts also stress the sexual anomalies described.

22. *Richmond and Louisville Medical Journal*, May 1868, p. 194, cited by Edward Turnipseed, "Some Facts in Regard to the Anatomical Differences between the Negro and White Races," *American Journal of Obstetrics* 10 (1877): 32–33.

23. C. H. Fort, "Some Corroborative Facts in Regard to the Anatomical Difference between the Negro and White Races," *American Journal of Obstetrics* 10 (1877): 258–59. Paul Broca was influenced by similar American material concerning the position of the hymen, which he cited from the *New York City Medical Record* of 15 September 1868 in *Bulletins de la société d'anthropologie de Paris* 4 (1869): 443–44. Broca, like Cuvier before him, supported a polygenetic view of the human races.

24. William Turner, "Notes on the Dissection of a Negro," *Journal of Anatomy and Physiology* 13 (1878): 382–86; "Notes on the Dissection of a Second Negro," 14 (1879): 244–48; "Notes on the Dissection of a Third Negro," 31 (1896): 624–26. This was not merely a British anomaly. Jefferies Wyman reported the dissection of a black male suicide victim in the *Proceedings of the Boston Society of Natural History* on 2 April 1862 and 16 December 1863 and did not refer to the genitalia at all. *The Anthropological Review* 3(1865):330–35.

25. H. Hildebrandt, *Die Krankheiten der äusseren weiblichen Genitalien*, in Theodor Billroth, ed., *Handbuch der Frauenkrankheiten III* (Stuttgart: Enke, 1877), pp. 11–12. See also Thomas Power Lowry, ed., *The Classic Clitoris: Historic Contributions to Scientific Sexuality* (Chicago: Nelson-Hall, 1978).

26. Havelock Ellis, *Studies in the Psychology of Sex*, vol. 4, *Sexual Selection in Man* (Philadelphia: F. A. Davis, 1920), pp. 152–85.

27. Willem Vrolik, *Considérations sur la diversité du bassin des différentes races humaines* (Amsterdam: Van der Post, 1826); R. Verneau, *Le bassin dans les sexes et dans les races* (Paris: Baillère, 1876), pp. 126–29.

28. Charles Darwin, *The Descent of Man and Selection in Relation to Sex* (1871; Princeton: Princeton University Press, 1981), 2:317 on the pelvis, and 2:345–46 on the Hottentot.

29. John Grand-Carteret, *Die Erotik in der französischen Karikatur*, trans. Cary von Karwarth and Adolf Neumann (from the manuscript), Gesellschaft Österreichischer Bibliophilen XVI (Vienna: C. W. Stern, 1909), p. 195.

30. *The Memories of Dolly Morton: The Story of a Woman's Part in the Struggle to Free the Slaves: An Account of the Whippings, Rapes, and Violences That Preceded the Civil War in America with Curious Anthropological Observations on the Radical Diversities in the Conformation of the Female Bottom and the Way Different Women Endure Chastisement* (Paris: Charles Carrington, 1899), p. 207.

31. Sigmund Freud, *The Standard Edition of the Complete Psychological Works of Sigmund Freud*, trans. James Strachey (London: Hogarth, 1953–74), 7:186–87, especially the footnote added in 1920 concerning the "genital apparatus" of the female. Translations from other works are mine except where otherwise stated.

32. The best study of the image of the prostitute is Alain Corbin, *Les filles de noce: Misère sexuelle et prostitution aux 19e et 20e siècles* (Paris: Aubier, 1978). On the black prostitute see Khalid Kistainy, *The Prostitute in Progressive Literature* (New York: Schocken, 1982), pp. 74–84. On the iconography associated with the pictorial representation of the prostitute in nineteenth-century art see Hess and Nochlin, eds., *Woman as Sex Object,* as well as Linda Nochlin, "Lost and Found: Once More the Fallen Woman," *Art Bulletin* 60 (1978): 139–53, and Lynda Nead, "Seduction, Prostitution, Suicide: *On the Brink* by Alfred Elmore," *Art*

History 5 (1982): 310–22. On the special status of medical representations of female sexuality see the eighteenth-century wax models of female anatomy in the Museo della Specola (Florence), reproductions of which are in Mario Bucci, *Anatomia come arte* (Firenze: Edizione d'arte il Fiorino, 1969), esp. plate 8.

33. A. J. B. Parent-Duchatelet, *De la prostitution dans la ville de Paris* (Paris: J. B. Baillière, 1836), 1:193–244.

34. *On Prostitution in the City of Paris* (London: T. Burgess, 1840), p. 38. It is of interest that it is exactly the passages on the physiognomy and appearance of the prostitute which this anonymous translator presents to an English audience as the essence of Parent-Duchatelet's work.

35. Freud, *Standard Edition,* 7:191.

36. V. M. Tarnowsky, *Prostitutsija i abolitsioniszm* (St. Petersburg: n.p., 1888); *Prostitution und Abolitionismus* (Hamburg: Voss, 1890).

37. Pauline Tarnowsky, *Etude anthropométrique sur les prostituées et les voleuses* (Paris: E. Lecrosnier et Bebé, 1889).

38. Pauline Tarnowsky, "Fisiomie di prostitute russe," *Archivio di Psichiatria, scienze penali ed antropologia criminale* 14 (1893): 141–42.

39. Cesare Lombroso and Guglielmo Ferrero, *La donna deliquente* (Turin: Roux, 1893). On the photographs of the Russian prostitutes, pp. 349–50; on the fat of the prostitute, pp. 361–62; and on the labia of the Hottentots, p. 38.

40. Adrien Charpy, "Des organes génitaux externes chez les prostituées," *Annales des Dermatologie* 3 (1870–71): 271–79.

41. *Congrès international d'anthropologie criminelle* (1896) (Geneva: Georg et Co., 1897), pp. 348–49.

42. Ellis, *Psychology of Sex,* 4:164.

43. Guglielmo Ferrero [Guillaume Ferrero], "L'atavisme de la prostitution," *Revue scientifique* (Paris), 1892, pp. 136–41.

44. Abele De Blasio, "Steatopigia in prostitute," *Archivio di psichiatria* 26 (1905): 257–64.

45. Jefferson commented on the heightened sensuality of the black in slavery in his *Notes from Virginia* (1782); Diderot, in his posthumously published fictional *Supplément au voyage de Bougainville* (1796), represented the heightened sexuality of the inhabitants of Tahiti as examples of the nature of sexuality freed from civilization. See the general discussion of this theme in Alexander Thomas and Samuel Sillen, *Racism and Psychiatry* (New York: Brunner/Mazel, 1972), pp. 101 ff.

46. On Bachofen's view of primitive sexuality see the Introduction, Chapter 9, and selections by Joseph Campbell to J. J. Bachofen, *Myth, Religion & Mother Right,* trans. Ralph Manheim (Princeton, N.J.: Princeton University Press, 1973).

47. See Winthrop Jordan, *White over Black: American Attitudes toward the Negro, 1550–1812* (New York: W. W. Norton, 1977), pp. 3–43.

48. Iwan Bloch, *Der Ursprung der Syphilis,* 2 vols. (Jena: Gustav Fischer, 1901–11).

49. Reff, *Manet: Olympia,* pp. 57–58, also p. 118.

50. See Auriant, *La véritable histoire de "Nana"* (Paris: Mercure de France,

1942). See also Demetra Palamari, "The Shark Who Swallowed His Epoch: Family, Nature and Society in the Novels of Émile Zola," in Virginia Tufte and Barbara Myerhoff, eds., *Changing Images of the Family* (New Haven: Yale University Press, 1978), pp. 155–72, and Robert A. Nye, *Crime, Madness, and Politics in Modern France: The Medical Concept of National Decline* (Princeton: Princeton University Press, 1984).

51. All the quotations are from Charles Duff's translation of *Nana* (London: Heineman, 1953), here, p. 27. The position described by Zola mirrors Manet's image of Nana. It emphasizes her state of semi-undress (echoing the image of the half-dressed "Hottentot Venus"). In Manet's image she is in addition corseted, and the corset stresses her artificially narrowed waist and the resultant emphasis on the buttocks. Both Manet's and Zola's images recall the bustle that Nana would have worn once dressed. (Nana is, for Zola, a historical character, existing at a very specific time in French history, in the decade leading up to the Franco-Prussian War of 1872.) The bustle (or *tounure*) was the height of fashion between 1865 and 1876 (and again in the mid-1880s). Worn with a tightly laced bodice, the bustle gave the female a look of the primitive and the erotic while staying safely within the bounds of middle-class fashion. Both the woman wearing a bustle and those who observed her knew the accessory was artificial but they were also aware of its symbolic implications. The "bum rolls" of the seventeenth century and the "cork rumps" of the eighteenth century had already established a general association. But the bustle of the late nineteenth century, stretching out at the rear of the dress like a shelf, directly echoed the supposed primitive sexuality of the Hottentot. Thus the dress implied by Nana's state of semi-undress and by her undergarments, in Manet's painting and in Zola's description, also points to the primitive hidden within. See Bryan S. Turner, *The Body and Society: Explorations in Social Theory* (Oxford: Blackwell, 1985).

52. August Barthelemy, trans., *Syphilis: Poème en deux chants* (Paris: Béchet junior et Labé & Bohaire, 1840). This is a translation of a section of Fracastorius's Latin poem on the nature and origin of syphilis. The French edition was in print well past mid-century.

53. Cited by Bataille, *Manet*, p. 65.

54. Ellis, *Psychology of Sex*, 4:176.

55. Abel Hermant, *Confession d'un enfant d'hier*, cited in ibid., n. 1.

56. Joachim Hohmann, ed., *Schon auf den ersten Blick: Lesebuch zur Geschichte unserer Feindbilder* (Darmstadt: Luchterhand, 1981).

57. Freud, *Standard Edition*, 25:212. See also Renate Schlesier, *Konstruktion der Weiblichkeit bei Sigmund Freud* (Frankfurt: Europäische Verlagsanstalt, 1981), pp. 35–39.

4. Black Sexuality and Modern Consciousness

1. Amos Oz, *The Hill of Evil Counsel*, trans. Nicholas de Lang (London: Fontana, 1980), p. 189. Except where otherwise noted, other translations are mine.

2. Magnus Hirschfeld, *The Sexual History of the World War* (New York: Cadillac, 1941), p. 47.

3. Peter Altenberg, *Ashantee* (Berlin: S. Fischer, 1897). All citations are to this edition. On Altenberg the best overviews are: Camillo Schaefer, *Peter Altenberg: Ein biographischer Essay. Freibord,* special series, no. 10 (Vienna: Freibord, 1980), and Hans Christian Kosler, ed., *Peter Altenberg: Leben und Werke in Texten und Bildern* (Munich: Matthes & Seitz, 1981).

4. Friedrich Ratzel, *The History of Mankind,* trans. A. J. Butler (London: Macmillan, 1898), 2:352–57, 3:125–43.

5. *Die Fackel,* 806–9 (May 1929): 46 ff.

6. Bernadette Bucher, *La sauvage aux seins pendants* (Paris: Hermann, 1977). An older study that is, however, quite valuable in this context is Gustave-Jules Witkowski, *Tetoniana: Curiosités médicales, littéraires et artistiques sur les seins et l'allaitement* (Paris: A. Maloine, 1898).

7. Gustav Jaeger, *Die Entdeckung der Seele* (Leipzig: Ernst Günther, 1880), pp. 106–9.

8. Iwan Bloch, *Das Sexualleben unserer Zeit in seinen Beziehung zur modernen Kultur* (Berlin: Louis Marcus, 1907). Typical of the philosophical literature of the period for the resonance of this theme is Paul Ree, *Der Ursprung der moralischen Empfindungen* (Chemnitz: Ernst Schmeitzer, 1877), pp. 74–77.

9. John M. Eyler, *Victorian Social Medicine: The Ideas and Methods of William Farr* (Baltimore: Johns Hopkins University Press, 1979), p. 100. See also Alain Corbin, *Le miasme et la jonquille: L'ordorat et l'imaginaire social XVIIIe–XIXe siècles* (Paris: Aubier Montaigne, 1982).

10. Johann Wolfgang von Goethe, *Wilhelm Meister's Apprenticeship,* trans. Thomas Carlyle (Boston: S. E. Cassino, 1884), p. 60.

11. John Ritchie Findlay, *Personal Recollections of Thomas De Quincey* (Edinburgh: A. & C. Black, 1886), p. 36.

12. Havelock Ellis, *Studies in the Psychology of Sex,* vol. 7 (Philadelphia: F. A. Davis, 1928), pp. 171–72. See Phyllis Grosskurth, *Havelock Ellis: A Biography* (New York: Knopf, 1980).

13. Bernard C. Meyer, "Some Observations on the Rescue of Fallen Women," *Psychoanalytic Quarterly* 53 (1984): 224. Compare the discussion in Nina Auerbach, *Woman and the Demon: The Life of a Victorian Myth* (Cambridge: Harvard University Press, 1982), pp. 150–84.

14. Jan Goldstein, "The Hysteria Diagnosis and the Politics of Anticlericalism in Late Nineteenth-Century France," *Journal of Modern History* 54 (1982): 209–39.

15. Ratzel, *History of Mankind,* 2:283.

16. Cited in Schaefer, *Altenberg,* plate 2.

17. Walter Rathenau, "Höre, Israel!" *Die Zukunft* 18 (1897): 454–62. On the iconography of the "feminine male" see James D. Steakley, "Iconography of a Scandal: Political Cartoons and the Eulenberg Affair," *Studies in Visual Communication* 9 (1983): 20–51.

18. Alexander Pilcz, *Beitrag zur vergleichenden Rassen-Psychiatrie* (Leipzig and Vienna: Franz Deuticke, 1906), pp. 40–41. For a psychoanalytic parallel see

Arrah B. Evarts, "Dementia praecox in the Colored Race," *Psychoanalytic Review* 7 (1913–14): 388–403.

19. See, for example, the essays from 1912–1913 reprinted in the volume *Untergang der Welt durch schwarze Magie* (Munich: Kösel, 1960), pp. 308–11, 327–30.

20. D. H. Lawrence, *Lady Chatterley's Lover* (Paris: Odyssey Press, 1935), p. 240.

21. Henry Miller, *Tropic of Capricorn* (New York: Grove, 1961).

22. George Wickes, ed., *Lawrence Durrell and Henry Miller: A Private Correspondence* (New York: E. P. Dutton, 1963), p. 80.

23. Lawrence Durrell, *The Black Book* (London: Faber & Faber, 1973), p. 123. Laughter is the mark of the black. In Sherwood Anderson's *Dark Laughter* (New York: Grosset & Dunlop, 1925), the sexual ineptitude of the white world evokes "dark laughter," the laughter of "Negro women [who] have an instinctive understanding. They say nothing, being wise in women-lore" (233). Anderson, like Durrell, wrote a novel that contained numerous references (both overt and covert) to Joyce's *Ulysses* (1922). Its narrative form, like that of the later *Black Book*, was largely interior monologue, patterned after Molly Bloom's in *Ulysses*. The inner monologue became a favored medium for exploration of human sexuality for the moderns. Anderson in *Dark Laughter*, like Durrell in *The Black Book*, incorporates a stereotype of black sexuality as an ambiguous marker for the nature of white sexuality: "Such a strange feeling in me—something primitive like a nigger woman in an African dance. That was what they were after when they got up the show. You strip all away, no pretense. If I'd been a nigger woman—good night—something exotic. No chance then—that's sure" (184).

24. Durrell, *Black Book*, p. 123.

25. Ibid., p. 124.

26. Ibid., pp. 124–25.

27. James Joyce, *Ulysses* (New York: Random House, 1961), pp. 738 ff. See also Lindsey Tucker, *Stephen and Bloom at Life's Feast: Alimentary Symbolism and the Creative Process in James Joyce's "Ulysses"* (Columbus: Ohio State University Press, 1984), and Richard Brown, *James Joyce and Sexuality* (Cambridge: Cambridge University Press, 1985).

28. James Joyce, *Finnegans Wake* (New York: Viking, 1947), p. 622. In general on this question see the detailed discussion of this image in James Joyce, *Chamber Music*, ed. William York Tindall (New York: Columbia University Press, 1954), pp. 71 ff.

29. G. S. Fraser, *Lawrence Durrell: A Study* (London: Faber & Faber, 1973), pp. 46 ff.

30. Durrell, *Black Book*, p. 125.

31. Fredric Jameson, *Fables of Aggression: Wyndham Lewis, the Modernist as Fascist* (Berkeley: University of California Press, 1979), p. 39. Contrast the excellent essay by Allan Sekula, "Dismantling Modernism, Reinventing Documentary (Notes on the Politics of Representation)," *Massachusetts Review* 19 (1978): 859–83.

32. Otto Kernberg, "Paranoid Regression and Malignant Narcissism," in his *Severe Personality Disorders: Psychotherapeutic Strategies* (New Haven: Yale University Press, 1985), 290–314.

33. See my *On Blackness without Blacks: Essays on the Image of The Black in Germany* (Boston: G. K. Hall, 1982), pp. 125 ff.

34. Giacomo Leopardi, *Pensieri,* trans. W. S. Di Piero (Baton Rouge: Louisiana State University Press, 1981), p. 111.

5. On the Nexus of Blackness and Madness

1. Arrah B. Evarts, "Color Symbolism," *Psychoanalytic Review* 6 (1919): 156. See also Richard Sterba, "Some Psychological Factors in Negro Race Hatred and in Anti-Negro Riots," *Psychoanalysis and the Social Sciences* 1 (1974): 411–27.

2. Frantz Fanon, *Black Skin, White Masks* (New York: Grove, 1967), p. 188. A less polemical presentation is Urs Bitterli, *Die 'Wilden' und die 'Zivilisierten': Grundzüge einer Geistes- und Kulturgeschichte der europäisch-überseeischer Begegnung* (Munich: C. H. Beck, 1976).

3. Of importance for the present study were: Harold Beaver, " 'Run, Nigger, Run': The Adventures of Huckleberry Finn as a Fugitive Narrative," *Journal of American Studies* 8 (1971): 88–96; Michael Egan, *Mark Twain's "Huckleberry Finn": Race, Class and Society* (London: Sussex University Press, 1977), esp. pp. 66–102.

4. All references to the text are to the edition of *The Adventures of Huckleberry Finn* edited by Sculley Bradley et al. (New York: W. W. Norton, 1977), here, p. 126.

5. See Twain's volume of essays *Is Shakespeare Dead?* (New York: Harper Brothers, 1909). The relationship between Twain's lifelong interest in the exotic and his social consciousness is documented in Philip S. Fouer, *Mark Twain: Social Critic* (New York: International Publishers, 1958).

6. Mark Van Doren, *Shakespeare* (Garden City, N.Y.: Doubleday, 1939), p. 210.

7. Richard Bernheimer, *Wild Men in the Middle Ages: A Study in Art, Sentiment, and Demonology* (Cambridge: Harvard University Press, 1952), remains the standard study of this theme.

8. See Bo Lindberg, "William Blakes Nebuchadnezzar och Mänskodjuret," *Konsthistoriska stüdior* 1 (1974): 10–18, for an illustrated history of the theme from the Middle Ages through Blake.

9. J. Huizinga, *The Waning of the Middle Ages* (Garden City, N.Y.: Doubleday, 1954), pp. 271–72. See also J. P. Heather, "Color Symbolism," *Folklore* 59 (1948): 165–83; 60 (1949): 208–16, 266–76, 316–31; and Don Cameron Allen, "Symbolic Color in the Literature of the English Renaissance," *Philological Quarterly* 15 (1936): 81–92.

10. Concerning the alteration of meaning see both the *OED* ("Moor") and Grimm's *Wörterbuch* ("Mohr" and "Neger"). See also Lemuel A. Johnson, *The*

Devil, the Gargoyle, and the Buffoon: The Negro as Metaphor in Western Literature (Port Washington, N.Y.: Kennikat Press, 1971) and Hans Bächtold-Stäubli, ed., *Handwörterbuch des deutschen Aberglaubens* (Berlin: De Gruyter, 1934), 6:452–53.

11. Daniel G. Hoffman, *Form and Fable in American Fiction* (1961; reprinted in Bradley et al., *Huckleberry Finn*, p. 434). See also his "Jim's Magic: Black or White?" *American Literature* 32 (1960): 47–54; Ray W. Frantz, Jr., "The Role of Folklore in 'Huckleberry Finn,'" *American Literature* 28 (1956): 314–27; and Victor Royce West, *Folklore in the Works of Mark Twain*, University of Nebraska Studies in Language and Literature, 10 (Lincoln: University of Nebraska Press, 1930). Concerning the general background see Harry Levin, *The Power of Blackness* (New York: Random House, [1958]), esp. pp. 245–46.

12. The background for this problem is sketched by John S. Haller, *Outcasts from Evolution: Scientific Attitudes of Racial Inferiority, 1859–1900* (Urbana: University of Illinois Press, 1971), esp. pp. 40–69.

13. Richard K. Crallé, ed., *The Works of John C. Calhoun* (New York: D. Appelton, 1874), 5:337–38.

14. The most recent and most complete discussion is in Gerald W. Grob, *Edward Jarvis and the Medical World of Nineteenth-Century America* (Knoxville: University of Tennessee Press, 1978), pp. 70–75. See also Eric T. Carlson, "Nineteenth Century Insanity and Poverty," *Bulletin of the New York Academy of Medicine* 48 (1972): 539–44, which presents data on earlier statistical surveys of insanity. Carlson omits the Parkman survey of the insane in Massachusetts undertaken in 1817.

15. Other reactions to the census are: C. B. Hayden, "On the Distribution of Insanity in the United States," *Southern Literary Messenger* 10 (1844): 180; Samuel Forrey, "Vital Statistics Furnished by the Sixth Census of the United States, Bearing upon the Question of the Unity of the Human Race," and "On the Relative Proportion of Centenarians, of Deaf and Dumb, of Blind, and of Insane, in the Races of European and African Origin, as Shown by the Censuses of the United States," *New York Journal of Medicine and the Collateral Sciences* 1 (1843): 151–67; 2 (1844): 310–20. Jarvis published his first answer in the *Boston Medical and Surgical Journal* 27 (1842): 116–21.

16. "Startling Facts from the Census," *American Journal of Insanity* 8 (1851): 154, reprinted from the *New York Observer*. Jarvis immediately published a rejoinder, "Insanity among the Coloured Population of the Free States," *American Journal of Insanity* 8 (1852): 268–82.

17. "Report on the Diseases and Physical Peculiarities of the Negro Race" (Part 1), *New Orleans Medical and Surgical Journal* 8 (1851): 692–713. Cartwright's views quickly became the subject of much debate. See his letter to Daniel Webster on this subject published in *DeBow's Review* 11 (1851): 184–97. Concerning Cartwright see James Denny Guillory, "The Pro-Slavery Arguments of Dr. Samuel A. Cartwright," *Louisiana History* 9 (1968): 209–27; Thomas S. Szasz, "The Sane Slave: A Historical Note on the Use of Medical Diagnosis as Justificatory Rhetoric," *American Journal of Psychotherapy* 25 (1971): 228–39, as well as his "The Negro in Psychiatry: An Historical Note on Psychiatric Rhetoric,"

American Journal of Psychotherapy 25 (1971): 469–71; and Benjamin Malzberg, "Mental Disease among American Negroes: A Statistical Analysis," in Otto Klineberg, ed., *Characteristics of the American Negro* (New York: J. & J. Harper, 1944), pp. 371–99.

18. Quoted from Szasz, "The Sane Slave," pp. 233–34.

19. J. B. Andrews, "The Distribution and Care of the Insane in the United States," *Transactions of the International Medical Congress,* Ninth Session, 1887, 5:226–37, cited by George Rosen, *Madness in Society: Chapters in the Historical Sociology of Mental Illness* (Chicago: University of Chicago Press, 1968), pp. 190–91.

20. J. F. Miller, "The Effects of Emancipation upon the Mental and Physical Qualifications of the Negro in the South," *North Carolina Medical Journal* 38 (1896): 287, cited by Haller, *Outcasts from Evolution,* p. 45.

21. Quoted in Henry M. Hurd, ed., *The Institutional Care of the Insane in the United States and Canada* (Baltimore: The Johns Hopkins Press, 1916), pp. 372–73.

22. Ibid., p. 376.

23. Benjamin Pasamanick, "Myths Regarding Prevalence of Mental Disease in the American Negro: A Century of Misuse of Mental Hospital Data and Some New Findings," *Journal of the National Medical Association* 56 (1964): 17. See also William D. Postell, "Mental Health among the Slave Population on Southern Plantations," *American Journal of Psychiatry* 110 (1953): 52–54.

24. Pasamanick, "Myths," p. 6.

25. Peter L. Thorslev, Jr., "The Wild Man's Revenge," in Edward Dudley and Maximillian E. Novak, eds., *The Wild Man Within: An Image from the Renaissance to Romanticism* (Pittsburgh: University of Pittsburgh Press, 1972), pp. 298–99.

26. All references are to the edition by Ernst Schwarz (Darmstadt: Wissenschaftliche Buchgesellschaft, 1967), here, l. 3309. For a survey of the literature see Peter Wapnewski, *Hartmann von Aue,* Sammlung Metzler 17 (Stuttgart: Metzler, 1967). A philological introduction to some of the complexities of this question is given by Francis B. Gummere, "On the Symbolic Use of the Colors Black and White in Germanic Tradition," *Haverford College Studies* 1 (1889): 112–62.

27. Cited from J. M. N. Kapteyn, ed., Wirnt von Gravenberc, *Wigalois der Ritter mit dem Rade.* Rheinische Beiträge und Hilfsbücher zur germanischen Philologie und Volkskunde 9 (Bonn: Fritz Klopp, 1926): ll. 6279–91. The translation is from J. W. Thomas, trans., *Wigalois: The Knight of Fortune's Wheel* (Lincoln: University of Nebraska Press, 1977), p. 174. My emphasis.

28. Cited from Justus Lunzer Edler von Lindhausen, ed., *Orneit und Wolfdietrich nach der Wiener Piaristenhandschrift.* Bibliothek des litterarischen Vereins 239 (Tubingen: Litterarischer Verein, 1906), verses 1352–54. See also the discussion of this passage in Hermann Schneider, *Die Gedichte und die Sage von Wolfdietrich* (Munich: Beck, 1913), pp. 266–67.

29. One of the most puzzling presentations of the figure of the black in medieval German literature is the multicolored Feirefiz, Parzifal's half-brother, the son of a black heathen and a Christian knight. It is evident that this figure represents

the merging of two stereotypes, that of the black and that of the heathen. This figure and his color may reflect an Islamic rather than a Western tradition. See Marilyn Robinson Waldman, "The Development of the Concept of *Kufr* in the Qur'ān," *Journal of the American Oriental Society* 88 (1968): 442–55, and Bernard Lewis, *Race and Color in Islam* (New York: Harper & Row, 1971), for the background of this contamination of medieval Christian belief.

30. Bernheimer, *Wild Men*, p. 15.

31. Cited by Margaret T. Hodgen, *Early Anthropology in the Sixteenth and Seventeenth Centuries* (Philadelphia: University of Pennsylvania Press, 1964), p. 362.

32. Alfred Dunston, Jr., *The Black Man in the Old Testament and Its World* (Philadelphia: Dorrance, 1974).

33. See Winthrop Jordan, *White over Black: American Attitudes toward the Negro, 1550–1812* (New York: W. W. Norton, 1977), p. 16, and Joel Kovel, *White Racism: A Psychohistory* (New York: Pantheon, 1970), pp. 63–64. See also David Brion Davis, *The Problem of Slavery in the Age of Revolution, 1770–1823* (Ithaca, N.Y.: Cornell University Press, 1975), pp. 523–56.

34. Following the interpretation by Friedrich Ohly, *Hohelied-Studien: Grunzüge einer Geschichte der Hoheliedauslegung des Abendlandes bis um 1200* (Wiesbaden: Steiner, 1958). All references to commentaries are, for the sake of simplicity, to the *Patrologiae Cursus Completus: Series Latina* (PL), ed. J. P. Minge, 221 vols. (Paris: n.p., 1844–64), except where texts are not present. The Index (PL 219, cols. 107–8) lists thirty commentaries on the Song of Songs alone; other interpretations of this passage are to be found in other exegetical writings. A general summary of the complex medieval interpretations of this passage is to be found in Cornelius a Lapidé, *Commentarius in Scripturam Sacram* (Paris: Ludovicus vives, 1868), 7:492–96.

35. G. N. Bonwetsch and Hanns Achelis, eds., *Hippolytus: Werke I. Die griechischen christlichen Schriftsteller der ersten drei Jahrhunderte* (Leipzig: J. C. Hinrich, 1897), p. 359.

36. PL 14: 508. The translation is by Michael P. McHugh, *St. Ambrose: Seven Exegetical Works*, The Fathers of the Church (Washington: Catholic University Press, 1972), 65:19–20.

37. PL 183: 794–95. The translation is by A Priest of Mount Melleray, *St. Bernard's Sermons on the Canticle of Canticles* (Dublin: Browne & Nolan, 1920), 1:21–22.

38. Penelope B. R. Doob, *Nebuchadnezzar's Children: Conventions of Madness in Middle English Literature* (New Haven: Yale University Press, 1974), p. 140.

39. The classic discussion of melancholy and blackness, Raymond Klibansky, Erwin Panofsky, and Fritz Saxl, *Saturn and Melancholy: Studies in the History of Natural Philosophy, Religion and Art* (London: Nelson, 1964), pp. 289–90, identifies five different phrases that point to the blackness of the melancholic's countenance.

40. Cited in ibid., p. 59. Compare Lynn Thorndike, "De Complexionibus," *Isis* 49 (1958): 404, and his reference to the *luteique coloris* of the melancholic. The

basic introduction to the history of the classical physiognomies is Elizabeth C. Evans, *Physiognomics in the Ancient World,* Transactions of the American Philosophical Society n.s. 59, 5 (Philadelphia: American Philosophical Society, 1969), esp. p. 29. A recent study of this motif in literary studies is Helen Watanabe-O'Kelly, *Melancholie und die melancholische Landschaft. Ein Beitrag zur Geistesgeschichte des 17. Jahrhunderts* (Bern: Lang, 1978).

41. Cited from the edition and translation by W. S. Hett, *Aristotle: Minor Works* (Cambridge: Harvard University Press, 1936), pp. 125, 131. Compare Thorndike, "De Complexionibus," p. 402.

42. Compare the discussion of the change in visual image of the black in the Middle Ages in Jean Vercoutter et al., *The Image of the Black in Western Art* (New York: William Morrow, 1976 ff.).

43. See Frank M. Snowden, Jr., *Blacks in Antiquity: Ethiopians in the Greco-Roman Experience* (Cambridge: Harvard University Press, 1970), and Benjamin N. Azikiwe, "The Negro in Greek Mythology," *Crisis* 41 (1934): 65–66.

44. A parallel view of the nature of the black's perception of the world is given by the thirteenth-century monk Witelo, who concludes his chapter on aesthetic perception with observations about the different aesthetic norms of the blacks and the Northern Europeans. See Alessandro Parronchi, ed., *Vitellione, Teorema della Belleza* (Milan: All'insegna del pesce d'oro, 1967), p. 25.

45. The association of blackness and illness reappears often. Robert Burton believed that bad air might be a cause of melancholy among the inhabitants of Africa as "hot countries are most troubled with melancholy," *The Anatomy of Melancholy* (1621), ed. Holbrook Jackson (London: J. M. Dent, 1932), 1:237–38. Benjamin Rush saw the skin color of the black as a result of a form of leprosy, again associating blackness with disease. See Donald J. D'Elia, "Dr. Benjamin Rush and the Negro," *Journal of the History of Ideas* 30 (1969): 413–22; Howard Feinstein, "Benjamin Rush: A Child of Light for the Children of Darkness," *The Psychoanalytic Review* 58 (1971): 209–22; and B. L. Plummer, "Benjamin Rush and the Negro," *American Journal of Psychiatry* 127 (1970): 793–98.

46. Leslie Fiedler, "Come Back to the Raft Ag'in, Huck Honey," *Partisan Review* (1948), reprinted in Bradley et al., *Huckleberry Finn,* p. 420.

47. Susan Sontag, *Illness as Metaphor* (New York: Farrar, Straus & Giroux, 1977).

48. Harold R. Isaacs, "Blackness and Whiteness," *Encounter* 21 (1963): 8–21.

6. The Madness of the Jews

1. Cited in S. S. Prawer's translation from his *Heine's Jewish Comedy* (Oxford: Oxford University Press, 1983), p. 433.

2. See my "Nietzsche, Heine and the Rhetoric of Anti-Semitism," *London German Studies* 2 (1983): 76–93.

3. Leon Poliakov, *The History of Anti-Semitism,* trans. Richard Howard (New York: Vanguard, 1965), 1:143, and Joshua Trachtenberg, *The Devil and the Jews:*

The Medieval Conception of the Jew and Its Relationship to Modern Antisemitism (New Haven: Yale University Press, 1943), pp. 88–96. For the broader context see Lionel Rothkrug, "Peasant and Jew: Fears of Pollution and German Collective Perceptions," *Historical Reflections/Réflexions historiques* 10 (1983): 59–78.

4. F. L. de La Fontaine, *Chirurgisch-Medicinische Abhandlungen verschiedenen Inhalts Polen betreffend* (Breslau: Korn, 1792), pp. 145–55.

5. See R. P. Neuman, "Masturbation, Madness, and the Modern Concepts of Childhood and Adolescence," *Journal of Social History* 8 (1975): 1–27.

6. Henri Grégoire, *Essai sur la régénération physique, morale et politique des juifs* (Metz: Lamort, 1789), pp. 44–64.

7. Jacob Katz, *From Prejudice to Destruction. Anti-Semitism, 1700–1933* (Cambridge: Harvard University Press, 1980), pp. 56–57.

8. Karl Wilhelm Friedrich Grattenauer, *Über die physische und moralische Verfassung der heutigen Juden* (Leipzig: n.p., 1791).

9. Stephen Wilson, *Ideology and Experience: Antisemitism in France at the Time of the Dreyfus Affair* (Rutherford, N.J.: Fairleigh Dickinson University Press, 1980).

10. M. Boudin, "Sur l'idiote et l'aliénation mentale chez les Juifs d'Allemagne," *Bulletins de la société d'anthropologie de Paris* (1863): 386–88.

11. Richard M. Goodman, *Genetic Disorders among the Jewish People* (Baltimore: Johns Hopkins University Press, 1979), pp. 421–27.

12. "À Propos du Procès-verbal," *Bulletins de la société d'anthropologie de Paris* 7 (1884): 698–701. All translations mine unless otherwise noted.

13. J. M. Charcot, *Leçons du Mardi à la Salpêtrière* (Paris: Progrès médical, 1889), 2:11–12.

14. Charcot's influence was felt immediately. See "Sur la race juive et sa pathologie," *Académie de médecine,* (Paris), Bulletin 3, ser. 26 (1891), pp. 287–309.

15. Richard Krafft-Ebing, *Text-Book of Insanity,* trans. Charles Gilbert Chaddock (Philadelphia: F. A. Davis, 1905), p. 143. A detailed summary of these views can be found in Alexander Pilcz, *Beitrag zur vergleichenden Rassen-Psychiatrie* (Leipzig and Vienna: Deuticke, 1906), pp. 26–32.

16. Krafft-Ebing, *Text-Book of Insanity,* p. 143.

17. Richard Krafft-Ebing, *Nervosität und neurasthenische Zustände* (Vienna: Hölder, 1895), p. 96. For the context, see T. J. Jackson Lear, *No Place of Grace: Anti-Modernism and the Transformation of American Culture* (New York: Pantheon, 1981).

18. Martin Engländer, *Die auffallend häufigen Krankheitserscheinunge der jüdischen Rasse* (Vienna: J. L. Pollak, 1902), p. 12.

19. Cesare Lombroso, *L'antisemitismo e la scienze moderne* (Turin: L. Roux, 1894), p. 83.

20. *Max Nordaus Zionistische Schriften* (Cologne: Jüdischer Verlag, 1909), pp. 379–81. The answer to Nordau and to the various Jewish uses of this image of the Eastern Jew as the diseased Jew was very late in coming. See *Hygiene und Judentum: Eine Sammelschrift* (Dresden: Jac. Sternlicht, 1930). Recently it has been argued that the Eastern European Jewish community, at least in the United States, was *healthier,* rather than more diseased. See Jacob Jay Lindenthal, "*Abi

Gezunt: Health and the Eastern European Immigrant," *American Jewish History* 70 (1981): 420–41.

21. On the historical importance of incest in nineteenth-century thought see Herbert Maisch, *Inzest* (Reinbeck: Rowohlt, 1968), pp. 27–30. See also Mary Douglas, *Purity and Danger: An Analysis of Concepts of Pollution and Taboo* (Harmondsworth: Penguin, n.d.), pp. 94–113, on the power of the symbols of defilement and taboo.

22. See Peter de Mendelssohn, *Der Zauberer: Das Leben des deutschen Schriftstellers Thomas Mann* (Frankfurt: Fischer, 1975), 1:662–73, and Marie Walter, "Concerning the Affair Wälsungenblut," *Book Collector* 13 (1964): 463–72.

23. Adolf Hitler, *Mein Kampf,* trans. Ralph Manheim (Cambridge: Houghton Mifflin, 1943), p. 306.

24. Rafael Becker, *Die jüdische Nervosität: Ihre Art, Entstehung und Bekämpfung* (Zurich: Speidel & Wurzel, 1918). On the nervousness of the Germans see Observator, *Über die Nervosität im deutschen Charakter* (Leipzig: Neuer Geist, 1922).

25. Fritz Wittels, *Der Taufjude* (Vienna: Breitenstein, 1904).

26. Rafael Becker, *Die Nervosität bei den Juden: Ein Beitrag zur Rassenpsychiatrie für Ärzte und gebildete Laien* (Zurich: Orell Füssli, 1919).

27. Ibid., p. 96.

28. A. Myerson, "The 'Nervousness' of the Jew," *Mental Hygiene* 4 (1920): 65–72. Compare *Medical Record* (New York), 16 February 1918, pp. 269–75.

29. See Richard W. Fox, *So Far Disordered in Mind: Insanity in California, 1870–1930* (Berkeley: University of California Press, 1978), for further nineteenth-century examples.

30. Monika Richarz, *Der Eintritt der Juden in die akademischen Berufe* (Tübingen: J. C. V. Mohr, 1974), pp. 28–43.

7. Race and Madness in I. J. Singer's *The Family Carnovsky*

1. The best attempts to place I. J. Singer in the broader context of Yiddish letters are Clive Sinclair, *The Brothers Singer* (London: Allison & Busby, 1983), and Charles Madison, *Yiddish Literature: Its Scope and Major Writers* (New York: Schocken, 1968), pp. 449–78. See also Irving Howe, "The Other Singer," *Commentary* 41 (March 1966), pp. 78, 80–82, and N. Mayzl, *Forgeyer un Mittsaytler* (New York: Cyco, 1946), pp. 372–91.

2. Important references to Berlin in fiction of the twentieth century have been examined by Marilyn Sibley Fries, *The Changing Consciousness of Reality: The Image of Berlin in Selected German Novels from Raabe to Döblin* (Bonn: Bouvier, 1980). On I. J. Singer see Susan A. Slotnik, "Concepts of Space and Society: Melnits, Berlin and New York in I. J. Singer's *Die Mishpokhe Karnovski,*" *German Quarterly* 54 (1981): 33–43.

3. All references are to the English translation by Joseph Singer, *The Family Carnovsky* (New York: Harper & Row, 1969), here, p. 119. On the novel see the

essay by M. Ravitsch in *Tsukunft* (March 1944): 87 ff., as well as the following reviews of the English translation: P. Adams, *Atlantic Monthly*, February 1969, p. 133; J. Bauke, *Saturday Review*, 22 March 1969, p. 66; A. Bezanker, *Nation*, 23 June 1969, p. 800; H. Roskelenko, *New York Times Book Review*, 16 November 1969, pp. 72–73; S. Simon, *Library Journal*, 1 January 1969, p. 97.

4. Keith L. Nelson, "The 'Black Horror on the Rhine': Race as a Factor in Post–World War I Diplomacy," *Journal of Modern History* 42 (1970): 618–19.

5. The question was initially raised by Ernst Bertram in his essay "Das Problem des Verfalls," *Mitteilungen der Literarhistorische Gesellschaft Bonn* 2 (February 1907): 72–79. See also Gerhard Loose, "Thomas Mann and the Problem of Decadence," *University of Colorado Studies* 1 (1941). 345 75.

6. Cited from Adolf Hitler, *Mein Kampf*, trans. Ralph Manheim (Cambridge: Houghton Mifflin, 1943), here, p. 301.

7. Cited in the translation by Walter Kaufmann, *Basic Writings of Nietzsche* (New York: Modern Library, 1966), p. 599.

8. Bruno Bettelheim, *The Informed Heart: Autonomy in a Mass Age* (New York: The Free Press, 1960), p. 121.

8. Sigmund Freud and the Jewish Joke

1. Gershom Scholem, *From Berlin to Jerusalem: Memories of My Youth*, trans. Harry Zohn (New York: Schocken, 1980), p. 40. On Scholem and his relationship to the growth of German-Jewish thought in the twentieth century see David Biale, *Gershom Scholem: Kabbalah and Counter-history* (Cambridge: Harvard University Press, 1979).

2. Manuel Schnitzer [M. Nuél], *Das Buch der jüdischen Witz* (Berlin: Hesperus, 1907). The influence of Buber's "model" of the Germanization of the tradition of Eastern Jewry can be seen in the structure of Schnitzer's later collection, *Rabbi Lach und seine Geschichten* (Berlin: Hesperus, 1910). Similar to Schnitzer's collection are: Richard Schmidt, *O diese Juden!* (Berlin: Koszius, 1906), and Simon Joseph Rügenwald, *Humor aus dem jüdischen Leben* (Frankfurt: Kauffmann, 1903).

3. The only study of the image of the comic Jew which attempts to explore this image synchronically is Sig Altman, *The Comic Image of the Jew: Explorations of a Pop Culture Phenomenon* (Rutherford, N.J.: Fairleigh Dickinson Press, 1971). This volume is marred by the lack of firsthand historical information on the tradition of the comic Jew in Europe. For a Freudian reading see Theodor Reik, *Jewish Wit* (New York: Gamut, 1962).

4. Schnitzer, *Das Buch der Witz*, p. 9. All translations mine except where otherwise noted.

5. Ibid., p. 7.

6. Ibid., pp. 59–60.

7. Ibid., p. 10.

8. Manuel Schnitzer [M. Nuél], *Das Buch der jüdischen Witze: Neue Folge* (Berlin: Gustav Riecke, 1908?), p. 98.

9. On this topic see my essay "The Rediscovery of the Eastern Jews: German Jews in the East, 1890–1918," in David Bronsen, ed., *Jews and Germans from 1860 to 1933: The Problematic Symbiosis* (Heidelberg: Carl Winter, 1979), pp. 338–66, and Steven E. Aschheim, *Brothers and Strangers: The East European Jew in German and German Jewish Consciousness, 1800–1923* (Madison: University of Wisconsin Press, 1982).

10. Avrom Reitzer, *Gut Jontev: Rituelle Scherze und koscher Schmonzes für unsere Leut* (Vienna: Deubler, 1899); *Nebbach: Rituelle Scherze, Lozelech, Maisses und koschere Schmoznes für unsere Leut* (Vienna: Deubler, 1901): *Solem Alechem, Nix für Kinder: E Waggon feiner, vescher, safter Lozelach, Schmonzes takef pickfeiner Schmüs für unsere Leit* (Vienna: Deubler, 1902); *500 lozelech Maisses koschere Schmonzes pickfeine Schmüs für unsere Leut* (Vienna: J. Deubler, n.d.).

11. Reitzer, *Solem*, p. 3.

12. Richard Wagner, *Prose Works*, trans. William Ashton Ellis (London: Kegan Paul, Trench, Trubner, 1894), 3:84; Theodor Billroth, *Über das Lehren und Lernen der medicinischen Wissenschaften* . . . (Vienna: Carl Gerolds Sohn, 1876), p. 153.

13. L. M. Büschenthal, *Sammlung witziger Einfalle von Juden, als Beytrage zur characteristik der Jüdischen Nation* (Elberfeld: H. Buschler, 1812).

14. Sabattja Josef Wolff, *Streifereien im Gebiete des Ernstes und des Scherzes*, 2 vols. (Berlin: Ernst Siegfr. Mittler, 1818–19).

15. Büschenthal, *Witziger Einfalle*, p. iv.

16. Immanuel Kant, *Anthropology from a Pragmatic Point of View*, trans. Victor Lyle Dowdell (Carbondale: Southern Illinois Press, 1978), p. 219.

17. Büschenthal, *Witziger Einfalle*, p. 5.

18. Julius von Voss, *Der travestierte Nathan der Weise* (Berlin: Joh. Wilh. Schmidt, 1804), p. xiii.

19. The most recent studies that focus on the question of Freud's Jewish identity are: Ernst Simon, "Sigmund Freud, the Jew," *Leo Baeck Institute Yearbook* 2 (1957): 270–305; David Bakan, *Sigmund Freud and the Jewish Mystical Tradition* (New York: Van Nostrand, 1958); John Murray Cuddihy, *The Ordeal of Civility: Freud, Marx, Lévi-Strauss, and the Jewish Struggle with Modernity* (New York: Basic Books, 1974); Marie Balmary, *Psychoanalyzing Psychoanalysis: Freud and the Hidden Fault of the Father*, trans. Ned Lukscher (Baltimore: Johns Hopkins University Press, 1982); Martha Robert, *From Oedipus to Moses: Freud's Jewish Identity*, trans. Ralph Manheim (London: Routledge & Kegan Paul, 1977); Reuben M. Rainey, *Freud as a Student of Religion* (Missoula, Mont.: American Academy of Religion, 1975); Peter Gay, "Six Names in Search of an Interpretation: A Contribution to the Debate over Sigmund Freud's Jewishness," *Hebrew Union College Annual* 53 (1982): 295–308; Peter Gay, "Sigmund Freud: A German and His Discontents," in his *Freud, Jews and Other Germans* (New York: Oxford University Press, 1978), pp. 29–92; Marianne Krull, *Freud und sein Vater: Die Entstehung der Psychoanalyse und Freuds ungelöste Vaterbindung* (Munich: C. H. Beck, 1979); Dennie B. Klein, *Jewish Origins of the Psychoanalytic Movement* (New York: Praeger, 1981); Justin Miller, "Interpretation of Freud's Jewishness, 1924–

1974," *Journal of the History of the Behavioral Sciences* 17.(1981): 357–74 (the best overview); Theo Pfrimmer, *Freud: Lecteur de la Bible* (Paris: Presses Universitaires de France, 1982); Max Kohn, *Freud et le Yiddish: Le préanalytique* (Paris: Christian Bourgois, 1982). The latter work, the first book-length study of Freud's book on humor, badly confuses Yiddish with the image of the Yiddish-accented speaker in Germany. All of the recent studies draw heavily on the anecdotal material presented in Max Schur, *Freud: Living and Dying* (New York: International Universities Press, 1972). See also Stanley Rosenman, "The Late Conceptualization of the Self in Psychoanalysis: The German Language and Jewish Identity," *Journal of Psychohistory* 11 (1983): 9–42. A more general recent study of Freud's concept of wit is Elliott Oring, *The Jokes of Sigmund Freud: A Study in Humor and Jewish Identity* (Philadelphia: University of Pennsylvania Press, 1984).

20. Ernst Freud et al., *Sigmund Freud* (New York: Harcourt Brace Jovanovich, 1978), p. 53.

21. Breuer's casenotes are published in Albrecht Hirschmüller, *Physiologie und Psychoanalyse in Leben und Werk Josef Breuers. Jahrbuch der Psychoanalyse*, Beiheft 4 (Bern: Hans Huber, 1978). This fact is mentioned in a letter to Robert Binswanger of 4 November 1881 reprinted by Hirschmüller. The case is reprinted in Freud, *The Standard Edition of the Complete Psychological Works of Sigmund Freud*, trans. James Strachey (London: Hogarth, 1953–74), here, 2:21–47.

22. *Allerlei Geschichten; Maase-Buch*, trans. Bertha Pappenheim (Frankfurt: Jüdischer Frauenbund, 1929) and *Zeenah u-Reenah: Frauenbibel*, trans. Bertha Pappenheim (Frankfurt: Jüdischer Frauenbund, 1930).

23. Hirschmüller, *Werk Josef Breuers*, p. 354.

24. Frank J. Sulloway, *Freud, Biologist of the Mind: Beyond the Psychoanalytic Legend* (New York: Basic Books, 1979), "Myth 2", pp. 57 ff.

25. Freud, *Standard Edition*, 14:13–15.

26. Sigmund Freud, *The Complete Letters of Sigmund Freud to Wilhelm Fliess, 1887–1904*, trans. and ed. Jeffrey Moussaieff Masson (Cambridge, Massachusetts: The Belknap Press of Harvard University Press, 1985), p. 254. The centrality of the Jewish joke to Freud's thought at this point in his development cannot be underestimated, nor should the Jewish joke's relationship to mauscheln be ignored. As early as July 14, 1894, and October 31, 1895, Freud uses Jewish jokes as commonplaces, repeating only their punchlines, in letters to the Berlin ear, nose, and throat specialist Wilhelm Fliess, like Freud an acculturated Jew. Evidently such jokes were for them a common ground. The joke in the latter case actually reappears in full in Freud's study of the nature of humor. Thus his comment, in his letter of June 22, 1897, that "I must admit that I have recently started a collection of profound Jewish stories," follows a period of interest in Jewish humor. Indeed this very statement concludes a paragraph in which Freud compares himself and Fliess to two figures in a Jewish joke, "two beggars, one of whom gets the province of Posen" (p. 254). In this letter Freud, for the first time, uses a Yiddishism. (He employs the word *Schnorrer* for beggar.)

After this introduction Freud laces his letters with Yiddishisms for comic effect: *meschuge* = crazy (December 3, 1897; December 29, 1897; March 23,

1900); *Parnosse* = sustenance (December 12, 1897); *Dalles* = poverty (June 9, 1898); *Knetscher* = wrinkles (December 5, 1898); *Tomer doch* = maybe? (August 20, 1898); *Stuss* = bunk (September 6, 1898); *Shigan* = craziness (November 9, 1899; March 23, 1900).

Without a doubt the most telling moment in the Freud/Fliess exchange is the letter of September 21, 1897, in which Freud acknowledges that his earlier seduction theory of the origin of neurosis was wrong. He casts his sense of loss in "a little story from my collection . . . 'Rebecca, take off your gown, you are no longer a bride' " (p. 266). This rather enigmatic punchline has had a number of interpretations. What is important, however, is that Freud uses a punchline known to himself and Fliess as the appropriate discourse to convey his disappointment. The punchline is even more telling in that it contains the Yiddishism *Kalle,* a sexual *double-entendre* meaning both bride and prostitute.

What is striking about all the Yiddishisms Freud uses in his exchange with Fliess is that they are part of the urban slang of the period. Freud distinguishes between his own comic use of Yiddish (which is employed for effect and does not mark him as a "bad" Jew) and that of the Eastern Jew when, in the letter of April 27, 1898, he refers to his brother-in-law Moriz Freud (a distant cousin who married his sister Marie) as a "half-Asian" who suffers from "pseudologica fantastica" (p. 311). He is a "half-Asian" because he is an Eastern Jew (he comes from Bucharest), and the "disease" he is said to suffer from is, in fact, the psychiatric diagnosis for those mythomaniac patients who lie in order to gain status. For Freud it is the damaged, comic discourse of the Eastern Jew which approximates the anti-Semitic image of the lying Jew.

27. Freud, *Standard Edition,* 8:49.

28. I rely here on two insightful essays: Jeffrey Mehlman, "How to Read Freud on Jokes: The Critic as *Schadchen,*" *New Literary History* 6 (1975): 439–61, and Mary Jacobus, "Is There a Woman in This Text?" *New Literary History* 14 (1982): 117–41.

29. See my discussion of Balmary's work, "Psychoanalyzing *Psychoanalyzing Psychoanalysis,*" *Contemporary Psychiatry* 2 (1983): 213–15.

30. *Der jüdische Spassvogel, oder Jocosus hebricosus. Ahne Versammlung von aller mit ahner pauetischen Vorred* (Munich: A. L. Berend, 1877; 2d ed., 1890). See Freud, *Standard Edition,* 8:57.

31. Freud, *Standard Edition,* 8:108, 114.

32. Ibid., p. 16.

33. Otto Weininger, *Sex and Character* (New York: G. P. Putnam's Sons, 1906), p. 146.

34. Ibid., p. 324.

35. Freud, *Standard Edition,* 23:33.

9. Sexology, Psychoanalysis, and Degeneration

1. Of special help in formulating this paper was Annemarie Wettley, *Von der "Psychopathia sexualis" zur Sexualwissenschaft,* Beiträge zur Sexualforschung 17 (Stuttgart: Enke, 1959). This work appeared in abridged form in Annemarie and

Werner Leibbrand, *Formen des Eros: Kultur- und Geistesgeschichte der Liebe* (Freiburg: Karl Alber, 1972), pp. 569–86. Two essays by Wettley-Leibbrand were also of interest: "Bemerkungen zum Entartungsbegriff im Hinblick auf den Alkoholismus und die sexuellen Perversionen," Archivo ibero-americano de historia de la medicina 9 (1957): 539–42, and "Zur Problemgeschichte der 'degenerescence,' " *Sudhoffs Archiv* 43 (1959): 193–212. Other useful works on the concept of degeneration were: Georges Genil-Perrin, *Histoire des origines et de l'évolution de l'idée de dégénérescence en médecine mentale* (Paris: Alfred Leclerc, 1913); Richard D. Walter, "What Became of the Degenerate? A Brief History of a Concept," *Journal of the History of Medicine and the Allied Sciences* 11 (1956): 422–29; Francesco Parenti, "Psiche e degenerazione (Nascita ed evoluzione di una teoria)," *Pagine di storia della medicina* (Rome) 9 (1965): 45–53; Françoise Castel, "Dégénérescence et structures: Réflexions méthodologiques à propos de l'oeuvre de Magnan," *Annales médico-psychologiques* 125 (1967): 521–36; Emilo Balaguer Perigüell, "El somaticismo y la doctrina de la 'degeneración' en la psiquiatria valenciana del siglo XIX," *Medicina Espagnola* 62 (1969): 388–94; Colin Martindale, "Degeneration, Disinhibition, and Genius," *Journal of the History of the Behavioral Sciences* 7 (1971): 177–82.

2. On the relationship of the history of sexuality to the concept of degeneracy see Michel Foucault, *The History of Sexuality*, vol. 1, *An Introduction*, trans. Robert Hurley (New York: Vintage, 1980), and Peter Gay, *The Bourgeois Experience: Victoria to Freud* (New York: Oxford University Press, 1984). See also Eugen Holländer, *Äskulap und Venus: Eine Kultur- und Sittengeschichte im Spiegel des Arztes* (Berlin: Propyläen, 1928); Jill Conway, "Stereotypes of Femininity in a Theory of Sexual Evolution," *Victorian Studies* 14 (1970): 47–62; Milton Rugoff, *Prudery and Passion* (London: Rupert Hart-Davis, 1972), pp. 98–102; Norbert Elias, *The Civilizing Process: The History of Manners*, trans. Edmund Jephcott (New York: Urizen, 1970), pp. 169–89; Vern L. Bullough, *Sex, Society and History* (New York: Science History Publishers, 1976), pp. 112–25; Eric Trudgill, *Madonnas and Magdalens: The Origins and Development of Victorian Sexual Attitudes* (New York: Holmes & Meier, 1976); Steven Marcus, *The Other Victorians: A Study of Sexuality and Pornography in Mid-Nineteenth Century England* (New York: Meridian, 1974); Vern L. Bullough, *Sexual Variance in Society and History* (New York: John Wiley, 1976), Georges Lanteri-Laura, *Lecture des perversions: Histoire de leur appropriation médicale* (Paris: Masson, 1979); Fraser Harrison, *The Dark Angel: Aspects of Victorian Sexuality* (London: Sheldon Press, 1977); Dietrich von Engelhardt, "Sittlichkeitsdeliquenzen in Wissenchaft und Literatur der 2. Hälfte des 19. Jahrhunderts," in H. Hess, ed., *Sexualität und soziale Kontrolle* (Heidelberg: Kriminalistik Verlag, 1978), pp. 141–68; G. Williams, "Unclean Sex and the Unclean Sex: Some Victorian Paradoxes," *Trivium* 13 (1978): 1–17; J. J. Sauri, "Nacimiento del concepto de perversion," *Revista neuropsiquiatrica* 42 (1979): 71–85; J. A. Banks, "The Attitude of the Medical Profession to Sexuality in the 19th Century," *Society for the Social History of Medicine* 22 (1978): 9–10; Esther Fischer-Homberger, *Krankheit Frau und andere Arbeiten zur Medizingeschichte der Frau* (Bern: Hans Huber, 1979). The basic interrelationship between models of human sexuality and the model of degeneracy as perceived

during the nineteenth century is discussed by Phyllis Grosskurth, *Havelock Ellis: A Biography* (New York: Knopf, 1980), pp. 116 ff. See also R. A. Padgug, "Sexual Matters: On Conceptualizing Sexuality in History," *Radical History Review* 20 (1979): 3–24.

3. E. H. Hare, "Masturbatory Insanity: The History of an Idea," *Journal of Mental Science* 108 (1962): 2. See also Karl-Felix Jacobs, "Die Entstehung der Onanie-Literatur im 17. und 18. Jahrhundert" (diss., Munich, 1963).

4. Heinrich Kaan, *Psychopathia sexualis* (Leipzig: Leopold Voss, 1844). See Foucault, *History of Sexuality*, pp. 63, 118. My translation. In general, quotations are from translations indicated in the notes; other translations are mine.

5. Kaan, *Psychopathia Sexualis*, pp. 47–48.

6. See my essay "Hegel, Schopenhauer, and Nietzsche See the Black," *Hegel-Jahrbuch* 16 (1981): 163–88.

7. Central to any contemporary reading of Morel is the comprehensive study by Ruth Friedlander, "Bénédict-Augustin Morel and the Development of the Theory of Dégénérescence (The Introduction of Anthropology into Psychiatry)" (diss., University of California, San Francisco, 1973). Friedlander stresses the break that Morel's work made with earlier uses of the term *degeneration*. As this is simply a shift within the same paradigm, I have maintained the older term *degeneration* here. See also Peter Burgener, *Die Einflüsse des zeitgenössischen Denkens in Morels Begriff der "dégénérescence,"* Züricher Medizingeschichtliche Abhandlungen, N. R. 16 (Zurich: Juris, 1964).

8. This passage is a contemporary English translation and paraphrase from Morel's 1857 *Traité des dégénérescences physiques, intellectuelles et morales de l'espèce humaine,* which appeared as a series during 1857 in *The Medical Circular* (London), here, 25 March 1857, ed. and trans. Edwin Wing. This represents the contemporary impression of what was important within Morel's work.

9. The merger of theological and medical literature during the nineteenth century was possible only by virtue of the presumed agreement of these basic models. See P. J. C. Debreyne, *Essai sur la théologie morale, considérée dans ses rapports avec la physiologie et la médecine* (Brussels: M. Vanderborght, 1846), pp. 62–69, and Felix Antoine Philabert Dupanloup, Bishop of Orleans, *De l'éducation* (Paris: Charles Douniol, 1863), 3:399–402. Both texts use contemporary scientific material for their theological discussions of the nature of childhood sexuality.

10. Friedlander, pp. 134 ff. F. Merke, in *Geschichte und Ikonographie des endemischen Kropfes und Kretinismus* (Bern: Hans Huber, 1971), gives a detailed discussion of the central role played by the model of the cretin in nineteenth-century medical thought.

11. Johannes Häussler, *Über Beziehungen des Sexualsystems zur Psyche überhaupt und zum Cretinismus ins Besondere* (Wurzburg: Strecker, 1826). For some reason Merke does not discuss Häussler's work, but it plays a role in Hans-Giese, ed., *Die sexuelle Perversion* (Frankfurt: Akademische Verlagsgesellschaft, 1967).

12. On this confusion of cause and effect see my essay "Den Geisteskranken sehen: Henry Mackenzie, Heinrich von Kleist, William James," *Confinia psychiatrica* 22 (1979): 127–44.

13. Morel, *Traité des dégénérescences,* p. 22.

14. Jakob Santlus, *Zur Psychologie der menschliche Triebe* (Neuwied: J. H. Heuser, 1864), pp. 68–69. On the politics of sexuality see Carl E. Schorske, *Fin-de-siècle Vienna: Politics and Culture* (New York: Vintage, 1981), pp. 181–207; Richard Hamann and Jost Hermand, *Stilkunst um 1900* (Frankfurt: Fischer, 1977), pp. 26–178; George L. Mosse, "Nationalism and Respectability: Normal and Abnormal Sexuality in the Nineteenth Century," *Journal of Contemporary History* 17 (1982): 221–46; Reinhard Koselleck and Paul Widmer, eds., *Niedergang, Sprache und Geschichte* 2 (Stuttgart: Klett/Cotta, 1981); as well as Isabel V. Hull, "Reflections on George L. Mosse's 'Nationalism and Respectability,'" *Journal of Contemporary History* 17 (1982): 247–68.

15. See the English translation by Frank Chance, *Cellular Pathology as Based upon Physiological and Pathological Histology* (New York: Robert M. De Witt, [1860]), p. 40. Virchow rejected the rhetoric of degeneracy throughout his later work; see especially his essay "Descendenz und Pathologie," *Archiv für pathologische Anatomie und Physiologie* 103 (1886): 1–14. Virchow's views are in no way unique. The key term *atavism* was later coined by the economist Walter Bagehot, *Physics and Politics* (1875; Boston: Beacon, 1956), to describe the Hobbesian return to the primitive state. This view was continued within medical biology by John Hughlings Jackson. See James Taylor, ed., *The Selected Writings of John Hughlings Jackson* (New York: Staples, 1958).

16. All references are to the English translation by Ralph Manheim, *Myth, Religion and Mother Right: Selected Writings of J. J. Bachofen,* Bollingen Series 84 (Princeton: Princeton University Press, 1967), here, p. 105. See Berta Eckstein-Diener [Sir Galahad], *Mütter und Amazonen: Ein Umriss weiblicher Reiche* (Munich: Albert Langen, 1932), pp. 239, 276–90, for a major political critique of Bachofen's concept of the Amazon.

17. Bachofen, *Selected Writings,* p. 105.

18. Ibid., pp. 105–6.

19. Mill's *Subjection of Women* (1869; written in 1861) simply continued a view which was basic to early nineteenth-century thought; see M. H. Abrams, *Natural Supernatural: Tradition and Revolution in Romantic Literature* (New York: W. W. Norton, 1971), pp. 356–72. The power of this image is suggested by the fact that Friedrich Nietzsche evidently rediscovered it in his reading of Mill's essay in Sigmund Freud's 1880 translation.

20. G. W. F. Hegel, *Lectures on the Philosophy of Religion,* trans. E. B. Spiers (New York: Humanities Press, 1962), 1:101.

21. This reference is in Hegel's *Philosophie des Geistes* in Hermann Glockner, *Sämtliche Werke* (Stuttgart: Fromann, 1927 ff.), 10:73–74.

22. Bachofen, *Selected Writings,* p. 105.

23. Eduard Reich, *Geschichte, Natur- und Gesundheitslehre des ehelichen Lebens* (Cassel: J. C. Krieger, 1864).

24. Eduard Reich, *Ueber Unsittlichkeit: Hygienische und politisch-moralische Studien* (Neuwied: J. H. Heuser, 1866).

25. Eduard Reich, *Ueber die Entartung des Menschen: Ihre Ursachen und Verhütung* (Erlangen: Ferdinand Enke, 1868). Other works of interest by Reich are: *Studien*

über die Frauen (Jena: Hermann Costenoble, 1875); *Die Abhängigkeit der Civilisation von der Persönlichkeit des Menschen und von der Lebensbedürfnisse* (Minden: J. C. C. Bruns, 1883); *Geschichte der Seele, die Hygiene des Geisteslebens und die Civilisation* (Minden: J. C. C. Bruns, 1884).

26. Prostitution became the central point about which major questions of the "private" versus the "public" sphere were focused.

27. Reich, *Entartung,* pp. 519–22.

28. Gordon W. Allport, *The Nature of Prejudice* (New York: Doubleday Anchor, 1958), p. 315. My discussion of Gobineau is indebted to the unpublished book manuscript by Professor Annette Smith of the California Institute of Technology, "Gobineau et l'histoire naturelle" (1981).

29. Richard von Krafft-Ebing, *Psychopathia Sexualis: A Medico-Forensic Study,* rev. trans. by Harry E. Wedeck (New York: G. P. Putnam, 1965), here, p. 24. "Shamelessness" is a major category in Bachofen's tracing of the development of civilized sexual behavior. He interprets Hyginus's description of Oedipus as *impudens* as referring to the "unregulated tellurian sexuality of the swamp" (180). Here, too, some type of control is called for.

30. Westermarck's *History of Human Marriage* (London: Macmillan, 1903) is the major conservative document of the nineteenth century concerning human sexuality. He so wished to project European sexual standards on history that he argued that promiscuity, postulated by such thinkers as Bachofen as the original form of human sexuality, is an aberration among "savages" caused by the influence of "civilization" (66–70).

31. Krafft-Ebing, *Psychopathia Sexualis,* p. 25.

32. Ibid., pp. 25–26.

33. Engels, basing his work on Bachofen and on Morgan's anthropological studies among the Iroquois, saw the development of human sexuality in three stages: wildness, with unlimited sexual partners (promiscuity); barbarism, with a limited number of sexual partners (*Paarungsehe*); and civilization, with one sexual partner (monogamy). He saw this history, however, as a destruction of the productivity of the gens with the state replacing the gens, and the abrogation of the rights of the woman and her reduction to the role of the producer of children as heirs for the male. See the detailed introduction by Eleanor Burke Leacock to Friedrich Engels, *The Origin of the Family, Private Property and the State,* trans. Alec West (New York: International, 1972).

34. Krafft-Ebing, *Psychopathia Sexualis,* pp. 27–28.

35. Compare R. G. Collingwood, *The Idea of Nature* (Oxford: Oxford University Press, 1945), p. 13, for a discussion of history as a model for nineteenth-century biology.

36. The literature on the homosexual emancipation movement of the late nineteenth century is extensive. See the following bibliographies for a general overview: J. Foster, *Sex Variant Women in Literature: A Historical and Quantitative Survey* (New York: Vantage, 1956); N. Garde, *The Homosexual in Literature: A Chronological Bibliography, Circa 700 B.C.–1958* (New York: Village Press, 1959); W. Legg and A. Underwood, *An Annotated Bibliography of Homosexuality* (Los

Angeles: Institute for the Study of Human Resources, 1967); *A Gay Bibliography: Eight Bibliographies on Lesbian and Male Homosexuality* (New York: Arno, 1975); Gene Daman, *The Lesbian in Literature: A Bibliography* (Reno: The Ladder, 1975); Linda C. Dowling, *Aestheticism and Decadence: A Selective Annotated Bibliography* (New York: Harper & Row, 1972); Vern Bullough et al., *An Annotated Bibliography of Homosexuality* (New York: Garland, 1976); William Parker, *Homosexuality Bibliography: Supplement 1970–1975* (Metuchen, N.J.: Scarecrow, 1977). Of importance for this present study has been James D. Steakley, *The Homosexual Emancipation Movement in Germany* (New York: Arno, 1975). The debate concerning the applicability of degeneracy to the homosexual was central to such writers as Magnus Hirschfeld. See his "Ursachen und Wesen des Uranismus," *Jahrbuch für sexuelle Zwischenstufen* 5:1 (1903): 142–59, for his rebuttal of Möbius. However, Hirschfeld did share the "biologistic" paradigm of sexuality discussed in this essay, to the extent that he named the lecture hall in his Institute for Sexual Science (Berlin) the Ernst Haeckel Hall.

37. The idea of the "basic drives" as elements of "natural law" is discussed by Otto von Gierke, *Das deutsche Genossenschaftsrecht,* vol. 4, *Die Staats- und Korporationslehre der Neuzeit* (Berlin: Weidmann, 1913).

38. "Degeneration" as a label is rarely used today except within the limited area of cell pathology. The concept has been absorbed into modern medicine and biology with the label "endogenous," which was introduced into psychiatric terminology by Möbius in 1892. The parallel terminology (degenerate/endogenous) made it possible for the concept of degeneration to exist even after the political associations of the term made its use in post–World War II science an impossibility. See Achim Mechler, "Degeneration und Endogenität," *Der Nervenarzt* 34 (1963): 219–26, and James C. King, *The Biology of Race,* 2d ed. (Berkeley: University of California Press, 1981).

39. George M. Beard, *American Nervousness: Its Causes and Consequences* (New York: G. P. Putnam, 1881), p. 5.

40. Ibid., pp. 7–8.

41. Voltaire, "Onan, Onanisme," *Oeuvres complètes,* vol. 20, *Dictionnaire philosophique* (Paris: Garnier, 1879), 4:133–35.

42. George M. Beard, *Sexual Neurasthenia,* 5th ed. (New York: E. B. Treat, 1902), p. 118.

43. Ibid., p. 343.

44. Eduard Reich, *Die Nervosität bei den Frauen: Ihre Ursache und Verhütung,* 2d ed. (Berlin: A. Zimmer, 1882), p. 109.

45. Ibid., p. 52.

46. Beard, *American Nervousness,* pp. vi–vii.

47. Otto Dornblüth, *Nervöse Anlage und Neurasthenie* (Leipzig: H. Hartung, 1896), p. 28.

48. Wilhelm Erb, *Ueber die wachsende Nervosität unserer Zeit* (Heidelberg: Gustav Koester, 1894), p. 17. Erb's essay seems to have functioned as a classic polemical presentation of neurasthenia, as it is referred to in most discussions of the illness after 1894.

49. Rudolph von Hösslin, "Symptomatologie," in Franz Carl Müller, ed., *Handbuch der Neurasthenie* (Leipzig: Voigel, 1893), 159–90.

50. Paul Julius Möbius, *Die Nervosität* (Leipzig: J. J. Weber, 1882), p. 87. The literature on Möbius is not as extensive as it should be. Recently, however, a major study of his work has been published: Francis Schiller, *A Möbius Strip: Fin-de-siècle Neuropsychiatry and Paul Möbius* (Berkeley: University of California Press, 1982).

51. Christian Ufer, *Nervosität und Mädchenerziehung in Haus und Schule* (Wiesbaden: J. F. Bergmann, 1890), p. 23.

52. Between 1890 and 1905 neurasthenia was almost universally accepted by the medical profession as an important disease. One notable renegade was Willy Hellpach, who, in *Nervosität und Kultur* (Berlin: Johannes Räde, 1902), pp. 184–99, criticized the perception of modern culture within the model of degeneration.

53. Max Nordau, *Degeneration* (New York: D. Appleton, 1895). Nordau's book introduced the concept of "degeneracy" into public dialogue. The response to this critique of fin-de-siècle culture, dedicated to Cesare Lombroso, was extraordinary. The concept of abulia upon which Nordau based his argument is, of course, nothing more than the medieval sin of acedia in nineteenth-century dress. Acedia, or sloth, became a psychopathological category in the Middle Ages and Renaissance. See my study *Seeing the Insane* (New York: John Wiley, 1982), pp. 13 ff. The most recent discussion of Nordau is to be found in Shlomo Avineri, *The Making of Modern Zionism: The Intellectual Origins of the Jewish State* (New York: Basic Books, 1981), pp. 101–11.

54. August Forel, *The Sexual Question: A Scientific, Psychological, Hygienic and Sociological Study*, trans. D. F. Marshall (New York: Physicians and Surgeons Book Co., 1925), pp. 331–32. I am grateful for an unpublished essay by Ruth Rinard, "Two Views of the Sexual Question: The Cultural Use of Biological Assumptions," which was written during my NEH seminar on the 1890s, Summer 1981.

55. This section and the next are intended to serve as a corrective to Frank J. Sulloway's *Freud, Biologist of the Mind: Beyond the Psychoanalytic Legend* (New York: Basic Books, 1979), esp. pp. 289–97, 423. Sulloway's attempt to present nineteenth-century biology as "science" in spite of its pseudoscientific aspects draws his very conclusions into question. But even more centrally, he rarely attempts to offer reasons for Freud's myth-making, and when he does they are often simplistic. In addition to Sulloway's work, the following essays were of importance in the formulation of this section: Hermann Glaser, "Die 'kulturelle' Sexualmoral und die moderne Nervosität," in his *Sigmund Freuds Zwanzigstes Jahrhundert* (Munich: Carl Hanser, 1976), pp. 51–168; Alexander Schusdek, "Freud's 'Seduction Theory': A Reconstruction," *Journal of the History of the Behavioral Sciences* 2 (1966): 159–66; Heinz Schott, "Traum und Geschichte: Zur Freudschen Geschichtsauffassung im Kontext der *Traumdeutung*," *Sudhoffs Archiv* 64 (1980): 298–312; Samuel Jaffe, "Freud as Rhetorician: *Elocutio* and the Dream-Work," *Rhetorik* 1 (1980): 42–69. Of little use, despite its title, is the speculative essay by Jean-Marc Dupen, "Freud and Degeneracy: A Turning Point," *Diogenes*

97 (1977): 43–64. The longer work announced in the essay has evidently not appeared.

56. See Emanuel Radl, *Geschichte der biologischen Theorien seit dem Ende des siebzehnten Jahrhunderts* (Leipzig: Engelmann, 1905), and Roderick Stackelberg, *Idealism Debased: From völkisch Ideology to National Socialism* (Kent, Ohio: Kent State University Press, 1981).

57. The appearance of the hybrid theory in Chamberlain's *Die Grundlagen des neunzehnten Jahrhunderts*, 14th ed. (Munich: Bruckmann, 1899), 1:406–9, as a way of denying the Jews the claim of being a "pure race" by labeling them as a hybrid with blacks continues an identification between blackness and Otherness which has very old historical roots in Germany, but which is here given biological form. See my *On Blackness without Blacks: Essays on the Image of the Black in Germany* (Boston: G. K. Hall, 1982). Chamberlain cites "Siegmund" Freud in his discussion of the nature of sexual repression in the formation of neurosis in a virulently anti-Catholic discussion of Loyola. A recent major study of Chamberlain is Geoffrey G. Field, *Evangelist of Race: The Germanic Vision of Houston Stewart Chamberlain* (New York: Columbia, 1981).

58. Sigmund Freud, *The Standard Edition of the Complete Psychological Works of Sigmund Freud*, trans. James Strachey (London: Hogarth, 1953–74), 1:8.

59. Ibid., p. 52.

60. Paul Julius Möbius, *Geschlecht und Entartung* (Halle: Carl Marhold, 1903), is a typical summary of these earlier views. See Esther Fischer-Homburger, *Krankheit Frau*, pp. 32–48, on the image of the hysteric, and the brilliant new work by Patricia Meyer Spacks, *The Adolescent Idea: Myths of Youth and the Adult Imagination* (New York: Basic Books, 1981).

61. Hermann Smidt, *Über das Vorkommen der Hysterie bei Kindern* (diss., Strasbourg, 1880). See K. Codell Carter, "Infantile Hysteria and Infantile Sexuality in Late 19th-Century German Language Medical Literature," *Medical History* 26 (1983): 186–96.

62. See Freud, *Standard Edition*, 2:87, 104, 294; 3:21, 46, 51, 249; 11:21; 12:207. See also the general discussion in Henri F. Ellenberger, *The Discovery of the Unconscious: The History and Evolution of Dynamic Psychiatry* (New York: Basic Books, 1970).

63. Freud, *Standard Edition*, 3:48.

64. Ibid., 12:207, but compare 7:254, 263.

65. Fliess's influence on Freud's thought was far reaching but fitted very much within the general "pseudoscience" tradition of nineteenth-century biology; see Peter Heller, "A Quarrel over Bisexuality," in Gerald Chapple and Hans H. Schulte, eds., *The Turn of the Century: German Literature and Art, 1890–1915* (Bonn: Bouvier, 1981), pp. 87–116.

66. Freud, *Standard Edition*, 1:240–41.

67. See Iwan Bloch's *Beiträge zur Aetiologie der Psychopathia sexualis* (Dresden: H. R. Dohrn, 1902–3) and his *Das Sexualleben unserer Zeit in seinen Beziehung zur modernen Kultur* (Berlin: Louis Marcus, 1907), as well as the work of Magnus Hirschfeld. These volumes are part of an attempt to achieve a political solution to

the question of homosexuality by recruiting science onto the side of liberalism.

68. Freud, *Standard Edition*, 7:160.

69. The great debate about prostitution in the nineteenth century was between the economic determinists, who relied on the work of Parent-Duchatelet, *De la prostitution dans la ville de Paris* (Paris: J. B. Baillière, 1836), and the biological determinists, represented by Lombroso. On Lombroso see Klaus Hofweber, *Die Sexualtheorien des Cesare Lombroso* (diss., Munich, 1969).

70. Freud, *Standard Edition*, 7:192.

71. Ibid., 18:47. For the context of these remarks see Fredrick B. Churchill, "Sex and the Single Organism: Biological Theories of Sexuality in Mid-19th Century," *Journal of the History of Biology* 12 (1979): 139–77.

72. Freud, *Standard Edition*, 18:55; see also 1:187.

73. Ibid., 16:307; see also 16:320; 18:243; 23:152.

74. Ibid., 14:275. See Larry Stewart, "Freud before Oedipus: Race and Heredity in the Origins of Psychoanalysis," *Journal of the History of Biology* 9 (1977): 215–28, and King, *The Biology of Race*.

75. The pressures involved in understanding stereotyping as a dynamic process are best described in David Brion Davis, *The Slave Power Conspiracy and the Paranoid Style* (Baton Rouge: Louisiana State University Press, 1970). A survey concerning the various approaches to anti-Semitism in recent scholarship is Alphons Silbermann, *Der ungeliebte Jude: Zur Soziologie des Antisemitismus* (Zurich: Interfrom, 1981). Of great value on the linkage of images of Otherness is Hans Mayer, *Aussenseiter* (Frankfurt: Suhrkamp, 1975).

76. See Burton Pike, *The Image of the City in Modern Literature* (Princeton: Princeton University Press, 1981).

77. My reference here is to Sulloway, *Freud, Biologist of the Mind*, p. 592, and his references, tabulated in his index, to the twenty-six "myths" concerning Freud. Sulloway does not even attempt to understand the necessity of such myth-building as a means of existing in the world. This is especially true of the second "myth," "The Myth of Anti-Semitism."

10. The Mad as Artists

1. See R. D. Laing, *The Divided Self: An Existential Study in Sanity and Madness* (London: Tavistock, 1960), as well as Robert Boyers and Robert Orrill, eds., *Laing and Anti-Psychiatry* (Harmondsworth: Penguin, 1971).

2. Michel Foucault, *Histoire de la folie à l'âge classique* (Paris: Gallimard, 1972), pp. 56 ff.

3. Mary Barnes and Joseph Berke, *Mary Barnes: Two Accounts of a Journey through Madness* (New York: Harcourt Brace Jovanovich, 1971). The best critique of *Mary Barnes* is U. H. Peters, "Mary Barnes. Psychopathologische Literaturinterpretation am Beispiel einer literarischen Gattung: Psychose-Fikton," in Bernd Urban and Winfried Kudszus, eds., *Psychoanalytische und psychopathologische Literaturinterpretation* (Darmstadt: Wissenschaftliche Buchgesellschaft, 1981), pp. 280–99.

4. See the discussion in Bennett Simon, *Mind and Madness in Ancient Greece* (Ithaca, N.Y.: Cornell University Press, 1978), pp. 228–37.

5. Philippe Pinel, *Traité médico-philosophique sur l'aliénation mentale, ou la manie* (Paris: Richard, Caille & Ravier, IX [1801]).

6. Benjamin Rush, *Medical Inquiries and Observations upon the Diseases of the Mind* (Philadelphia: Kimber & Richardson, 1812), and Eric Carlson et al., eds., *Benjamin Rush's Lectures on the Mind* (Philadelphia: American Philosophical Society, 1981).

7. Eric Carlson and Jeffrey L. Wollock, "Benjamin Rush on Politics and Human Nature," *Journal of the American Medical Association* 236 (1976): 73–77.

8. Pliny Earle, "The Poetry of Insanity," *American Journal of Insanity* (1845): 193–224. Other nineteenth-century works on the "poetry of the insane" are: R. G. Brunet, *Les fous littéraires* (Brussels: Gay et Doucé, 1880), and its continuation, Av. Iv. Tcherpakoff, *Les fous littéraires* (Moscow: W. G. Gautier, 1883).

9. Forbes Winslow, "On the Insanity of Men of Genius," *Journal of Psychological Medicine* 2 (1848): 262–91; *On Obscure Diseases of the Brain and Disorders of the Mind* (Philadelphia: Blanchard & Lea, 1860); "Mad Artists," *Journal of Psychological Medicine* n.s. 6 (1880): 33–75. The best overview of the literature on the medical use of the art of the insane is Maria Mcuer-Keldenich, *Medizinische Literatur zur Bildnerei von Geisteskranken* (Cologne: Institut für Geschichte der Medizin, 1979). See also Peter Gorsen, *Kunst und Krankheit: Metamorphosen der ästhetischen Einbildungskraft* (Frankfurt: Europäische Verlagsanstalt, 1980), 317–42.

10. Cesare Lombroso, *Genio e follia* (Milan: Chiusi, 1864).

11. Ambrose Auguste Tardieu, *Étude médico-légale sur la folie* (Paris: J.-B. Baillière et fils, 1872).

12. On the Romantic fascination with the nightside and the function of poetry see Mario Praz, *The Romantic Agony*, trans. Angus Davidson (New York: Meridian, 1956).

13. Max Simon, "L'imagination dans la folie," *Annales médico-psychologiques* 16 (1876): 358–90.

14. E. Regis, "Les aliénés peints par eux-mêmes," *Encephale* 2 (1882): 184–98, 373–82, 557–64; 2 (1883): 642–55.

15. Marcel Réja, "L'art malade: Dessins de fous," *Revue universelle* 1 (1901): 913–15, and *L'art chez les fous: Le dessin, la prose, la poésie* (Paris: Soc. du Mercure de France, 1907).

16. Aleš Hrdlička, "Art and Literature in the Mentally Abnormal," *American Journal of Insanity* 55 (1899): 385–404.

17. Manfred Bleuler, "Forschungen und Begriffswandlungen in der Schizophrenielehre, 1941–1950," *Fortschritte der Neurologie und Psychiatrie* 9/10 (1951): 385–453; Werner Janzarik, *Themen und Tendenzen der deutschsprachigen Psychiatrie* (Berlin: Springer, 1974).

18. Joseph Rogues de Fursac, *Les écrits et les dessins dans les maladies nerveuses et mentales; essai clinique* (Paris: Masson, 1905).

19. Friedrich Justinus Mohr, "Über Zeichnungen von Geisteskranken und ihre diagnostische Verwertbarkeit," *Jahrbuch der Psychologie und Neurologie* 8 (1906–7):

913–15; "Zeichnungen von Geisteskranken," *Zeitschrift für angewandte Psychologie* 2 (1908–9): 291–300.

20. The best overview is Werner Janzarik, "100 Jahre Heidelberger Psychiatrie," in his *Psychopathologie als Grundlagenwissenschaft* (Stuttgart: Thieme, 1979).

21. Karl Jaspers, *Allgemeine Psychopathologie* (1913; Berlin: Springer, 1973).

22. Hans Prinzhorn, "Das bildnerische Schaffen der Geisteskranken," *Zeitschrift für die Gesamte Neurologie und Psychiatrie* 52 (1919): 307–26. One evidence of Lombroso's influence on many of these later studies is the fact that, just as Lombroso followed his studies of the insane with studies of the drawings and graffiti found in prisons, Prinzhorn followed his study of the art of the insane with *Bildnerei der Gefangenen* (Berlin: Axel Juncker Verlag, 1926), art of the prisoners.

23. The best overviews in German on Prinzhorn are the three postwar catalogues of exhibitions selected from the collection: Wolfgang Rothe, *Bildnerei der Geisteskranken aus der Prinzhorn-Sammlung* (Heidelberg: Galerie Rothe, 1967); *Bildnerei von psychisch Kranken, aus der Sammlung Prinzhorn* (Bonn: Rheinland-Verlag, 1973); and Hans Gercke and Inge Jarchov, eds., *Die Prinzhornsammlung* (Königstein: Athenäum, 1980). An English translation of Prinzhorn's 1922 monograph *Bildnerei der Geisteskranken* (Berlin: J. Springer, 1922) is *Artistry of the Mentally Ill*, trans. Eric von Brockdorff (New York: Springer-Verlag, 1972). There is also a monograph by Roger Cardinal, *Outsider Art* (New York: Praeger, 1972), which deals with most of the Prinzhorn material.

24. Paul Schilder, *Wahn und Erkenntnis: Eine psychopathologische Studie* (Berlin: J. Springer, 1918).

25. These texts are now collected in Thomas Anz, ed., *Phantasien über den Wahnsinn: Expressionistische Texte* (Munich: C. Hanser, 1980). See also Wolfgang Rothe, "Der Geisteskranke im Expressionismus," *Confinia psychiatrica* 15 (1972): 195–211.

26. In Anz, *Phantasien über den Wahnsinn*, p. 58. My translation.

27. Ibid., 127–32.

28. Walter Morgenthaler, *Ein Geisteskranker als Künstler* (Bern: E. Bircher, 1921).

29. See my and Wolf Von Eckardt's *Bertolt Brecht's Berlin* (New York: Doubleday, 1974).

30. *Mein Kampf*, trans. Ralph Manheim (Cambridge: Houghton Mifflin, 1943), pp. 258–59.

31. See Franz Roh, *"Entartete" Kunst: Kunstbarbarei im Dritten Reich* (Hannover: Fackelträger-Verlag, 1962), and Henry Grosshans, *Hitler and the Artists* (New York: Holmes & Meier, 1983), pp. 95–116.

32. See the translation by William C. Bunce, *Degenerate "Art"* (Redding, Conn.: Silver Fox Press, 1972).

33. Carl Schneider, "Entartete Kunst und Irrenkunst," *Archiv für Psychiatrie und Nervenkrankheit* 110 (1939): 135–64. The link between the Jews, the insane, and "degenerate art" was one of the standard associations of the *Reich* Ministry for Propaganda. See Franz-Josef Heyen, ed., *Parole der Woche: Eine Wandzeitung im Dritten Reich, 1936–1943* (Munich: dtv, 1983), p. 44.

34. Alexander Mitscherlich, *Doctors of Infamy: The Story of the Nazi Medical Crimes,* trans. Heinz Norden (New York: H. Schuman, 1949).

Conclusion

1. Walter Benjamin, *Illuminations,* ed. Hannah Arendt, trans. Harry Zohn (New York: Harcourt, Brace & World, 1969), p. 255.
2. Louis Althusser, *Lenin and Philosophy and Other Essays,* trans. Ben Brewster (New York: Monthly Review Press, 1971), p. 165.
3. Albert Einstein, "On the Method of Theoretical Physics," *Philosophy of Science* 1 (1934): 162.
4. Donald M. Lowe, *History of Bourgeois Perception* (Chicago: University of Chicago Press, 1982).
5. Blaise Pascal, *Pensées* (Paris: Garnier frères, 1961), 1:7.

Index

Library of Congress Cataloging in Publication Data

Gilman, Sander L.
  Difference and pathology

  Bibliography: p.
  Includes index.
  1. Stereotype (Psychology)—Social aspects—History. 2. Sex
differences—Social aspects—History. 3. Ethnopsychology—Social aspects—
History. 4. Mental illness—Social aspects—History. I. Title.
BF323.C5G55 1985   305   85-7809
ISBN 0-8014-1785-6 (alk. paper)
ISBN 0-8014-9332-3 (pbk. : alk. paper)